CRYPTOCURRENCY
The Next Level For Banking Reform

Sir Patrick Bijou

**Copyright © 2022 by Sir Patrick Bijou All rights reserved.
Cover design: Copyright © 2022 by Sir Patrick Bijou
All rights reserved**

This document is geared towards providing exact and reliable information about the topic and issue covered. The publication is sold with the idea that the publisher is not required to render accounting, officially permitted, or otherwise, qualified services. If advice is necessary, legal, or professional, a practiced individual in the profession should be retained.

In no way is it legal to reproduce, duplicate, or transmit any part of this document in either electronic means or printed format. Recording of this publication is strictly prohibited and any storage of this document is not allowed unless with written permission from the publisher. All rights reserved.

The information provided herein is stated to be truthful and consistent, in that any liability, in terms of inattention or otherwise, by any usage or abuse of any policies, processes, or directions contained within is the responsibility of the recipient reader. Under no circumstances will any legal responsibility or blame be held against the publisher for any reparation, damages, or monetary loss due to the information herein, either directly or indirectly.

Respective authors own all copyrights not held by the publisher.

The information herein is offered for informational purposes solely and is universal as so. The presentation of the information is without a contract or any type of guarantee assurance.

The trademarks that are used are without any consent, and the publication of the trademark is without permission or backing by the trademark owner. All trademarks and brands within this book are for clarifying purposes only and are owned by the owners themselves, not affiliated with this document.

Published by BIJOUBOOKS

Table of Contents

ABOUT THE AUTHOR 1
DESCRIPTION 5
INTRODUCTION 7
CHAPTER 1 9
How Does Cryptocurrency Like Bitcoin Happens? 9
Cypherpunks, Libertarianism, And Digital Money 14
The Development Of Cryptography 20
So How Does It Work With Bitcoin? 22
The Birth Of Bitcoin 24
Highlighting The Important Of Cryptocurrencies 28
CHAPTER 2 31
Cryptocurrency Community 31
From Cryptocurrency To Blockchain 32
The Analog Stone-Block-Chain 33
Security Model Of The Stone-Block-Chain 37
Is Cryptocurrency The New Money? 39
Basis Of Money 42
Traditional Money 44

No Or Limited Role For A Central Authority: Intrinsic Value 44

Government Authority: Fiat Money 45

Banks: Transferring Value Through Intermediaries 47

The Electronic Exchange of Money 49

The Price and Usage of Cryptocurrency 51

Cryptocurrency Values 54

CHAPTER 3 55

Components Of Cryptocurrency Technologies 55

Core Data Structures And Concepts 57

BLOCKCHAIN... 61

The Types Of Blockchain 68

SMART CONTRACT 69

Ethereum: Redemption And Birth Of Blockchain 2.0 72

The Traditional Financial Market Reborn 75

The Future Of Smart Contracts. 76

ICO: Bubble Or Extra Bonus? 77

Mining As Gold Rush 79

The Changing Value Of Bitcoins 84

ICO—Initial Coin Offering – The New IPO 87

The Traditional Financial Industry Tries …
Something New 93

CHAPTER 4 97

Decentralizing Financial Services 97

From Offline Banking To Blockchain Banking .. 98

Vocean Is Ready For This Market 105

The Future Of Blockchain In The Financial
Industry. 106

The Top Of The Food Chain And The Birth Of
Crypto Exchanges 108

The Fight Between Centralization And
Decentralization 110

The Future Of Exchanges: The Coexistence Of
Centralization And Decentralization. 113

Some Secrets Of Exchanges 115

The Future Of Crypto Exchanges: External
Regulation And Self-Regulation 119

The Secondary Market: Low-Lying Land 120

The Secondary Market Of Low Liquidity 121

The Unregulated Market Maker 124

Hot Money In The Secondary Market 125

OTC—Big Players 127

The Future Of The Secondary Market 130

Leading Currencies In The Field 131

Is Blockchain Technology Just for Cryptocurrencies? 133

CHAPTER 5 137

Key Actors in Digital Technology 137

Benefits And Risks Of Digital Currencies 142

Risks of Digital Currencies 143

U.S. Government Agencies' Risks Advisories .. 144

Consumer Financial Protection Bureau (CFPB) 145

Government Services Administration (GSA) ... 146

Securities and Exchange Commission (SEC) .. 147

Immigration and Customs Enforcement (ICE) .. 148

Federal Reserve Board (FED) 149

European Union Agency for Network and Information Security (ENISA) 149

Nobel Laureates' Concerns 151

Banks And Blockchain Technology 151

Types Of Cryptocurrencies 152

Other Variations of Cryptocurrencies 161

CHAPTER 6 175

Issues of Digital Technology 175

Jurisdiction 175

SEC v. Shavers 179

Virtual Currencies as Money 181
Smart Contracts 183
Intellectual Property 186
Federal Regulation of Virtual Currencies 189
U.S. Government Agencies Concerned With
Virtual Currencies 192
SEC Warnings to Social Media 204
Consumer Protection Resource Page 220
Financial Crimes Enforcement Network (FinCEN)
.... 220
Requirements When Designated as a Money
Services Business 229
Additional Agencies That May Regulate Virtual
Currencies 233
Consumer Financial Protection Bureau (CFPB) 234
Office of Comptroller of the Currency (OCC) 235
Federal Trade Commission (FTC) 236
North American Securities Administrators
Association (NASAA) 238
International Regulation 239
International Organizations And Entities 240
European Union 241

European Securities and Markets Authority (ESMA) 245
The key challenges, accordinsg to the 2016 discussion paper are: 248
European Union's New Blockchain Initiative . 249
European Court of Justice Ruling 250
Organisation For Economic Co-operation And Development (OECD) 251
United Nations (UN) 252
G20 252
IOSCO 253

CHAPTER 7 254
Actions Taken By Uk Authorities And The Government 254
Policy Approach 257
Overarching Approach And Related UK Initiatives 259
Expanding The Regulatory Perimeter 262
Scope Of Regulation And Requirements 267
Actors, Activities And Requirements 269
DLT-Based Financial Market Infrastructures ... 282

CHAPTER 8 287
A Central Bank Issuing Digital Currency 287

Public Sector Mandates For CBDC And
Stablecoin Governance 289
Mandates For Public Sector Financial Institutions
 291
Bitcoin Questions 293
Antifragility 312
CONCLUSION **329**

ABOUT THE AUTHOR

Sir Patrick Bijou is Senior Judge for the ICJ-ICC, Ambassador for the United Nations, a British investment banker, philanthropist, and a published author. Sir Patrick specializes in the debt capital markets, private placements, equities, derivatives and futures trading. He has worked with multiple leading banks such as Wells Fargo, Deutsche Bank, Credit Agricole CIB, Merrill Lynch and others, apart from trading on Wall Street.

He has over three decade's experience in the financial markets and has worked with numerous prolific clients, including governments, banking institutions, and corporations. He is also a renowned author and has published over 25 books across several genres.

Sir Patrick was born in Georgetown, Guyana, South America. At the age of five, he came to Britain. Having been brought up in London, he spent part of his education in England and completed his education in the USA, where he obtained his degrees in Business Studies and later an MBA in Economic and International banking.

Cyptocurrency: The Next Level for Banking Reform

As a notable level 17 investment banker, he has also worked on Wall Street, and is a skillful and highly experienced Tier 1 trader in the derivative and bond markets, and he also established MTN desks within various significant banks. He became responsible for the setup of the MTN & Private Placement Desk and dealer functions within Lloyds Bank PLC, and was the first trader for Lloyd's treasury for increasing the portion of self-led deals significantly from 4% to 32% in 2002.

Sir Patrick has tailored funding and investments for many different clients, including governments, banks and financial institutions, and has implemented over $16.B funding for socio-economic and humanitarian projects.

He has excelled as an investment banker and was awarded many accolades such as the Multiple Recipient, of the Wells Fargo "Valley of the Stars" award throughout his illustrious career. He was also distinguished by receiving the Wells Fargo "Circle of Stars" award, and was a Member of Wells Fargo's "Millionaire Club" and "Champion Circle". This further propelled him to become the notable banker he is today. He was finally awarded his most distinguished accolade of all, a knighthood, for his services to banking and philanthropy.

His expertise is so profound that he was selected for a position within the International Court of Justice Redemption Department for his finance and international law proficiency to become a member of the Panel of Arbitrators of the International Centre for the Settlement of Investment Disputes. He currently sits as a

Sir Patrick Bijou

Senior Judge of the ICJ-ICC. Sir Patrick manages to fit all these activities into his current role as Fund Manager for LWP Capital, and is also distinguished as being a U.N. Ambassador.

He is also a Global Ambassador for the International Rights and Welfare Association (IRAWA), and Ambassador of the Royal Diplomatic Club. In May 2021, he was appointed Ambassador by The Academy of Universal Global Peace USA as a member of the governing board/trustees and awarded The Human Excellency Award and Presidency of the Commonwealth Entrepreneurs Club.

One of his most significant career achievements was creating a line of credit for international supply chains and SMEs for the public sector and government funding through PPP. He also helped create the Contract for Difference (CFD) economic phenomena and credit leverage ratio concepts, regarded as hugely pioneering, which all banks and trading institutions have adopted today.

His journey into content writing has allowed him to become an exceptionally motivated and enthusiastic author and professional communicator, experienced in proactive campaign-driven and responsive communications.

His trading platforms are at Credit Suisse Geneva and DBS Singapore, where he manages high yield investments with attractive returns for selective high net worth clients.

"Coming together is a beginning, keeping together is progress, and working together is success."

- Sir Patrick Bijou

DESCRIPTION

If you want to try **CRYPTOCURRENCY**, this book will help you understand the **FUNDAMENTALS OF CRYPTOCURRENCY**. It also discusses the various pros and cons of Cryptocurrency and the Banking Industry and shows you how you can put the knowledge to good use. It aims at describing how cryptocurrency works and understanding the different types of cryptocurrency. It has taken the public a while to migrate from digital money (transferring digital dollars online) to using cryptocurrency that is, money created using cryptography. However, that migration is now occurring and often leads to a discussion on cryptocurrency in the economy. The Book describes extensively the discoveries about the digital world of banking and its fundamentals and **as you read this book, you will discover the different terminology and language and all you will ever be required to know in one book this exciting new world of banking. Some call it the NEW WORLD ORDER OR THE GREAT RESET.**

Cyptocurrency: The Next Level for Banking Reform

Note: Once you have a clear understanding of the fundamentals of cryptocurrency and its role in the banking industry and monetary system, you have then stepped into the world of cryptocurrency and that's just the beginning!

INTRODUCTION

In 2008, an anonymous computer programmer or group of programmers operating under the pseudonym Satoshi Nakamoto developed a computer platform that will allow users to make legitimate transactions of digital representations of value. The system, known as Bitcoin, is the first cryptocurrency. A cryptocurrency is digital money used in an electronic payment system where payments are confirmed by a decentralized network of system users and cryptographic protocols rather than a centralized middleman (such as a bank).

Since 2009, cryptocurrencies have gone from little-known, niche technological curiosities to rapidly proliferating financial instruments that are the subject of intense public interest. Recently, they have been incorporated into a variety of other financial transactions and products. For example, cryptocurrencies have been sold to investors to raise funding through initial coin offerings (ICOs), and the terms of certain derivatives are now based on cryptocurrencies. Some government central banks have examined the possibility of issuing cryptocurrencies or other digital currency. Media coverage of cryptocurrencies has been widespread, and various observers have characterized cryptocurrencies as either the future of monetary and payment systems that will displace government-backed currencies or a fad with little real value.

When analyzing the public policy implications posed by cryptocurrencies, it is important to keep in mind what these currencies are expressly designed and intended to be—alternative electronic payment systems. The purpose of this report is to assess how and how well cryptocurrencies perform this function, and in so doing to identify possible benefits, challenges, risks, and policy issues surrounding cryptocurrencies. The report begins by reviewing the most basic characteristics and economic functions of money, the traditional systems for creating money, and traditional systems for transferring money electronically. It then describes the features and characteristics of cryptocurrencies and examines the potential benefits they offer and the challenges they face regarding their use as money. The report also examines certain risks posed by cryptocurrencies when they are used as money and related policy issues, focusing in particular on two issues: cryptocurrencies' potential role in facilitating criminal activity and concerns about protections for consumers who use these currencies. Finally, the report analyzes cryptocurrencies' impact on monetary policy and the possibility that central banks could issue their own, government-backed digital currencies.

CHAPTER 1

How Does Cryptocurrency Like Bitcoin Happens?

In late 2008, under the long shadow cast by the most severe economic crisis in generations, a revolutionary new form of currency was quietly being shaped. Initially, there was no clue that an obscure form of electronic money would prove to be the most important financial innovation of the 21st century, a tool that would soon be widely adopted by people, economies, and companies all across the world. In October of that year, in a white paper issued by an anonymous person or group calling itself Satoshi Nakamoto now known to the world as "the creator of Bitcoin" the digital currency known as Bitcoin, and the technologies underpinning it, were laid out for the first time. There were few clues in this initial description that made anyone think Bitcoin had the power to upend and revolutionize the world's financial system. Bitcoin's success was far from assured.

In its early days, Bitcoin was mostly seen as an oddity something that was only around to amuse experts in cryptography. Just ten years ago, the general public was still mostly unfamiliar with cryptocurrency. It was only for specialists and eccentrics. Today, of course, Bitcoin has become a household name. It has the highest market value of any cryptocurrency. Moreover, it has drawn an enormous amount of attention to blockchain, the technology on which, it is built. (If you've ever been to a blockchain conference, you will truly feel the "electricity in the air" of the great expectations people now hold for the future of blockchain technology. Bitcoin has had its ups and downs, but this enthusiasm has not abated.) Blockchain was originally developed as a sort of "storage room" for Bitcoin something that would record transactions and avoid the possibility of the currency being used inappropriately. The focus of this book will be the technical backbone of cryptocurrency and the crypto economies it makes possible. But before we get into the thick of it, we need to spend a moment on Bitcoin and its history, because Bitcoin was the driver of it all. It's just that important.

The disaster of the subprime mortgage crisis in 2008 shook the public's confidence in banks, governments, and other powerful institutions. Suddenly, everything was in doubt. Entities that had been seen as rock-solid and trustworthy for generations appeared to have abruptly let us down. They had been revealed as empty facades. The emperors had no clothes. Now, the world was looking for new solutions. And into this environment, Bitcoin arrived like a magic bullet, seemingly designed to solve the very issues that had caused the financial crisis in the first place. Bitcoin would decentralize power. There would be no external arbiter or regulator that might fail us. To the contrary, the people the users of the cryptocurrency themselves would truly hold the power.

But perhaps Bitcoin was not only successful because it arrived on the scene at just the right time. One must admit that it also has a sense of mystery about it, an allure that many found romantic and daring. Bitcoin was exclusive at first, like a club that people wanted to join. It was initially introduced to a very small group of people experts in cryptography and "tech nerds" who were obsessed with the concept of individual liberty. (Some called these people "cypherpunks.") Just as one sees in the trajectory of any exclusive brand, Bitcoin gradually made itself more available to the masses. Yet even as consumers scrambled to get in on the hip, new "Bitcoin rush," many did not truly understand what the currency was, and the transformative power it held. But for us to discuss that here, we need to take a brief look at the history of money.

Sumer is an ancient civilization that was founded in Mesopotamia around the year 3000 BC. Sumerians have generally understood to be the first people who used money as a medium to facilitate exchange. Before the Sumerians, humans mostly used a barter system to make exchanges trading things for other physical things. There are many disadvantages to a barter system.

For example, say it's winter, and you'd like some wood to heat your house. You raise sheep and cows. Your neighbor grows trees, and he would like to have some meat for his family. You and your neighbor have to work out a barter arrangement say, one sheep for twenty wood blocks. You give him your sheep, and he gives you his blocks. Sure, it works, but it's not as easy as using money.

The direct exchange of goods without a universally accepted medium brings all kinds of inefficiencies and issues. If you don't have anything your neighbor wants, for example, then a trade cannot happen. As a way around these issues, we invented money and credit, which remain the foundations of our economy today. Today, if you want wood blocks, you can use credit or debt to borrow twenty wood blocks from your neighbor which puts you in his debt but allows you to pay him in the future. You can also simply pay him for the wood blocks in cash, which he can then spend any way he likes. Either works if your neighbor trusts you and/or trusts the currency you give him. Credit and money enable trade and make it more efficient.

And now, after 3000 years of financial and technological evolution, the Internet has brought us to a digital version of ancient Sumer. Since the Internet was first invented in 1969, half a century has gone by. In the intervening time, the Internet has become an inextricable part of our lives. Many of us can live without our girlfriends or boyfriends, but not without access to the Internet! The Internet connects people wirelessly and instantly through emails, social media, online businesses, and more. The extent of the social and financial engagements we are forging through the Internet reveal just how much we rely upon it in every aspect of our lives.

The benefits of the Internet are clear. But there are also downsides. Some of the biggest downsides that we really can't ignore involve privacy and security. Namely, how can we protect our privacy and stay safe when all of our photos and personal information are all over the web?

For most of us, the answer has been to allow centralized, trusted authorities to verify and safely enable activities conducted online. In a way, it's similar to how we've decided to let governments and banks oversee, manage, and control our economic transactions. Companies like Facebook, Google, Microsoft, and IBM have all in different ways become part of the apparatus we trust to provide safety online. The information we use is stored in central servers owned by powerful Internet companies. These companies provide services we value, and in return we trust them with our personal information. Yet once our information is in their hands, we have very little control over how they may use or exploit it. Think of how frequently we learn that a web company has been selling user information without permission. Think of how frequently websites change their terms of service, allowing customer data to be sold or used in other ways. Facebook's recent scandal is an excellent example of the violations of privacy and abuses of power that many users feel are unfairly foisted on them month after month.

Yet no matter how one feels about the Internet, it's undeniably the major force pushing us into the future. Much like banks, Internet-based giants have become too big to fail. Google dominates information exchange through the prevalence of its search engine. Dominant social media platforms such as Facebook control personal connections and public information exchange.

E-commerce has also become a part of our lives, with Amazon and Alibaba the unshakable giants in the field.

Theft of personal information is one thing, but the potential for the theft of online financial information presents a whole new ball game. For many people across the world, the ritual of going to the bank in person has been replaced by completing our financial transactions online. As the hard times in retail evince, we also now buy and sell merchandise online with increasing frequency. And instead of picking up the phone and calling restaurants to place our orders, we now browse menus and make orders on the web. This increase in online financial activity demands better security and efficiency. Cryptocurrency was created for this. It provides better security and is easier to use. We don't need to reveal our identities when we make purchases using cryptocurrencies. And that fact, vitally, means we can choose to remain anonymous.

Cypherpunks, Libertarianism, And Digital Money

It took the public a while to migrate from digital money (transferring digital dollars online) to using cryptocurrency that is, money created using cryptography. But that migration is now happening. Yet to truly understand a phenomenon like this, we need to ask why it is happening. Why did people want to create a currency separate from the fiat money controlled by the central governments and central banks?

Diners Club is generally considered to have been the birth of the credit card. In 1974, Roland Moreno invented the IC card as a medium to store digital currency. In 1982, the United States created the electronic funds transfer system (EFTS), with Great Britain and Germany creating similar institutions shortly thereafter. Credit cards issued by banks were an instant hit, expanding exponentially as demand increased. This was the first digitizing of fiat money. It was important because it changed our perception of money in a way it had not been in centuries. For the first time, most of us didn't need to carry cash around. Everything could be done virtually.

Even though digital money is very different from and exists in a different form from fiat money, it still relies on the centralized oversight of powerful banks and governments. Not everybody likes this because of the inherent requirements and regulations. Namely, unlike cash, you can't use your credit card anonymously. You're charged a special rate to use your credit card in another country. Some cards are not accepted at all in certain countries. And middlemen such as banks and finance companies play major roles in the transactions. PayPal and Ali Pay likewise present themselves as "trusted third-party payment options," yet their presence removes our ability to make many transactions discreetly or anonymously. International money transactions from one bank to another are also impossible without going on the public record.

To better capture customer and seller information, online middlemen have also attempted to introduce invasive technologies like Public Key that require both buyer and seller to go through complicated processes to verify their identities whenever they make a transaction. However, the birth of Bitcoin has largely derailed the adoption of these new systems.

The ability to make anonymous payments and transactions online has always had the support of certain communities, such as IT elites, cryptographers (the so-called cypherpunks), advocates of decentralization, and people on the libertarian side of the political spectrum. There is something of a communal identity involved some shared worldview between these groups. They feel part of a fraternity influenced by thinkers like Friedrich August von Hayek. When barriers to free commerce like Public Key appeared on the horizon, cypherpunks and their kin aimed to create a new way of exchanging information (financial and otherwise) that would have little or no interference from the new regulators. They wanted to enhance privacy and protect personal freedom. They also wanted to actively subvert the government and its attempts at regulation.

All of these desires seemed to actualize themselves in Bitcoin.

Back in the 1980s, Timothy May proposed an idea for digital money that he called "Crypto Credits." David Chaum was the first to apply cryptography to E-cash. Yet one of the major issues that E-cash faced was called "Double Spend." This, more or less, is what it sounds like. Money is spent twice. Transactions are redeemed twice. It's like taking a check to one bank and cashing it, and then being able to take it to another bank and cash it again. For example, say that the User A issues $1 in E-cash through an E-signature to User B. The risk is that User B will then duplicate User A's E-signature to get two dollars instead of one.

An early solution calculated to solve the Double Spend problem was printing a unique serial number on each note issued. When the note was sent out from User A, User B would check the signature and make a phone call to User A, asking him or her for the serial number, and if the E-cash note had been used previously. If the note had, not been cashed before, User B would accept the note. User A would then document that the note had been used. Whew, Is it any wonder that a system like this did not catch on?

In today's the digital world, servers complete all the work, including documenting every signature and serial number involved in financial transaction. Using serial numbers solved the Double Spend problem, but it did not allow individuals to transact anonymously, since each transaction (and corresponding personal information) could be tracked through the serial number. To try and make each transaction anonymous, David Chaum then proposed a work-around known as "Blind Signature," which basically solves two problems at once anonymity and double spend. It allows the user to perform any monetary exchange that actual, physical money would allow (except perhaps physically flipping coins). How does Blind Signature work? It all takes place in an "envelope." User A puts a note with a serial number into the "envelope," which no one has access to except for

User A. But then how does User B sign the note without his or her identity becoming known? The answer is to insert a carbon paper into the "envelope"—the signature will then appear on the note through the carbon paper. However, User B doesn't know the serial number, and User A doesn't know who signed the note.

The bottom line is that a transaction will take place with two parties not knowing each other's identity. Using this technology, David Chaum started two companies. One, DigiCash, was created to provide digital payments online using E-cash. The other, Cyberbucks, was designed to provide support for banks.

E-cash was a very refreshing solution, but like a cool drink enjoyed too quickly, the refreshment it provided lasted only for a few moments! Despite its advantages, it was never able to get mainstream acceptance. Even though it was designed to help buyers and sellers facilitate transactions, few sellers saw a benefit in using it. It's a different story when it comes to Bitcoin and we'll discuss those differences later in this book. But regardless of the failure to commercialize its E-cash service, the concept of Blind Signature was a vital and important milestone in the history of digital currency.

David Chaum applied for patents for the technologies related to E-cash, including Blind Signature, a move that received some criticism as hindering the advancement of e-payments. However, this did not stop cypherpunks, who continued using Blind Signature to develop better payment solutions. Ten years after DigiCash went into bankruptcy, Satoshi revealed the birth of Bitcoin to the world. And most of the people on Satoshi's email list were these very cypherpunks. Let's spend a little more time thinking about these cypherpunks, and what exactly they wanted to accomplish. Julian Assange might be a good example of a "distinguished cypherpunk," but he's, not the only one. Cypherpunks share a passion for individual liberty. Assange was passionate about making information available and accessible to the public. Cypherpunks feels the same way about cryptocurrency. They believe private financial transactions should be available to the public, decentralizing the existing banking system, avoiding inflation, and improving security. Cypherpunks also seeks to avoid the calamities that have hit the world economy in recent years. The crisis of 2008 shook global confidence in the ability of governments and major financial institutions to effectively control the economy. To cypherpunks, Bitcoin presented a new hope by proposing a solution that would allow users to avoid the mistakes of the past entirely. But despite the fondest wishes of the cypherpunk crowd back in 2008, Bitcoin and other cryptocurrencies have yet to be accepted as widely as fiat money. Yet, at the same time, Bitcoin has generated tremendous global awareness through its disruptive spirit and its astronomical increase in value. Because its benefits are so clear, and it is so appealing to so many people, many governments are actively trying to establish ways to work with it. Next, I'd like us to consider cryptocurrency against regular currencies by looking at how currencies are issued.

The Development Of Cryptography

For hundreds of years, central banks have been playing one of the most critical roles in the financial system by managing how much money is released into the market, and controlling when this release happens. This is true for fiat money, and also for traditional digital money. In order to be accepted as a legitimate currency, digital money needs to represent value and be able to carry value. As I mentioned earlier, digital money is merely another form of fiat money. It is, essentially, the same thing. It relies on a trusted third party to verify every transaction. Cryptocurrency, however, has no need for a third party. Another way to put this is that it cuts out the middleman. Cryptocurrencies are also different from fiat money in that they are backed up by cryptography. Cryptography has two critical functions, encryption, and verification, which are accomplished through coding and decoding.

Cryptography as a science was widely applied during World War II. Fighting alongside the soldiers of the the allied armies were mathematicians and engineers who used cryptography to wage a silent war of information. As the Germans used their famous Enigma machine to transfer coded orders, allied cryptographers fought against time to decipher it. Today, cryptography is widely applied in a variety of economic functions and situations. Cryptography has become especially useful in computer science, and notably in the area of Internet security. With every single browser click, we interact with pages running on a complicated system of codes. Cryptography secures the input and output of information on these pages.

In the 1970s, the field of cryptography saw major innovations. Whitfield Diffie and Marty Hellman invented the so-called "Diffie and Hellman Key Exchange" in 1976, which enabled modern e-commerce and encrypted communication. In 1977, Ron Rivest, Adi Shamir, and Leonard Adelman came up with the RSA—a powerful encryption engine of great commercial value. And in 1985, Neal Koblit and Victor Miller introduced ECC—an approach to public-key cryptography based on the algebraic structure of elliptic curves over finite fields.

Encryption is the backbone of Internet security, telecommunication, and also of cryptocurrencies like Bitcoin. In their earliest stages, the government had absolute control over encryption algorithms. The NSA kept a close eye on who was using them. It was only in the 1990s that these algorithms were released to the public. Interestingly enough, the NSA is known to have planted backdoor entryways into the technologies released to the public to enable the NSA weaken or disorient certain content at will.

Bitcoin is lucky enough to have avoided the backdoor "way in" planted by the NSA. Satoshi Nakamoto, the father of Bitcoin, went with an algorithm that was not popular enough to be on the NSA's radar. As confirmed by no less than Vitalik Buterin, the founder of Ethereum, Satoshi made many lucky decisions when crafting his creation, and among them was choosing the right algorithm to avoid the traps planted by the NSA. There are only few programs existing today that have been able to successfully avoid the NSA loophole. The sense of security this gives user may be yet another reason for Bitcoin's success. Bitcoin is the best example of the value of blockchain technology. In Satoshi's white paper from 2008, it's made clear that blockchain will be the backbone of the exchange system for Bitcoin users. It will be, as Satoshi puts it, "a purely peer-to-peer version of electronic cash [allowing] online payments to be sent directly from one party to another without going through a financial institution." Using cryptographic technology to secure payment has eliminated the need for banks—or other institutions—to act as middlemen.

So How Does It Work With Bitcoin?

A person making transactions with Bitcoin uses an electronic wallet, which has an IP address containing that person's public "key" and other identification. It is this wallet that allows the person to send and receive Bitcoins, and to document each transaction. Beside the public key, the Bitcoin user also has her or his own private key to which only they have access. This double encryption helps users of Bitcoin to remain anonymous. In order to verify a Bitcoin transaction, users have to contribute computer power to the blockchain to achieve a consensus. Transactions are then documented into blocks spread across the entire chain. One way to think of this is that blockchain allows a permanent record to be kept of each Bitcoin transaction and eliminates the possibility of so-called double payments. Blockchain is essential to Bitcoin and is what allows for the cryptocurrency's decentralization and disintermediation. Each block in the chain nests information that cannot be altered. Trust is created by the technology itself and the way it provides total transparency. But how exactly does blockchain prevent people from cheating or committing fraud? It's a fair question.

I don't want to get too technical here, but cryptography is the key. In the chain of blocks that is the blockchain, every block has something called a Hash Pointer, which points to and reveals the Hash Value contained in the block in the front of the chain. With this Hash Pointer in place, it is impossible to hack the blockchain. Once a block is created and accepted, it is almost impossible to alter. At a primordial, technical level, this means the blocks and the transactions they record are virtually inalterable. We've already discussed some of the issues involved in preserving anonymity when conducting transactions with digital money. Any truly anonymous transaction involves a public key and a private key. However, it also involves a digital signature and asymmetric cryptography, which we should also examine.

The terms might sound complicated, but the concept is not hard to explain. Asymmetric cryptography gives every user two keys, a public key and a private key. The public key presents the identification and the IP address of the account holder. It can also encrypt information. Whatever information the public key encrypts can only be decoded by the matching private key. If a user is using a private key to sign any information, only the matching public key can verify the authenticity of the signature. In this world of decentralization, there is no need for a centralized power like a bank or software company, or government entity to manage or secure any user's information. Users open their accounts and keep their private key. Bitcoin users (and users of any other cryptocurrencies) often use the word address to refer to the Hash Value of the public key. The private key stays in the control of each user. In this way, asymmetric cryptography cuts out the government and any other entities who, in the physical world, collect and manage our identification information to verify transactions. Peer-to-peer network technology was the final element that had to fall into place to ensure the birth of Bitcoin. When most people think of this kind of technology, they think of something like Napster.

Napster, founded by Sean Fanning and Shawn Parker in 1999, was the first music application that allowed people to share music from one computer to another, directly over the Internet. Due to copyright problems and lawsuits, Napster ceased to exist in the first year of the 21st century. Yet despite its ultimate failure, it was important because it proved that peer-to-peer technology works, and that it can be adopted and deployed on a massive scale.

The Birth Of Bitcoin

The nine-page white paper released by Satoshi Nakamoto in October of 2008 starts with the words "A purely peer-to-peer version of electronic cash would allow online payments to be sent directly from one party to another without going through a financial institution." With these words, Satoshi was throwing down the gauntlet. He had identified the problem and also proposed the solution. Bitcoin would be different from other digital money because it would be detached from centralized power.

For his project to work, Satoshi would have to get the world comfortable with the idea of decentralized power. It sounds daunting, but is it really such a radical shift? We experience decentralization in our daily lives each day. We use email all the time, for example, and the Simple Mail Transfer Protocol is a decentralizing system.

But in order to accomplish his goal of promulgating a system based on decentralization, Satoshi knew he would also have to solve the issue of distributed consensus.

What exactly is distributed consensus? The story of the Byzantine Generals has often been used to help explain the concept.

The story goes like this: Byzantium was once the most powerful empire in the world, but it was also very big, extending throughout Europe and Asia. The territory under its control was bigger than the United States. Whenever there was a war, armies were dispatched away from the central government. Each army was led by one general operating independently. The problem was how to ensure that the generals would stay loyal out in the field, and how to detect if a general had become a traitor. Things came to a head when generals were called upon to either make a coordinated attack or make a coordinated retreat. (The consequences of half of the generals doing one, and half the other, would be calamitous.) When the generals communicated with one another and one heard from another that an attack or retreat was called for how would each general know he was, not dealing with a traitor?

Cryptographers encountered the same problem. Namely, how to reach an agreement when there are many "generals" spreading out peer-to-peer information in the blockchain? Satoshi solved the problem of distributed consensus through something called Proof of Work. Simply put, honest work gets rewards. Proof of Work was first tested by Adam Back, a British cryptographer, who in 1996 developed software for fighting off junk emails. The system he designed required every received email to be sent with certain proof of how much time and effort had been put into creating the email. This gave spammers trying to send junk email a headache because they had to put work into meeting the standard in order for their emails to pass the test and land in the targeted recipient's email box. But since, not many people used email back in 1996 (at least not compared to now), the issue of junk spam email didn't get the attention it gets today. Consequently, Back's system did not get a chance to be widely adopted. However, the innovation that his software had created would go on to be very useful in the future.

From an economical point of view, Proof of Work increases the cost of inputting false information. To release a block into the chain of a blockchain takes a considerable amount of computer power. Being the first one to release a block into the system can be very time- and energy-intensive. When you hear about miners "mining Bitcoins," they are actually creating new blocks or verifying new transactions in the chain. The Bitcoin blockchain accordingly rewards these miners through Proof of Work for their efforts.

If 10,000 hours make a person an expert in a certain field as the adage goes then it is the same in the world of Bitcoin, where miners have to prove their work through Hash Function. In addition to being a long process, it's also a very complicated process. Miners need to solve all kinds of mathematical problems. The result of successfully solving those problems is receiving Bitcoins. Whenever a new block in a blockchain is created, the miner will be rewarded with a certain amount of Bitcoins. And when a new piece of transaction is put into blocks, then the miner will be rewarded with a certain amount of Bitcoins depending on who initiated the transaction.

Proof of Work runs in a space where there is no need for "trust" in the traditional sense, because everything is verified by the system. As long as you get your work done, you will be rewarded. It's almost impossible to cheat in this process. There are many types of cryptocurrencies currently using Proof of Work to validate transactions and create new blocks, including Bitcoin, Litecoin, Dogecoin, and Monero.

The more blocks in a chain, the more information released into blocks will make the system more solid and safer, yet at the same time, more energy will be consumed. This vicious cycle of energy consumption puts Proof of Work in an environmentally unfriendly situation. Thus, many seek viable alternatives to it. In this connection, Proof of Stake has emerged as another very popular way of reaching distributed consensus.

Proof of Stake is another way to determine value, but it has a much lower cost of input. Put in simple English, this approach can be summarized as "the rich get richer." Under Proof of Stake, the more Bitcoins you possess, the better the chance you are going to be assigned to solve the block. In Proof of Stake, miners are called validators. Validators needs to deposit a certain amount of cryptocoins to start with. The more they deposit, the better chance they have to solve the new block. Proof of Stake does not need as much as electricity as traditional mining, and it's catching on. For example, Ethereum recently switched from Proof of Work to Proof of Stake.

Highlighting The Important Of Cryptocurrencies

I've never been to Yap, an island in Micronesia, but I've heard that the money there is unique. Islanders on Yap use discs made from limestone as currency. If a disc is too big to move around as many are the owner has only to make a mark on that stone to indicate it has been used to settle a transaction. This is actually a somewhat similar concept to Bitcoin, at least in terms of how each transaction is documented. Marking on a Yap stone disc is not much different from keeping transaction information preserved in a blockchain. The exchange information for Bitcoins (and other cryptocurrencies) is not kept in one central server. Rather, every transaction is documented in each block of a chain. The blockchain spreads out and runs on millions of computers, which makes it hard for anyone to hack, since it is not being kept on any single large database. Rather, information is everywhere, all at the same time. In this way, blockchain is open and accessible to everyone in the Internet at any time. Privacy at least in terms of spending and receiving money is protected by use of the public and private keys. So Bitcoin is the asset of choice for the Internet, and the blockchain is the backbone protecting it by documenting and securing every single transaction.

It's been a decade since Satoshi laid down his vision for Bitcoin and Blockchain. From the early days of cypherpunks and tech nerds circulating a trendy new currency for insiders only, cryptocurrencies are now empowering the general public by providing a new way of participating in and conducting transactions. It may take a while for any cryptocurrency to rival traditional currency, but the idea is no longer science fiction. It could happen within our lifetimes. And if it does, we will realize new efficiencies in all kinds of transactions by undercutting third parties, creating fewer transaction costs, saving time, enjoying better security and safety, and preserving near-total anonymity. Blockchain separated from Bitcoin purely as a technology, is the next Internet.

The Internet brought us into the computer age (or information age) by making everything instant and available at the click of a mouse. Thanks, to the Internet, the world has become flat. Communication across great distances is fast and equal. Blockchain is going to enable us to embrace an even better and more connected world. It will be a world of trustworthiness through transparency, of information 24/7, and of increased openness that allows everybody to be involved. Blockchain opens the gate to new inventions and innovations, new applications, and youthful energy from the next generation. It's new to many of us, and it's also very exciting. With just a bit more patience, I believe we're going to see blockchain unfold even further in important ways during the very near future.

CHAPTER 2

Cryptocurrency Community

The cryptographic currency community is as diverse as the possible viewpoints on the topic. Cryptocurrencies are, as the name suggests, intended to be used as currencies. Therefore, they attract a variety of different people, including technology enthusiasts, businesses and investors, ideologists, researchers, cypherpunks, libertarians, public authorities and policy makers, financial regulators, banks, and also criminals, who exploit anonymity measures and make use of the fact that criminal investigation and de-anonymization techniques are lagging behind. In contrast to that, the distributed nature of Bitcoin-like cryptocurrencies also attracts activists and individuals living in oppressive regimes, as these enable them to manage their digital assets despite political sanctions. This highlights the important role that decentralized currencies can play for inhabitants of such countries.

This composition of the broader Bitcoin community as well as its loose structure, combined with a strong mindset of avoiding trusted single points of failure, might also be one reason why it is sometimes hard to reach consensus regarding the direction of Bitcoin's technological development, as interests might diverge. This book aims to not engage in currently ongoing debates (e.g., regarding the maximum block size) but rather to present a neutral, fact-based introduction to this broad topic. Following the traditional publication spirit of Satoshi Nakamoto, many papers in this field are self-published or made available online as pre-prints prior to their acceptance at scientific journals or conferences. Therefore, we opted to also reference online resources and pre-prints that have not yet been published in peer reviewed venues. The authors are furthermore maintaining a public bibliography where all references that are made in this book can be found.

From Cryptocurrency To Blockchain

Early works in the area of cryptographic currencies or cryptocurrencies mostly focused on required cryptographic primitives as well as the privacy guarantees that could be achieved in such systems. Thereby, these systems themselves still had to rely on trusted third parties (TTPs) to be able to guarantee correct operation. This necessity changed in 2009 when Bitcoin was launched as the first decentralized distributed currency that removed the dependency on TTPs. Bitcoin achieves this through a novel combination of well-known primitives and techniques, such as, for example, proof-of-work (PoW), to eventually establish agreement (or consensus) amongst all nodes on the state of the underlying transaction ledger. The resulting consensus approach, termed Nakamoto consensus, allows for permissionless participation by potentially anonymous actors.

One core element of Bitcoin and Nakamoto consensus is the blockchain. Originally the term blockchain was used to refer to the aggregation and agreement on transactions in an immutable ledger. Now blockchain is used as an umbrella term to refer to all kinds of cryptocurrency technologies. This set of technologies and techniques is also commonly referred to as blockchain technologies. Although the term blockchain is often, not well defined, a rough distinction can be made between permissionless blockchains, where participation in the consensus algorithm, at least in principle, is not restricted, and permissioned blockchain, where there is a closed set of nodes amongst which consensus has to be reached.

The Analog Stone-Block-Chain

Capturing and effectively conveying the basic principles of Bitcoin and other blockchain-based cryptocurrencies to novices, especially those without a technical background, can be a difficult task. When trying to explain the technological innovation and novel approach presented by Bitcoin, you are quickly faced with the problem of having to refer to complex elements such as consensus algorithms and cryptography. This section provides a completely analog example that may be helpful when trying to explain the fundamental mechanisms of blockchain technologies to people without the necessary technological background knowledge. The example of the stone-block-chain replaces Bitcoin's complex components with simple, real-world analogies, and while it is, of course, not able to accurately cover all the details, it should capture the basic ideas. Practicality aside, the described system should help illustrate the basic principles of blockchain-based cryptocurrencies.

Nakamotopia: In a land far away, there is a stone age village called Nakamotopia whose in- habitants are famous for their stone carvers and general obsession with stone blocks. Up until recently, the Nakamotopians relied upon small, round, intricately carved rocks as their currency and medium of exchange. However, crafty individuals found a process that allowed them to easily and quickly carve new rocks and subsequently both the value and trust in the currency was quickly lost in the wake of hyperinflation. In dire need of a new currency, the village elders called for an emergency meeting to discuss the future of the Nakamotopian financial system. Their solution was an ingenious idea for a stone-block-chain that combines the Nakamotopians' obsession with stone blocks and their attraction toward lottery systems. The following three-step scheme was devised, which the Nakamotopians called the block creation ceremony:

Miner selection: Every day, all Nakamotopians meet in the village square. In the first part of the block creation ceremony, every villager puts one small stone, engraved with their (unique) name, into a big wooden box. Thereby, the other villagers oversee the process and check that every villager acts honestly. This box is then placed on a geyser next to the village. During the selection ceremony, all villagers wait for the geyser to erupt and eject steam so that the box containing all the stones is propelled high up into the air and scatters its contents. The villager whose stone lands closest to the geyser wins the lottery and is elected as the miner of the next block.

Transaction processing: After a villager has been selected as miner for that day, she has the duty to collect all transactions from the villagers that have not yet been recorded. The villagers who want to perform transactions queue up in front of the miner to inform her about transactions that should be included in the stone-block-chain. A transaction transfers ownership of a certain number of currency units from one name to another and is only valid if the sender actually has at least as many units as he wants to transfer to the receiver. The only exception to this rule is the first transaction that is engraved into the block, which credits the miner with a predetermined number of units as a reward for her efforts. This special miner transaction is also the only way in which new currency units can be created. At the end of this session, the stone block will contain all the transactions the miner has decided to include. The remaining space of the stone block will be filled with the holy termination symbol 0x00 so that no additional transactions can be added, i.e., engraved, later on without being detected. If someone were to polish the entire surface of the stone block to engrave a completely new set of transactions, this would be detectable, since all blocks must have the same dimensions. During this whole process, the chosen miner is allowed to not includes a particular transaction. If this happens, the person who wants the transaction to be included into a stone block has to wait until the next day and hope that the next miner will include the transaction.

Chaining: After the miner has prepared the current stone block, it is heaved toward the town center. Because of the tremendous size and weight of such a stone block, it takes the combined effort of a large number of villagers to move it at all. If a miner were to engrave invalid transactions or otherwise create a stone block that does not obey the rules that were set out by the elders, no honest villager would help the miner move the block. This ensures that the miner sticks to the rules and does not forfeit her chance to receive the mining reward. Once a valid stone block has been moved by the villagers into the town center, they lift it on top of the towering stack of previous blocks. Only once a block is placed onto this stack is it considered valid by the Nakamotopians.

Stacking the stone blocks has several advantages: Not only does it establish a logical order of transactions, it also makes it much more difficult to change blocks that are further down in the past. An attacker would need to persuade a large number of villagers to start taking off blocks from the top, each requiring a significant amount of time and effort to be removed, which would not remain unnoticed by honest villagers for very long. On the other hand, if a large number of villagers come to the conclusion that one or several blocks should not belong on top of the chain, they can collectively remove these blocks and replace them, thereby ensuring that the majority always agrees upon the contents of their stone-block-chain.

Security Model Of The Stone-Block-Chain

We will now look at the security guarantees such a stone-block-chain can offer and how this analogy relates to the properties current cryptographic currency technologies aim to provide. Public transaction ledger As with Bitcoin, all transactions that take place in Nakamotopia are recorded in a publicly accessible chain of blocks. The key difference here is that Bitcoin is a pseudonymous system, whereas the Nakamotopians uses their real identities in their transactions. Proof-of-Work The basic requirement for a proof-of-work (PoW) should be that it is hard to produce but easy to verify. In Bitcoin, the PoW also functions as a leader election mechanism that randomly selects a new leader, i.e., creator of a valid PoW, on every new block.

In the stone-block-chain analogy, the properties of the proof-of-work are split into three parts.

1. The work that has been put into crafting the blank blocks beforehand and placing the current one at the top of the chain on town square aims to fulfill the "hard to produce" criterion.
2. Once a block has been placed onto the stone-block-chain, it is still easy to verify by reading the transactions engraved onto it and measuring its dimensions to verify that it complies with the rules defining a valid block layout.

3. The geyser in our example works as a random leader-election mechanism on every new stone-block. In Bitcoin, this is achieved through the probabilistic properties of computing a valid PoW for blocks.

Immutability, since every stone block is huge and has precisely defined dimensions, it is unlikely that the effort required for changing a previous stone block in the chain will go unnoticed by several honest Nakamotopians. Even if someone manages to craft a completely new stone block that includes malicious transactions, the effort of replacing an older block in the chain will be detected by some villagers living next to the town square and would also require the collaboration of many dishonest Nakamotopians to be feasible.

In Bitcoin, the blocks are chained together by cryptographic hash functions.

Honest majority Assuming that the majority of villagers are honest, a large portion of the stacked chain of blocks comes from honest villagers and will eventually cease to be in danger of being changed by malicious villagers. Initially there is a slight chance that some of the topmost blocks that have been added to the chain came from malicious villagers while the larger portion of honest Nakamotopians were occupied with other, more pressing issues. Once they returns, this honest majority can set about removing the invalid blocks and start replacing them. On the other hand, it takes time for the minority of dishonest villagers to remove or add blocks and both can be quickly detected by any honest villager. If there are enough new stone blocks stacked upon a particular block, it would take the dishonest villagers many days to remove them, making such an attack very unlikely to succeed. Therefore, stone blocks that have been included far enough in the past (i.e., lower in the chain) can be considered agreed upon. Bitcoin blocks that have a high number of confirmations, i.e., blocks appended after them, are unlikely to change and can, therefore, be considered agreed upon. Although the number of confirmation blocks depends on the value of the transaction in question, common wisdom is that six confirmation blocks are enough to consider a past transaction secure.

Is Cryptocurrency The New Money?

As noted above, cryptocurrency acts as money in an electronic payment system in which a network of computers, rather than a single third-party intermediary, validates transactions. In general, these electronic payment systems use public ledgers that allow individuals to establish an account with a pseudonymous name known to the entire network or an address corresponding to a public key and a passcode or private key that is paired to the public key and known only to the account holder. A transaction occurs when two parties agree to transfer cryptocurrency (perhaps in payment for a good or service) from one account to another. The buying party will unlock the cryptocurrency they will use as payment with their private key, allowing the selling party to lock it with their private key. In general, to access the cryptocurrency system, users will create a "wallet" with a third-party cryptocurrency exchange or service provider. From the perspective of the individuals using the system, the mechanics are similar to authorizing payment on any website that requires an individual to enter a username and password. In addition, certain companies offer applications or interfaces that users can download onto a device to make transacting in cryptocurrencies more user-friendly.

Cryptocurrency platforms often use blockchain technology to validate changes to the ledgers. Blockchain technology uses cryptographic protocols to prevent invalid alteration or manipulation of the public ledger. Specifically, before any transaction is entered into the ledger and the ledger is irreversibly changed, some member of the network must validate the transaction. In certain cryptocurrency platforms, validation requires the member to solve an extremely difficult computational decryption. Once the transaction is validated, it is entered into the ledger.

The History Of Money;

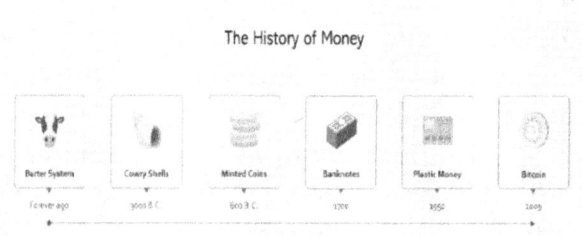

These protocols secure each transaction by using digital signatures to validate the identity of the two parties involved and to validate that the entire ledger is secure so that any changes in the ledger are visible to all parties. In this system, parties that otherwise do not know each other can exchange something of value (i.e., a digital currency) not because they trust each other but because they trust the platform and its cryptographic protocols to prevent double spending and invalid changes to the ledger.

Cryptocurrency platforms often incentivize users to perform the functions necessary for validation by awarding them newly created units of the currency for successful computations (often the first person to solve the problem is given the new units), although in some cases the payer or payee also is charged a fee that goes to the validating member. In general, the rate at which new units are created and therefore the total amount of currency in the system is limited by the platform protocols designed by the creators of the cryptocurrency. These limits create scarcity with the intention of ensuring the cryptocurrency retains value. Because users of the cryptocurrency platform must perform work to extract the scarce unit of value from the platform, much as people do with precious metals, it is said that these users mine the cryptocurrencies. Alternatively, people can acquire cryptocurrency on certain exchanges that allow individuals to purchase cryptocurrency using official government-backed currencies or other cryptocurrencies.

Cryptographers and computer scientists generally agree that cryptocurrency ledgers that use blockchain technology are mathematically secure and that it would be exceedingly difficult approaching impossible to manipulate them. However, hackers have exploited vulnerabilities in certain exchanges and individuals' devices to steal cryptocurrency from the exchange or individual.

Basis Of Money

Money exists because it serves a useful economic purpose: it facilitates the exchange of goods and services. Without it, people would have to engage in a barter economy, wherein people trade goods, and services for other goods and services. In a barter system, every exchange requires a double coincidence of wants each party must possess the exact good or be offering the exact service that the other party wants. Anytime a potato farmer wanted to buy meat or clothes or have a toothache treated, the farmer would have to find a particular rancher, tailor, or dentist who wanted potatoes at that particular time and negotiate how many potatoes a side of beef, a shirt, and a tooth removal were worth. In turn, the rancher, tailor, and dentist would have to make the same search and negotiation with each other to satisfy their wants. Wants are satisfied more efficiently if all members of a society agree they will accept money a mutually recognized representation of value for payment, be that ounces of gold, a government-endorsed slip of paper called a dollar, or a digital entry in an electronic ledger.

How well something serves as money depends on how well it serves as (1) a medium of exchange, (2) a unit of account, and (3) a store of value.

To function as a medium of exchange, the thing must be tradable, and agreed to have value. To function as unit of account, the thing must act as a good measurement system. To function as a store of value, the thing must be able to purchase approximately the same value of goods and services at some future date as it can purchase now.

Returning to the example above, could society decide potatoes are money? Conceivably, yes. A potato has intrinsic value (this report will examine value in more detail in the following section, "Traditional Money"), as it provides nourishment. However, a potato's tradability is limited: many people would find it impractical to carry around sacks of potatoes for daily transactions or to buy a car for many thousands of pounds of potatoes. A measurement system based on potatoes is also problematic. Each potato has a different size and degree of freshness, so to say something is worth "one potato" is imprecise and variable. In addition, a potato cannot be divided without changing its value. Two halves of potato are worth less than a whole potato the exposed flesh will soon turn brown and rot so people would be unlikely to agree to prices in fractions of potato. The issue of freshness also limits potatoes' ability to be a store of value; a potato eventually sprouts eyes and spoils, and so must be spent quickly or it will lose value.

In contrast, an ounce of gold and a dollar bill can be carried easily in a pocket and thus are tradeable. Each unit is identical and can be divided into fractions of an ounce or cents, respectively, making both gold and dollars effective units of account. Gold is an inert metal and a dollar bill, when well cared for, will not degrade substantively for years, meaning can both function as a store of value. Likewise, with the use of digital technology, electronic messages to change entries in a ledger can be sent easily by swiping a card or pushing a button and can be denominated in identical and divisible units. Those units could have a stable value, as their number stays unchanging in an account on a ledger. The question becomes how does a lump of metal, a thing called a dollar, and the numbers on a ledger come to be deemed valuable by society, as has been accomplished in traditional monetary systems.

Traditional Money

Money has been in existence throughout history. However, how that money came to have value, how it was exchanged, and what roles government and intermediaries such as banks have played have changed over time. This section examines three different monetary systems with varying degrees of government and bank involvement.

No Or Limited Role For A Central Authority: Intrinsic Value

Early forms of money were often things that had intrinsic value, such as precious metals (e.g., copper, silver, gold). Part of their value was derived from the fact that they could be worked into aesthetically pleasing objects. More importantly, other physical characteristics of these metals made them well suited to perform the three functions of money and so created the economic efficiency societies needed: these metals are elemental and thus an amount of the pure material is identical to a different sample of the same amount; they are malleable and thus easy divisible, and they are chemically inert and thus do not degrade. In addition, they are scarce and difficult to extract from the earth, which is vital to them having and maintaining value. Sand also could perform the functions of money and can be worked into aesthetically pleasing glass. However, if sand were money, then people would quickly gather vast quantities of it and soon even low-cost goods would be priced at huge amounts of sand.

Even when forms of money had intrinsic value, governments played a role in assigning value to money. For example, government mints would make coins of precious metals with a government symbol, which validated that these particular samples were of some verified amount and purity. Fiat money takes the government role a step further, as discussed below.

Government Authority: Fiat Money

In contrast to money with intrinsic value, fiat money has no intrinsic value but instead derives its value by government decree. If a government is sufficiently powerful and credible, it can declare that some thing a dollar, euro, a yen, for example shall be money. In practice, these decrees can take several forms, but generally they involve a mandate that the money be used for some economic activity, such as paying taxes or settling debts. Thus, if members of society want to participate in the relevant economic activities, it behooves them to accept the money as payment in their dealings.

In addition, to such decrees, the government generally controls the supply of the money to ensure it is sufficiently scarce to retain value yet in ample-enough supply to facilitate economic activity. Relatedly, the government generally attempts to minimize the incidence of counterfeiting by making the physical money in circulation difficult to replicate and creating a deterrence through criminal punishment.

Modern monies are generally fiat money, including the U.S. dollar. The dollar is legal tender in the United States, meaning parties are obligated to accept the dollar to settle debts, and U.S. taxes can (and generally must) be paid in dollars. This status instills dollars with value, because anyone who wants to undertake these basic economic activities in the largest economy and financial system in the world must have and use this type of money.

In the United States, the Board of Governors of the Federal Reserve System maintains the value of the dollar by setting monetary policy. Congress mandated that the Federal Reserve would conduct monetary policy in the Federal Reserve Reform Act of 1977 (P.L. 95-188), directing it to "maintain long run growth of the monetary and credit aggregates commensurate with the economy's long run potential to increase production, so as to promote effectively the goals of maximum employment, stable prices, and moderate long-term interest rates."

Under this system, money stock currently exceeding $15 trillion circulates in support of an economy that generates over $21 trillion worth of new production a year, and average annual inflation has not exceeded a rate of 3% since 1993.1

In addition, the Federal Reserve operates key electronic payment systems, including those involving interbank transfers. In this way, the Federal Reserve acts as the intermediary when banks transfer money between each other.

Banks: Transferring Value Through Intermediaries

Banks have played a role in another evolution of money: providing an alternative to the physical exchange of tangible currency between two parties. Verifying the valid exchange of physical currency is relatively easy. The payer shows the payee he or she is in fact in possession of the money, and the transfer is valid the moment the money passes into the payee's possession. This system is not without problems, though. Physically possessing money subjects it to theft, misplacement, or destruction through accident. A physical exchange of money typically requires the payer and payee be physically near each other (because both parties would have to have a high degree of trust in each other to believe any assurance that the money will be brought or sent later).

From early in history, banks have offered services to accomplish valid transfers of value between parties who are not in physical proximity and do not necessarily trust each other. Customers give banks their money for, among other reasons, secure safekeeping and the ability to send payment to a payee located somewhere else (originally using paper checks or bills of exchange). Historically and today, maintaining accurate ledgers of accounts is a vital tool for providing these services. It allows people to hold money as numerical data stored in a ledger instead of as a physical thing that can be lost or stolen. In the simplest form, a payment system works by a bank recording how much money an individual has access to and, upon instruction, making appropriate additions and reductions to that amount.

The mechanics of the modern payment system, in which instructions are sent and records are stored electronically, are covered in more detail in the following section, "The Electronic Exchange of Money." What can be noted here in this basic description is that participants must trust the banks and that ledgers must be accurate and must be changed only for valid transfers. Otherwise, an individual's money could be lost or stolen if a bank records the payer's account as having an inaccurately low amount or transfers value without permission. A number of mechanisms can create trust in banks. For example, a bank has a market incentive to be accurate, because a bank that does not have a good reputation for protecting customers' money and processing transactions accurately will lose customers. In addition, governments typically subject banks to laws and regulations designed in part to ensure that banks are run well and that people's money is safe in them. As such, banks take substantial measures to ensure security and accuracy.

The Electronic Exchange of Money

Today, money is widely exchanged electronically, but electronic payments systems can be subject to certain difficulties related to lack of scarcity (a digital file can be copied many times over, retaining the exact information as its predecessor) and lack of trust between parties. Electronic transfers of money are subject to what observers refer to as the double spending problem. In an electronic transfer of money, a payer may wish to send a digital file directly to a payee in the hopes that the file will act as a transfer of value. However, if the payee cannot confirm that the payer has not sent the same file to multiple other payees, the transfer is problematic. Because money in such a system could be double (or any number of times) spent, the money would not retain its value.

As described in the preceding section, this problem traditionally has been resolved by involving at least one centralized, trusted intermediary such as a private bank, government central bank, or other financial institution in electronic transfers of money. The trusted intermediaries maintain private ledgers of accounts recording how much money each participant holds. To make a payment, an electronic message (or messages) is sent to an intermediary or to and between various intermediaries, instructing each to make the necessary changes to its ledgers. The intermediary or intermediaries validate the transaction, ensure the payer has sufficient funds for the payment, deduct the appropriate amount from the payer's account, and add that amount to the payee's account. For example, in the United States, a retail consumer may initiate an electronic payment through a debit card transaction, at which time an electronic message is sent over a network instructing the purchaser's bank to send payment to the seller's bank. That banks then make the appropriate changes to their account ledgers (possibly using the Federal Reserve's payment system) reflecting that value has been transferred from the purchaser's account to the seller's account.

Significant costs and physical infrastructure underlie systems for electronic money transfers to ensure the systems' integrity, performance, and availability. For example, payment system providers operate and maintain vast electronic networks to connect retail locations with banks, and the Federal Reserve operates and maintains networks to connect banks to itself and each other. These intermediaries store and protect huge amounts of data. In general, these intermediaries are highly regulated to ensure safety, profitability, consumer protection, and financial stability. Intermediaries recoups the costs associated with these systems and earn profits by charging fees directly when the system is used (such as the fees a merchant pays to have a card reading machine and on each transaction) or by charging fees for related services (such as checking account fees).

In addition, intermediaries generally are required to provide certain protections to consumers involved in electronic transactions. For example, the Electronic Fund Transfer Act (P.L. 95-630) limits consumers' liability for unauthorized transfers made using their accounts. Similarly, the Fair Credit Billing Act (P.L. 93-495) requires credit card companies to take certain steps to correct billing errors, including when the goods or services a consumer purchased are not delivered as agreed. Both acts also require financial institutions to make certain disclosures to consumers related to the costs and terms of using an institution's services. Notably, certain individuals may lack access to electronic payment systems. To use an electronic payment system, a consumer or merchant generally must have access to a bank account or some retail payment service, which some may find cost prohibitive or geographically inconvenient, resulting in underbanked or unbanked populations (i.e., people who have limited interaction with the traditional banking system). In addition, the consumer or merchant typically must provide the bank or other intermediaries with personal information. The use of electronic payment services generates a huge amount of data about an individual's financial transactions. This information could be accessed by the bank, law enforcement (provided proper procedures are followed), or nefarious actors (provided they are capable of circumventing the intermediaries' security measures).

Cryptocurrencies such as Bitcoin, Ether, and Litecoin provide an alternative to this traditional electronic payment system.

The Price and Usage of Cryptocurrency

Analyzing data about certain characteristics and the use of cryptocurrency would be helpful in measuring how well cryptocurrency functions as an alternative source of payment and thus its future prospects for functioning as money. However, conducting such an analysis currently presents challenges. The decentralized nature of cryptocurrencies makes identifying authoritative sources of industry data difficult. In addition, the recent proliferation of cryptocurrency adds additional challenges to performing industry wide analysis. For example, as of March 10, 2020, one industry group purported to track 5,170 cryptocurrencies trading at prices that suggest an aggregate value in circulation of more than $231 billion.

Because of these challenges, an exhaustive quantitative analysis of the entire cryptocurrency industry is beyond the scope of this report. Instead, the report uses Bitcoin the first and most well-known cryptocurrency, the total value of which accounts for almost two-thirds of the industry as a whole as an illustrative example. Examining recent trends in Bitcoin prices, value in circulation, and number of transactions may shed some light on how well cryptocurrencies in general have been performing as an alternative payment system. The rapid appreciation in cryptocurrencies' value in 2017 likely contributed to the recent increase in public interest in these currencies. At the beginning of 2017, the price of a Bitcoin on an exchange was about $993.43 The price surged during the year, peaking at about $19,650 in December 2017, an almost 1,880% increase from prices in January 2017. However, the price then dramatically declined by 65% to $6,905 in less than two months. Since that time, the price of a Bitcoin remained volatile. Other major cryptocurrencies, such as Ether and Litecoin, have had similar price movements.

As of March 9, 2020, the price of one Bitcoin was $7,945 and approximately 18.3 million Bitcoins were in circulation, making the value of all Bitcoins in existence about $144 billion. Although these statistics drive interest in and are central to the analysis of cryptocurrencies as investments, they reveal little about the prevalence of cryptocurrencies' use as money. Recent volatility in the price of cryptocurrencies suggests they function poorly as a unit of account and a store of value, an issue covered in the "Potential Challenges to Widespread Adoption" section of this report. Nevertheless, the price or the exchange rate of a currency in dollars at any point in time (rather than over time) does not have a substantive influence on how well the currency serves the functions of money. The number of Bitcoin transactions, by contrast, can serve as an indicator though a flawed one of the prevalence of the use of Bitcoin as money. This number indicates how many times a day Bitcoins are transferred between accounts. One industry data source indicates that the number of Bitcoin transactions averaged about 328,000 per days globally in 2019. This is a very small number in comparison to established electronic payment networks. For example, the Automated Clearing House an electronic payments network operated by the Federal Reserve Bank and the private company Electronic Payments Networkprocessed more than 69 million transactions per day on average in the fourth quarter of 2019. Visa's payments systems processed on average nearly 379 million transactions per day globally in 2019

Cryptocurrency Values

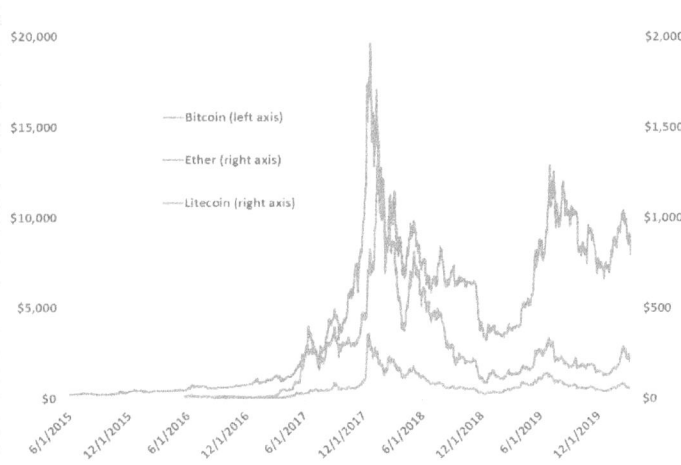

CHAPTER 3

Components of Cryptocurrency Technologies

There exist multiple approaches to decompose cryptocurrency technologies. Many described cryptocurrencies by separating them into different plains like network plane, consensus plane, storage plane, view plane, and a side plane. Inspired by this approach, it is decided to decompose cryptocurrencies on a two-level basis. On the first level we introduce a rough separation into two main components. On the second level, those two main components are decomposed into different subsystems. To avoid confusion with the "plains" concept defined in or the "layers" of the OSI model we use the terms components and subsystems in this context.

The operation of Bitcoin and most other cryptocurrencies can be broken down into two main components:

(I) Consensus management encompasses everything that is consensus relevant, e.g., consensus algorithms and communication aspects.

(II) Digital asset management refers to all applications that build upon the agreed state and act upon it, e.g., key and transaction management. For a more fine-grained separation, both main components can be divided into multiple subsystems.

- Consensus management component
  - Network subsystem
  - Storage subsystem
  - Consensus algorithm subsystem
- Digital asset management component
  - Key management subsystem
  - Transaction management subsystem

With this separation into two main components, it is also possible to view such systems as distributed operating systems with applications running on top of them. In this analogy the consensus management component can be viewed as the operating system which provides services (e.g., syscalls) to userland applications, i.e., the digital asset management component. This view highlights that both components can be replaced independently of each other. For example, if someone wants to use a different software for storing and using the public and secret key pairs related to her coins (i.e., a wallet) this would be possible without consensus critical changes. In other words, this would be the equivalent of changing the digital asset management component, which would not affect the other components as long as they can still communicate with each other, e.g., a wallet can run on any current instance of Bitcoin.

Distributed Network;

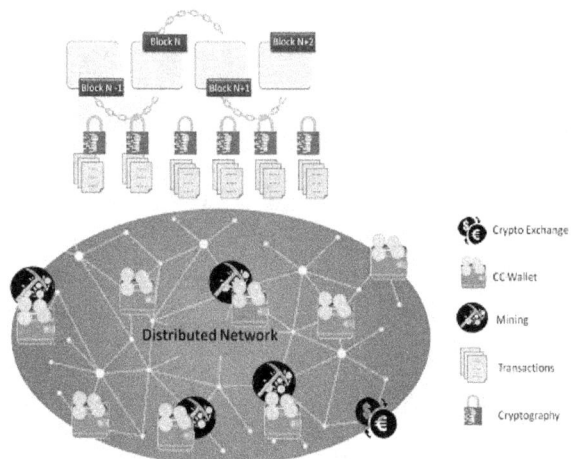

To the contrary, the subsystems within one component cannot be directly replaced without potentially influencing each other. For example, replacing the P2P networking implementation of Bitcoin with a different gossiping protocol would not directly touch the code on how to reach agreement, and hence the basic rules of Nakamoto consensus, however this change could alter message propagation times which in turn directly influence the achievable security and liveness properties of the consensus algorithm. Therefore, the subsystems are more contextualization to describe different parts more independently of each other.

Core Data Structures and Concepts

Addresses, transactions, and blocks are the three basic data structures used in Bitcoin. The need for these specific data structures arose from the fact that Bitcoin was designed as a distributed digital currency. All cryptographic currencies that are based on Bitcoin, whether they are direct forks of it (e.g., Namecoin, Litecoin, Zcash) or just conceptually based on it (e.g., Ethereum), also include variants of these core data structures with some small modifications. This section describes those structures and shows how they interlink with each other to outline the basic concepts of a cryptographic currency. Because of the data-centric view, the details on how consensus is reached in Bitcoin is deferred. For simplicity's sake, we assume in this section that the order of the blocks in the chain is agreed upon by every client and that each client knows at least the current head of the chain.

Over the lifetime of Bitcoin, there have been minor changes in the exact representation and interpretation of core data structures, e.g., the interpretation of the Version (nVersion) value of the block header, which originally just represented an increasing version number and is now interpreted as a bit vector so that miners can indicate whether they support features that require a soft fork. Most of the described constructs in this section have not been subject to major changes in the past.

Block Structure;

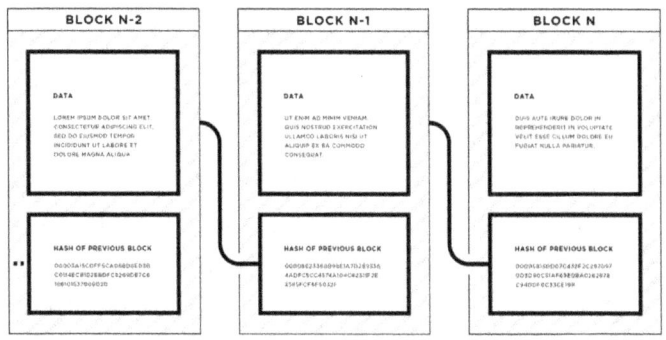

In this section, we focus on the core components and fundamentals of the Bitcoin protocol in a generalized way irrespective of the exact protocol version. The information presented here is intended as a practical example to illustrate the general concepts of cryptographic currencies.

For up-to-date details, we recommend consulting the Bitcoin developer guide, the respective Bitcoin improvement proposals (BIPs), and the source code of the reference implementation.

BLOCK

The most fundamental data structure in Bitcoin is a block. A block consists of a block header and the transactions associated with the respective block. These blocks are chained together by including cryptographic hashes of their predecessors to form a linked list commonly referred to as a blockchain. The current state of currency is represented by the order of the blocks in the chain. They represent a ledger of all performed transactions, in which the transactions are processed sequentially depending on their position in the block in which they occur.

Block Header

It shows the different fields of the block header (80 bytes) and the associated list of transactions. The most important field of the block header from the integrity point of view is the HashPrevBlock. It contains a cryptographic hash (SHA256) of the previous block in the chain. This ensures that the blocks are chained together to form an immutable data structure. The integrity of this blockchain can be checked by anyone who has access to the head, i.e., the last block in the chain. A client that has stored only the last block can verify that the chain up to this point has not been altered. Therefore, he requests all previous blocks of interest and recreates the hash chain up to the last block. If the final block hash matches, no past blocks have been changed after their inclusion into the chain.

The ordering of the list of transactions linked to every block is also vital, as they are processed in sequential order. This permits, for example, that the same funds can be moved several times by sequential transactions, all of which are associated with the same block. All transactions associated with a block are tied to the respective block via a Merkle tree root hash that is included in the block header (i.e., HashMerkleRoot). For a simplified explanation, it is also possible to think of this field as a hash value over all transactions. If the content of one transaction would be changed after linking it to a block header, this would be detectable due to the change in the Merkle tree root hash.

Bitcoin block header (80 bytes) and its associated transactions;

Block Header;

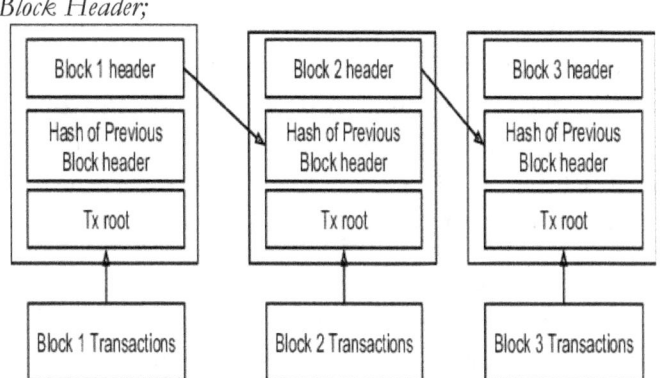

BLOCKCHAIN

The term blockchain, although not directly introduced by Satoshi Nakamoto in the original paper, is commonly used as an umbrella term to refer to concepts related to cryptographic currency technologies. There are two common spellings throughout the literature for this term, i.e., blockchain and blockchain. Although the later variant was used by Satoshi Nakamoto in a comment within the source code, the first one has been used frequently in recent academic literature. Therefore, we stick to this variant within this book. As with the spelling, there are also multiple definitions of the term blockchain. Therefore, we provide two possible interpretations for this term in this book: (I) the academic interpretation and (II) the colloquial interpretation.

Academic Interpretation

Since multiple definitions of the term blockchain also exist in the academic context, this book outlines several of those interpretations. The first definition is a broad one that is independent of the underlying consensus algorithm. Therefore it is applicable to all kinds of different types of blockchains and most accurately covers the broader usage of this term. We call this definition the Princeton definition, since it was first introduced informally in the Princeton Bitcoin book. We provide this definition more explicitly in this section.

The second set of definitions is more formal and also includes consensus related aspects. They are the result of various approaches toward more formally modeling such systems and include works. These works do not necessarily define the term blockchain directly. Kiayias et al. for instance use the term transaction ledger for their definition while Pass et al. use the term abstract definition. The evolution and details of these more formal analyses are outlined. For the remaining sections, up to but not including the entirety of the section, the Princeton definition as provided is sufficient to understand the concepts and follow the explanations.

A blockchain, according to the Princeton Definition, is defined as a linked list data structure, that uses hash sums over its elements as pointers to the respective elements.

By this definition, the construction of a blockchain ensures that as long as someone has stored or retrieved the correct block at the head of the chain, he is able to verify all other blocks of the chain when provided in their entirety.

Colloqoquial Interpretation

Colloquially the term blockchain refers to the category of distributed systems that are built using blockchain/cryptographic currency technologies, e.g., hash chains, asymmetric cryptography, game theory, etc. By this interpretation there exist two different versions of blockchains, namely: permissionless and permissioned blockchain.

Permissionless blockchains the central property of this type of blockchain is that the set of nodes, amongst which consensus over the state of the chain should be reached, is unknown. Vukolić et al. refers to this type as proof-of-work (POW) blockchains as permissioned blockchain The central property of this type of blockchain is that the set of nodes, amongst which consensus over the state of the chain should be reached, is known. Vukolic et al. refers to this type as Byzantine Fault Tolerant (BFT) blockchains. Further distinction can be made between permissioned blockchains and private blockchain regarding the composition and selection of the set of nodes.

ADDRESS

At the most basic level, Bitcoin addresses, like the addresses of many other cryptographic currencies, are cryptographic hashes of public keys. Therefore, each address actually consists of a public and a private part. The public part is the address, which can be compared to an account number in ordinary online banking. The private part is the corresponding secret key, which can be compared to the password or signature required to withdraw money from an ordinary savings account. Addresses can be generated by anybody as easily as public/private key pairs. This allows everyone to accept Bitcoins by handing out the public address without any deeper knowledge of the Bitcoin protocol itself or its consensus mechanisms.

In Bitcoin, addresses are an Elliptic Curve Digital Signature Algorithm (ECDSA) public/private key pair. More precisely, Bitcoin uses the elliptic curve secp256k1 specified and recommended by Certicom. To create a human-processable Bitcoin address, the public part is encoded as described in the Algorithm. In the process, the public key is hashed multiple times. Thereby, two different hash functions are used, i.e., RIPEMD160 and SHA256.

TRANSACTION

Transactions are used to transfer currency units from one address to another. They can be created by any entity that is in possession of currency units, i.e., bitcoins. Possession in this context means control over the private key of the respective address (i.e., public key) that currently holds the currency units that are to be transferred, i.e., an address that has received transactions in the past.

A transaction in Bitcoin consists of one or multiple inputs and one or multiple outputs. An input unlocks a previous output by providing a valid cryptographic signature. Thereby, the inputs serve as proof that the holder of the respective Bitcoin address that previously received the bitcoins is also in possession of the required private key. The private key is needed to generate the signature that unlocks the funds so that they can be used, i.e., transferred to another Bitcoin address.

For example, if Alice wants to transfer 5 bitcoins to Bob, she first requires Bob's Bitcoin address. For our example, we assume that this address is transferred over some trusted communication channel, e.g., displayed as payment information while shopping on a website that uses a valid certificate for TLS encryption. Alice places Bob's address in the output of the transaction she is constructing together with the number of coins she wants to transfer to this account, i.e. In the next step, Alice needs to prove that she is in possession of the required number of bitcoins and that she wants to transfer them to Bob. Therefore, Alice searches the blockchain for previous transactions where bitcoins were sent to addresses that are under her control, i.e., where she is in possession of the corresponding private keys. She then unlocks as many of these previous transactions as needed to cover the desired output of 5 bitcoins. In our example, she uses two previous transactions (outputs) for this, consisting of 4 and 3 bitcoins. Referring to the respective previous transactions, Alice creates an input in the current transaction for every output she wants to unlock. These inputs uniquely identify previous outputs by their transaction ID and number. To unlock those outputs, she has to prove that she is the rightful owner, which she does by providing cryptographic signatures along with every input. Alice now adds an output to the transaction which transfers 5 bitcoins to Bobs Bitcoin address. Since the two unlocked inputs sum up to more than the desired value of 5 bitcoins, Alice adds another output for transferring the change of 2 bitcoins back to a Bitcoin address that is under her control. As soon as the transaction is constructed, Alice broadcasts it to the Bitcoin peer- to-peer network and waits until it is included in a newly generated block. Once the transaction is included at the head of the blockchain, the transaction is called confirmed. The number of confirmations is defined by the number of blocks that build on top of the block that contains the transaction.

Transaction Validation

Generally a transaction in Bitcoin is considered valid if the following criteria hold:

- All unlocked inputs have not been spent (i.e., unlocked and used) in a previous transaction.
- All cryptographic signatures in the inputs are valid.
- The sum of all values unlocked in the inputs is greater than or equal to the sum of all values specified in the outputs of the transaction.

Blockchain Transformation—From 1.0 To 2.0

Will machines ever actually take over the world? Perhaps no one can say for sure. But the machines we create today are on many levels no different from the crude tools that were being created in the first days of human civilization.

What they share is an attempt to push the present into the future in hopes of creating something better. We are giving more power to the machine, and in return, we hope that the machine will make our lives easier and better.

At this stage, we have probably passed a "point of no return" when it comes to relying on technology. Blockchain does not exist if there is no power to supply computers or if there is no access to computers themselves. But is this really such a problem? To be honest, can we really live without our smartphones for a day? Technically, yes. But we'll probably feel terrible. We will want our smartphones back. We are dependent on the machines and the technology we have created, and that's okay.

Can you imagine the lives people had in the early 19th century before electricity was available? Can you even imagine life before people had TV? What about life before the Internet, smartphones, social media, and search engines? While many of you reading this may be able to remember that last one, would you actually want to live like that once more? Really? We cannot go back. We must march forward with technology.

If digital money was a gesture toward advancing the existing currency system, Bitcoin was the real breakthrough. Blockchain supports Bitcoin (and other cryptocurrencies) by storing all the transaction information into the chain (to avoid double spending and provide total transparency). It is also a decentralizing force that reshapes the power structure of regulation.

Essentially, blockchain is a database, a database that's distributed throughout the world instead of held on a central server. All transactions put into the block are validated by all the notes in the blockchain. It eliminates the need for trust by providing verification. It is impossible to change a block in the blockchain once is it created (and added to the public chain). Therefore, to fool the blockchain, you would need to control over 51 percent of the notes a feat that could technically be done, but whose cost would be unbearable.

The Types Of Blockchain

Depending on its uses, blockchain can be placed into one of three categories: a public blockchain, a private blockchain, or a consortium blockchain.

A public blockchain is basically open to everyone in the world. Everyone can participate in it and can and be part of the validation process for transactions. Data on a public blockchain are likewise accessible to everyone. Reaching a distributed consensus on this type of blockchain makes the whole system run transparently and securely. Examples of public blockchains is Bitcoin and Ethereum.

Private blockchains, in contrast, are usually built by large companies for their own use alone. In contrast to a public blockchain (which runs without the need for trust), a private blockchain relies very much on trust among authorized people who have been granted access. Unlike the decentralization offered with a public blockchain, this type of blockchain is centralized, with access provided only to a limited number of users. You might think of this category as a kind of customized "blockchain on demand." Many different institutes and organizations have designed private blockchains based on their unique needs and will continue to do so in the future.

Finally, a consortium blockchain is a sort of subtype of private blockchain. You might say that it's in between a public blockchain and a private blockchain partially decentralized. It enables two companies to share data that have been separately saved on each private blockchain.

These three types of blockchains find their best uses in different situations. Public blockchain creates a decentralized environment for information to flow without barriers. Private blockchain and consortium blockchains are more efficient in terms of privacy and purpose but are most applicable to organizations and companies that need their information made available only within certain limits.

SMART CONTRACT

So far, we have covered the basics of Bitcoin and blockchain. I hope I've given you the general sense that the blockchain for Bitcoin is sort of the "first generation" of blockchain. We could call it Blockchain 1.0. Ethereum and the smart contract are pushing blockchain into the next stage: Blockchain 2.0. Smart contract is critical to applying blockchain into broader use, so let's explore it further.

The computer scientist and cryptographer Nick Szabo first proposed the smart contract concept in a paper published in 1994. (It is worth noting that Szabo has been bandied about as the possible true identity of Satoshi, something he has denied.)

The smart contract created by Szabo is a computer system designed to facilitate and verify contracts between parties and people. The cryptocurrency Ethereum is a decentralized platform that runs smart contracts and allows developers to build their apps on the blockchain created by Ethereum. Smart contract is key in Ethereum, since it finally allows cryptocurrencies to be used in broader business activities. The smart contract can function in the absence of trust because it executes terms without intervention from the parties involved. Once a smart contract is generated, it cannot be reversed. Transactions is traceable but irreversible. A smart contract works on an "if-then" language. If A happens, then B will take place. So once a contract is set up, the terms will be executed automatically.

Vending Machine As Physical Smart Contract"

An example often used to help explain smart contracts is a vending machine. Everyone knows how they work. You go to a vending machine and put in a certain amount of money; in return, the machine dispenses a product. Say a vending machine sells sodas for $.25. Bob puts a quarter into the machine, and in return, it spits out a soda. Alice puts a dollar into the same machine, and it spits back $.75 and a soda.

Not a hard concept, right? Well, smart contract on blockchain functions similarly.

Smart contract on blockchain involves three steps:
1. Parties involved in the contract reach a consensus and formulate a smart contract.
2. The parties put the contract into the blockchain through a peer-to-peer network.
3. The smart contract is put into motion once it's accepted into the blockchain.

Let's look at a real-world example. Say I would like to lease my apartment to you. You, as renter, pay me an advance in Bitcoins through a blockchain. Once the transaction is done, I receive the payment. You will then get a contract and receipt. And I, as landlord, will give you a key to enter the apartment within a certain period of time. If the key is not delivered to you on time, the blockchain will return the advance to you. If the key is delivered before the agreed date, the blockchain will temporarily hold the key until you pay the advance.

The system works on these if-then propositions, and everyone on the blockchain is able to see the contract we've both agreed upon. Therefore, nobody has to worry about the authenticity of the contract. And after the rental period is over, the contract will be automatically terminated once the terms have been fulfilled.

Just as Bitcoin is decentralizing currency and business transactions, smart contract has the potential to decentralize the entire contract market. Assets in digital format are now able to be exchanged and traded in blockchain by adopting smart contract, so all kinds of interesting trades can happen on blockchain. Smart contract broadens the potential use of blockchain dramatically potentially bringing in almost the entire contractual landscape. And in my opinion, it's just getting started.

Ethereum: Redemption And Birth Of Blockchain 2.0

Vitalik Buterin is a name almost everyone in computer science, blockchain, and cryptocurrency is familiar with. His white paper, "Ethereum: A Next-Generation Cryptocurrency and Decentralized Application Platform," released in Bitcoin Magazine back in 2014, put him into the spotlight. At just 19 years old, he totally disrupted the existing crypto world.

One way to understand his innovation Ethereum is to appreciate how it aims to replace third parties on the Internet through the use of blockchain. What are third parties on the Internet? They're services like Google, Facebook, and Apple that hold our personal data, financial data, and professional data on their servers. The importance of replacing third parties is all about security. The third parties makes it easier for hackers to hack, since everyone's data are all in one place (or in just a few places). Also, under a third-party system, governments may be able to access your files without your knowledge.

Ethereum is an open software platform based on blockchain technology that developers can use to build and deploy decentralized applications. The first generation of applications on blockchain is, admittedly, quite limited. The blockchain Bitcoin uses merely focuses on transactions (and tracking of transactions) using Bitcoins. The use of first-generation blockchain is also very narrowly defined. However, Ethereum is offering a public blockchain that goes beyond a peer-to-peer electronic cash system. By implementing smart contracts, the use of blockchain has the potential to expand beyond cryptocurrency. Anything of value can now is exchanged with and through smart contracts. Agreements and exchanges of every sort can theoretically run on Ethereum.

Apps built using Ethereum are called DAPPs. Developers create their DAPPs using smart contracts. In keeping with the theme of decentralization, DAPPs are all decentralized and are not owned by individuals or organizations. Rather, they are owned by multiple people specifically, everyone on the blockchain.

Despite these innovations, it hasn't all been wine and roses. In the short history of Ethereum so far, it's had several major challenges. Probably, the biggest has been the DAO.

In May of 2016, the former CCO of Ethereum, Stephan Tual, founded Slock.it, along with a few members of the Ethereum team. In doing so, he also announced the concept of the DAO—the Decentralized Autonomous Organization. Despite very little information about what the DAO actually was, during its Initial Coin Offering (ICO), the DAO raised an amount of Ethereum equal to $150 million from over 20,000 investors.

Cyptocurrency: The Next Level for Banking Reform

However, on June 17, 2016, a hacker hacked the DAO through a loophole in the system. Within just a couple of hours, the DAO lost 3.6 million ETH, the equivalent of $70 million. The loophole facilitating this hacking did not come from Ethereum itself, but from an application on which it was built. However, the resulting mess was left to the Ethereum team and community to take care of. Several proposals were presented to get the stolen money back. Because transferred funds were always held in an account for twenty-eight days, the hacker could not simply take the money and run. Ethereum eventually proposed to "hard fork" the funds to an account available to the original owners. A hard fork involves making a primordial change to blockchain that can make previously invalid transactions valid, or vice versa. But by doing so, it subverts the shared goal of decentralization that so many people involved in cryptocurrency share. Eventually, even though 10 percent of the Ethereum community voted against it, Ethereum decided to hardfork 192 million blocks in order to retrieve the stolen funds. After this was done, a new blockchain was created called ETH (separate from the original blockchain, ETC).

There are many takeaways for the cryptocurrency and blockchain communities that come out of the DAO incident. If you're interested in getting granular, there are many articles on Google. However, as Einstein is supposed to have said, a person who never made a mistake is a person who never tried anything new. Smart contracts is something new, and so is everything related to blockchain. In my opinion, there are going to be bumps in the road like DAO along the way. But as long as we survive and learn from our mistakes, we shall all be stronger in the end.

The Traditional Financial Market Reborn

Smart contracts have been widely adopted across the digital world. Almost all active ICO projects are now using smart contracts. Tokens and the ownership of tokens will also always be written into a smart contract. For example, in a typical ICO, 10 percent of tokens are reserved to the ICO team, 50 percent of tokens go to private investors, and 40 percent go to public investors. And all of these conditions will be written into the smart contract, which is accessible to everyone in the community. Thus, once the ICO goes public, the smart contract will be put in motion to execute the terms automatically.

Smart contracts are expanding into other areas, as well. Clyde & Co. is a global law firm that recently formed a team to provide consulting services to clients who would like to set up smart contracts from technical, as well as legal, perspectives. And one of the world's largest insurance companies, AXA, recently announced the launch of Fizzy, the very first insurance product using both blockchain technology and smart contracts. (Fizzy mainly provides insurance covering flight delays.)

In October of 2017, Ernst & Young collaborated with blockchain developer Guardtime to explore applying blockchain to the marine insurance sector. PwC and Northern Trust announced an instant blockchain auditing service early this year. (PwC will be providing private equity auditors with instant access to data stored on a private blockchain.) In traditional auditing, auditors receive periodic reports from clients, which is not always an efficient way of doing things. But by having near-instant access to the data regarding actions taken by a fund manager (for example), the whole process can be audited in real time.

The Future Of Smart Contracts.

I'm confident that in the future, smart contracts will be put into even broader use in the financial sector. I think this for a number of reasons. To go back to PwC: in PwC's distributed accounting reports, there is now a thorough analysis of the future of blockchain and smart contracts. Since a smart contract is capable of self-executing contracts related to assets transfer, it, as a technology, definitely presents uses related to stock trading and other financial market trading.

Another reason for the growth of smart contracts will be the growth of the Internet of Things (IoT). According to Gartner Inc., the global research firm, worldwide IoT security spending will reach $1.5 billion in 2018. By 2021, it is expected to climb to $3.1 billion. Everything around us, including smartphones, cars, wearable products, and even furniture, is going to be connected to the Internet. This will create exponential data needs. What will we use to capture and store all of these new data? Blockchain.

Another trend in smart contracts' favor is that blockchain is cost-efficient and friendly. In traditional law firms and auditing firms, adopting blockchain and smart contracts will significantly lower the cost of doing business and improve efficiency. It will be a win-win.

ICO: Bubble Or Extra Bonus?

Ethereum brought ICO to startups as a new way to raise capital. Ethereum announced its own ICO on September 2, 2014, and it placed among the top five of all time in terms of the sheer amount of capital it raised. Ethereum raised $18.4 million, most of which was spent developing Ethereum blockchain and related applications. (The record for "largest ICO" has been consistently broken. The EOS cryptocurrency's token sales reached $4.1 billion over an one-year ICO, making it, for the moment, the number one ICO in history.)

The evolution of ICOs has happened in two stages. In the early days, speculators who hoped to make fast money were always there to try to take advantage of the situation somehow. An ICO is, of course, not a Ponzi scheme but rather a way for blockchain startups to raise money. But ICOs can be initiated by unsavory people who are only in it for quick profits at the expense of other people. These days, there is more awareness of this danger.

However, in the early days of ICOs, token sales were always great, but some of them were being sold by scammers. In the second stage the one we're in now as ICOs evolve into something more professional and transparent, they are attracting individuals and institutions from the traditional financial industry. There are advantages to this, yes, but it can also make things more standardized and slow things down. Blockchain, as an industry, is gathering experts and high-profile managers from across traditional industries and is improving every day and every hour.

ICO;

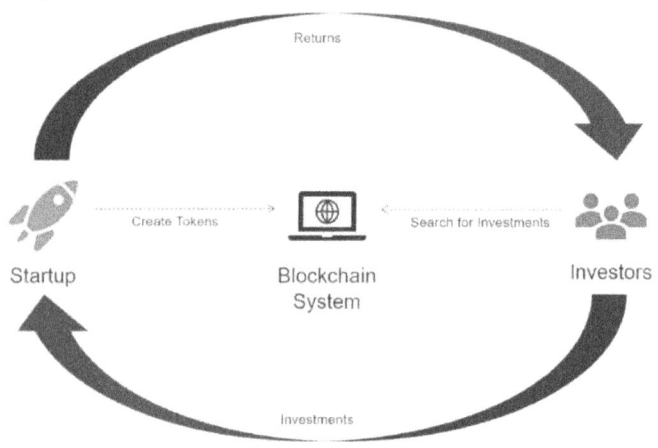

I believe that an ICO is soon going to be as accepted as an IPO is today. People make mistakes when they are young, and so do institutions. This was certainly true with ICOs. However, they have now become more consolidated and established. Launching an ICO is now as demanding as launching an IPO. It involves nearly everything that an IPO requires. Cryptocurrency and blockchain are interlinked so closely. Cryptocurrencies are supporting blockchain startups, and blockchain startups are relying on tokens to be issued and token sales to raise capital to grow bigger. At the same time, both are learning from traditional industries as well as bringing the latter more fully into the crypto economy.

Mining As Gold Rush

In 1848, after a local newspaper whispered that gold had been found in certain rivers in California, about 300,000 people from across United States left their homes and rushed west to follow their dreams of getting rich. The consequences were unexpected and the effects substantial. When the California Gold Rush took off in March of 1848, California was not even a state yet. (It makes me wonder what made Uncle Sam let California into the family: maybe the fact that approximately 3,700 tons of gold have been retrieved from the bottom of its rivers!)

History often repeats itself. Today, mining Bitcoin has become another Gold Rush. When Satoshi first "discovered" Bitcoin, he set a ceiling on the number of Bitcoins that could ever exist: 21 million units. And every four years, 210,000 new Bitcoins are released into the system. As the most valuable cryptocurrency, many people can't wait to get into Bitcoin mining. But how precisely does it work? Instead of picking up a pan, as most forty-niners did in California's Gold Rush, miners of Bitcoin use a far more sophisticated tool to dig for gold.

Satoshi created a decentralized network accessible through an open-source software available to everyone. In this network, people use Bitcoins to make exchanges. In order to avoid the double spending issue, Satoshi introduced blockchain, which will document every single transaction that happens, has ever happened, or is ever going to happen. But blockchain does not create itself. It depends on computer processing power to generate new blocks into the chain and maintain the system function. This is the true purpose of mining. Bitcoins are the reward for miners who either create new blocks or input transaction information into blockchain.

In order to become a miner, a person needs to join blockchain and get connected with other nodes. Once the connection is fully established, miners will need to fulfill six tasks:

1. Listen for transactions.
2. Listen for new blocks and maintain blockchain. If there is a new block, the miner needs to validate it.
3. Assemble a new valid block based on the transactions the miner has been hearing.
4. Find a nonce a.k.a. an arbitrary number that can be used only once to make the block valid.
5. Hope everyone in blockchain accepts the new block.
6. Enjoy profits! If everyone accepts the new block, the miner will be rewarded accordingly.

Miners need to validate new blocks (which means new transactions are coming into the network). This is the most critical work when it comes to maintaining the circulation of Bitcoin. But they also have to create new blocks, an activity that can be strikingly competitive. Miners compete with one another for new blocks. This part is not necessary to maintain the whole system of Bitcoin, but it functions as the incentive to encourage miners to fulfill the validation part of a job.

When Satoshi invented Bitcoin, he introduced this "motivating mechanism" to encourage miners to maintain the function of blockchain. But since the total number of Bitcoins is 21 million and only 210,000 Bitcoins are released every four years, the reward halves accordingly. Thus, in 2009, the reward was 50 Bitcoins in a block. But by 2016, it was down to 12.5 Bitcoins for each new block. When all Bitcoins are released into the system, the reward will drop to zero.

Even though the financial reward for creating new blocks is going away, the transaction fee remains an incentive to attract miners. In blockchain, users will be charged a certain fee in order to broadcast and document each transaction. The fee then goes to the miners who will put the information into the blocks. This generates a "bidding system." Bidding happens when there are many transactions waiting to be put into blocks. The higher a transaction fee you are willing to pay, the better chance you have of jumping ahead in the waiting line. As the fee for completing transactions keeps going up, miners will keep becoming more important in the world blockchain and cryptocurrency. (Miners is similar to the programmers working at Internet companies who maintain functions.)

Launched on May 21, 2018, a China-based cryptocurrency exchange called FCoin has proposed a new business model called "Trans-Fee Mining." This effectively turns the crypto trading itself into mining. For each transaction fee that users pay FCoin on its platform (in Bitcoin or Ethereum), users will be compensated 100 percent in FTs (a token issued by FCoin). Meanwhile, the platform will also allocate 80 percent of the transaction fee to FTs holders.

This model immediately boosted energy and created excitement among traders. Since trading and mining are the same thing on FCoin, if you trade on FCoin, the transaction fee is zero. But if you own FTs, you will be able to share the 80 percent of transaction fees generated from the platform proportional to the amount of FTs you hold. (This model has been defined by some as a "Token Economy.")

Since FCoin's launch, the volume of its trades has increased rapidly. Based on the success of the Trans-Fee Mining model, more and more new exchanges have come into the game. Users seem to love the approach to reimbursement and reward. However, the model itself has been criticized, with some alleging that "trans-fee mining" is just another form of ICO scheme.

Despite the criticism of the model, I think introducing a new rewarding system into blockchain is laudable and encourages people to explore the possibilities of using different reward methods. In the "Gold Rush" of Bitcoin, miners are trying their best to mine new blocks before others can, and many miners are now forced to tolerate a very high level of risk. Satoshi created the first block. (People call it "the genius block.") And every single block generated afterward is linked back to it. Blockchain is continuously growing as new transactions take place. But as I mentioned earlier, the fundamental architecture of blockchain requires a great amount of computing power. Computing power determines the speed of the mining, and the speed of the mining determines who is going be rewarded with Bitcoins for creating the next block faster than everyone else.

One of effects of the California Gold Rush was the improvement of gold-recovery techniques. At the beginning of the Gold Rush, because the gold was so richly concentrated in the gravel bed, using hands or pans or anything you could find in the kitchen was enough for forty-niners to retrieve those loose gold flakes and nuggets. But as more and more people joined in the search for their own California Dream, the tools had to become more advanced. In the first five years of Gold Rush, about 370 tons of gold were recovered—mostly by people digging with their hands. But from then until today, only about 3,700 tons of gold have been recovered in California. Getting gold got much harder as time went by.

Mining;

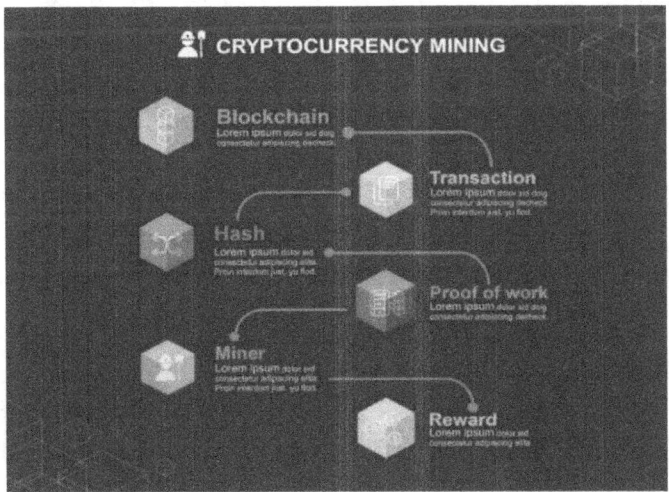

The same has held true with Bitcoin mining; early birds get more worms. A simple personal computer was enough for miners in the early stages. But now, the cost of input has increased significantly because mining demands consolidated resources. Putting aside the cost of the mining machine itself, just keeping a mining machine going can cost an enormous amount in electricity fees.

China has drawn a lot of attention in this connection from people looking at maps of electricity consumption. China is not only known for mining, but also as a leading computer chip manufacturer. It's estimated that over 80 percent of cryptocurrencies have been mined using computer chips manufactured in mainland China. Bitmain Technologies Ltd. (or Bitmain), with headquarters in Beijing, is the largest producer of Bitcoin mining chips in the world. According to Business Insider, Bitmain's founder, the cryptocurrency billionaire Jihan Wu, told Bloomberg that Bitmain was considering an initial public offering as it expands into producing hardware for artificial-intelligence computing.

The Changing Value Of Bitcoins

Here's a related question: if you are a miner, after you get your Bitcoins either through transaction fees or creating new blocks what do you do with them? You'd be surprised how the answer has changed over time.

On May 22, 2010, Laszlo Hanyeca, a computer programmer, bought two pizzas for the low, low price of only 10,000 Bitcoins. The purchase is widely considered to be the first transaction in the history of Bitcoin. As of the writing of this book, these two pizzas would be worth about $75 million, making them the most expensive pizzas in history.

From $20,000 per Bitcoin down to about $6,000, Bitcoin has been on a heck of ride recently. Ethereum, the second most valuable cryptocurrency, stands at $453.93 per unit at the time of this writing. And overall users of cryptocurrencies have increased from around 30,000 just a few years ago to over 1.3 million. So despite fluctuations in the market, there's evidence that the public is increasingly accepting of cryptocurrency.

The extreme up-and-down fluctuation we see in cryptocurrency trading prices corresponds to the confidence (or lack of it) that people hold in these currencies. The overall amount of a cryptocurrency is always fixed. If the demand-supply works effectively for cryptocurrency, more investment will always come in. It's the same idea with gold, diamonds, or works of art. The market sometimes sees the value of cryptocurrency as uncertain, but confidence overall continues to grow as more people become comfortable with the idea. Bitcoin has, of course, experienced extreme fluctuations in value. Yet, as time goes by, I'm confident the public will continue to develop better understandings of exchange platforms for cryptocurrencies. They will become more typical, "normal," and accepted, which will, in turn, help the value of cryptocurrencies overall.

The attitude of the government also plays a huge role in determining the future value of a cryptocurrency.

Cyptocurrency: The Next Level for Banking Reform

Though the technology of crypto is designed for decentralization the opposite of what has been going on with currency for thousands of years the opinion of a central government can still push things one way or the other (even if it feels left out). In the United States, some government officials and entities have issued consumer warnings regarding cryptocurrencies. Yet they've also said that cryptos are legal and should be allowed to exist. In some circles, this has counted as an endorsement of sorts. This brings us to the question of how to stabilize the value of cryptocurrency in the future. It's an important issue that will need to be resolved soon.

Dominant cryptocurrencies such as Bitcoin and Ethereum have already gained acceptance and (eventually) steady valuation. But not all cryptos have been as lucky. Almost a decade after the birth of Bitcoin, there are more and more people who are using, and investing in, Bitcoin, and it has been treated as a digital asset of great value globally. Along with Ethereum, Bitcoin has been seen as one of the strongest currencies in the world of cryptocurrency. In June of 2018, in an informal statement made at Yahoo Finance's "All Markets Summit Crypto," the SEC's director of finance stated that the SEC would not classify Bitcoin or Etherium as a security. Rather, the official said, both cryptocurrencies function more like commodities such as gold, silver, or oil. Will a decentralized cryptocurrency ever overtake a traditionally defined currency in status or value? It's hard to tell at this point. But with more and more activities and transactions happening online, the chance to cut out middlemen, use smart contracts, and purchase merchandise with cryptocurrency may be a temptation too strong to resist. With all the cost-effectiveness it is bringing us, I believe cryptocurrency will play a bigger and bigger role in all manner of scenarios.

ICO—Initial Coin Offering – The New IPO

Throughout most of recent history, an IPO has been the standard path for companies to attract investors through selling stocks. However, the process involves banks and venture capitalists who stand to make money on fees. An ICO undercuts intermediaries, such as venture capitalists and banks, removing them from the fundraising process.

We briefly talked about Ethereum's misadventure with the very first ICO on its platform, the DAO. I hope I can make the case to you here that times have changed since then, and that ICOs have changed. While they once felt like a Kickstarter or Indiegogo campaign, they now have about them the sober propriety of an IPO and then some.

During 2017, using ICOs, blockchain startups raised about $7 billion. Compare that to the capital raise of only $1 billion enjoyed by traditional VC for blockchain startups during that period. I think this makes the case that the ICO model is increasingly trusted, and also very hot. Over 200 ICOs have raised in excess of $10M with many going vastly above that. EOS, a blockchain system for supporting central business districts, attracted $4 billion; Filecoin took in $257 million; Tezos raised $232 million; and Bancor Protocal locked in $153 million.

The money changing hands in these ICOs has drawn a decent amount of attention from SEC. Mostly, these ICOs remain unregulated by the government. Some consumer advocates claim the rules are not clear when it comes to how investors will be properly protected. In June of 2018, the Chairman of the SEC, Jay Clayton, was interviewed by CNBC. In this interview, he stated that tokens and ICOs were securities. This issue is changing moment to moment, but based on these comments, it is reasonable to believe that ICOs will probably one day fall under SEC regulation to a greater degree.

Blockchain Participant;

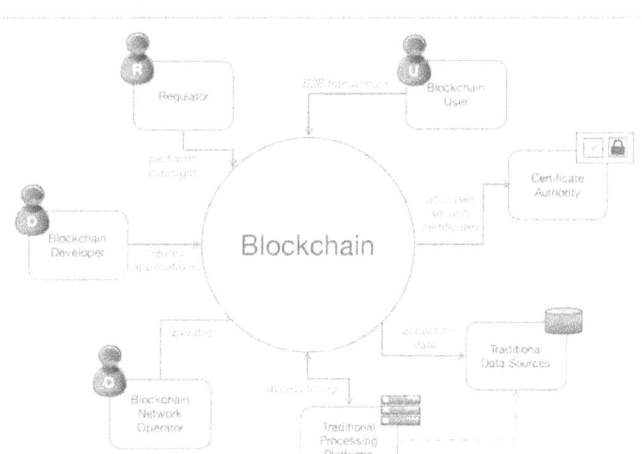

The Participants in a Blockchain Network

Yet there is always an alternative when regulation is forced upon us. The American startups that are looking for an ICO are learning from the Chinese Internet companies that typically raise capital overseas now. The

MIIT (Ministry of Industry and Information Technology) and Press and Publication Administration of China have stated that an Internet license can only be held by domestically funded companies. However, US-based startups are learning from these Chinese workarounds when launching their ICOs. For example, let's say that a domestic-based American company, Company A, is planning to launch an ICO. Company A will set up Company C in a cryptically friendly country. And another company, Company B, will be established to operate the ICO. But Company C will technically be the parent company of both A and B.

Perhaps such attention is being paid to ICOs because of the speculators in the market who, looking for a quick gain, had taken advantage of the unregulated system in its earliest days. Yet as more pump-and-dump schemes popped up in the ICO world, a self-cleaning mechanism was triggered. Investment banks, financial services providers, and technology companies based in Silicon Valley joined in to filter and vet projects looking for an ICO. The combination of all these forces raised the entry barrier by filtering out the unqualified or sketchy deals.

Any project going for an ICO is now being examined closely by multiple entities. Endorsements from qualified individuals or institutions are not given lightly. Further, the time frame of an ICO has been extended, allowing investors more time to conduct their due to diligence. And overall, the procedure for launching an ICO has become more standardized.

Cyptocurrency: The Next Level for Banking Reform

Perhaps some resistance should not be surprising. After all, the ICO is challenging the existing capital raising format. Because it is more barrier free than typical VC raises, people are jumping in. While not all ICOs have been successful and, yes, some have been scams there are many blockchain startups that have been wildly successful under the ICO model. The vast majority of these businesses are trying their best to bring genuine value to people's daily lives through the world of blockchain.

There are good apples, and there are bad apples. This will always be true. We cannot cut down the tree whenever a bad apple pops up. It would be unfair to the good ones. Yes, the ICO model probably needs a little bit more time to evolve into the best version of itself. Yet even in its current form, it can defend investors and offer great ideas and projects.

Martin Chen, founder of GDP Capital, a New York-based consulting firm, believes that most Internet-based services are suitable for an ICO. Blockchain and cryptocurrencies are born on the Internet, and they share the same "genes" you might say in that they both connect one person to another in a truly open world. In a token-centered community, information regarding the total number of tokens to be issued is always transparent and certain. Everyone in the community has access to this information, and the value of the token will go up as more and more people join that community. Obviously, there are tremendous benefits to this model. For the foreseeable future, I think it's reasonable to believe that token-centered communities will prove themselves superior to a traditional stock-based model.

Regionally imposed restrictions now have less of an influence on ICOs. Because of this, more and more Chinese companies seeking to go public are considering an ICO instead of an IPO. ICOs, through token sales, introduce firm advantages of liquidity to the stock. For many companies, an ICO is also appealing because it undercuts (or eliminates entirely) the costs and complicated paperwork usually involved in an IPO. Further, an ICO does not require companies to "open their books" to reveal their existing business performance. Many owners find this makes them more comfortable with the ICO model.

Have no doubt about it, the ICO is designed to challenge the traditional VC model. Yet whenever a company is in the process of launching an ICO, nothing prevents a venture capitalist from buying tokens and becoming a part of that community. In a way, this can open up new possibilities for traditional VC investors. For example, the valuation of a company is not restricted to the decrees or findings of a few specialized institutions but is based on the consensus of the whole community. The ICO model also offers solutions and opportunities for companies in industries that are usually ignored by VC.

Because the value of a company is determined by the whole community under the ICO model, we can see the promulgation of this model as another blow for decentralization (and against a small cluster of powerful regulating bodies). However it will always be pointed out that subverting the power of traditional regulating institutions has been a double-edged sword or at least it was in the early days of ICOs. Eight or nine years ago, there were definitely speculators who got in the game solely to rook people. Projects and companies turned out to be scams and schemes. This forced ICO investors to collectively become more savvy, and the learning curve was quick. But this early leaks did not sink the ship.

ICOs are also popular because they hold the potential for remarkably superior ROI (Return On Investment) when compared to other offerings. With traditional VC investments, it usually takes ten years to get one's initial investment back and then realize a profit. The rapid growth in blockchain and cryptocurrency has made this time horizon a relic of the past. In the world of blockchain, things move quickly. Things happens, and they don't stop to take a break. The energy is young and wild. Opportunities are everywhere. Investors now understand that people need to move fast in this world if they want to catch the early train before it leaves the platform and cash in on the benefits of being an early investor. In today's climate, it usually takes fewer than twenty-four hours for a major American fund to finish an investment deal made through an ICO. This is a remarkable change, and it isn't going to reverse itself anytime soon.

The Traditional Financial Industry Tries … Something New

Have you ever used a dating app?

In a lot of ways, blockchain now faces the same conundrum as a new "hot date" on Tinder. You could say that blockchain is receiving all kinds of "winks" and "likes" from traditional financial institutions. But are they ready to make a true connection and go out for coffee in real life? That remains to be seen. Relevant financial products are being developed by these institutions especially when it comes to Bitcoin but it may just be the equivalent of flirting on Tinder after a couple of cocktails.

In December of 2017, the Chicago Mercantile Exchange launched the the first trading instruments for Bitcoin futures. Yet so far, no European countries have followed suit and provided any Bitcoin or cryptocurrency-related financial products. Deutsche Boerse AG, the parent company of the Frankfurt Stock Exchange, appears to have begun work on a technology that will allow them to offer their clients Bitcoin and cryptocurrency-related products, but it remains in the early stages.

Back in the US, after rejecting the Winklevoss brothers' initial application for a Bitcoin Exchange-Traded Fund (ETF), the SEC has made statements recently that hint it may be changing its tune on the idea. If one thing is sure, it's that we're at a juncture in which governments' attitudes toward Bitcoin and crypto are largely unknowable and if they are known, they're revealed to vary widely from country to country. Some countries are very friendly when it comes to crypto, and some are the opposite. In Germany, for example, Bitcoin is now technically a "legal tender," meaning that Bitcoin is allowed to be used for tax purposes and for commercial trading. In the United States, Bitcoin can be used like regular money in many situations and many businesses accept it but it is not considered to be legal tender by the IRS. However, as we all know, this doesn't mean the IRS isn't "interested" in your Bitcoins. They are very interested. Bitcoins are considered to be your personal property, just like gold or a house, which means they have to comply with tax codes. According to the IRS, the value of a Bitcoin for US tax purposes is its fair market value in US dollars on the date it is received, and any transaction fees are added to that. If a person is trading Bitcoins as capital assest, then the gain is supposed to be taxed at capital gains rate.

As the appeal of crypto pushes the door wider and wider, traditional investment banks are catching on to the game. According to the New York Times, Goldman Sachs is about to open a Bitcoin trading operation on Wall Street. The operation will not buy or sell Bitcoins directly but is rather designed to meet the needs of their clients who may be exploring investments in cryptocurrency. Wall Street has generally shied away from Bitcoin and cryptocurrencies, but Goldman's decision to dip its toe in the water may be a bellwether. In a recent interview, Rana Yared, an executive involved in creating these offerings, said that Goldman Sachs "had concluded Bitcoin is not a fraud." Many clients of Goldman Sachs consider Bitcoin a commodity of value, and Goldman knows this. Because the amount of Bitcoins is forever set, a comparison to a commodity like gold makes sense for Goldman's clients. There is a finite amount of gold in the world. Barring an innovation by alchemists, there will never be more than there is right now. This connection to something real and finite is probably the quality that most makes Goldman comfortable moving forward.

For today's crypto "true believers," the appeal extends beyond the fact that big banks may have found Bitcoin semipalatable. Many users, including some Goldman clients, genuinely believe that blockchain is doing something good for the future of commerce and humanity. Others have no larger ideological drive but would simply like to sit at the table when the pie is being shared. If we're being frank, the investment banks probably fall into this latter group. But that doesn't mean their participation in growing the presence of crypto will not be meaningful or important.

There's a saying I like: "Get busy living or get busy dying."

I like this precisely because it helps me wrap my mind around the forces driving crypto today. That with faith in the currency have chosen to get busy promoting it, using it, and sharing it. They believe that it can help us go further and help our economic system become better. I think that's an inspiring view!

If you see blockchain as something inevitable something that's going to happen whether banks and governments like it or not then doubt in the marketplace can only be viewed as the age-old fear of change. If you see blockchain as an extension of how the Internet reached us and became a vital part of our lives whether we wanted it to or not then the eventual success of blockchain feels assured. And it also indicates that those who fail to evolve and accept blockchain may well fail to survive the future that is coming.

Blockchain is young. So is cryptocurrency and so are ICOs. But I, along with many experts in the field, see blockchain as the foundation of our financial future. It's a future that's going to include cryptocurrencies, tokens, ICOs, smart contracts, and many other applications that haven't even been invented yet! But as all of these elements continue to function together and grow stronger, the ecosystem of the crypto economy seems like it will soon have too much momentum to fail.

CHAPTER 4

Decentralizing Financial Services

Let's go back to 2008 again. The subprime mortgage crisis that flattened the economy that year proved a boon for storytellers, and not just in cryptocurrency books. I'm not sure if you've seen the 2011 movie Margin Call, but it's worth your time. I would especially recommend it if you're interested in the financial industries (dys)function, and how profoundly it influences every aspect of our daily lives. The movie limns the situation immediately prior to the financial crisis. A risk-management analyst has caught a mistake and suddenly understands the hit that his industry is about to take and what the impact may be for the rest of the world. The film is revealing because it lays bare the philosophy and attitude underpinning the whole of Wall Street, namely, that risk is usually not identified and acknowledged during times when the system seems to be working fine and everybody is making money. But as greed grows, things always spiral out of control. The financial industry manages trillions of dollars worth of assets. The whole world, in some fashion or another, relies on Wall Street to function correctly. When it doesn't, trust is shaken and everybody is impacted.

But what if there were new and different ways of doing things? What if there were new technologies that might allow us to avoid the Wall Street busts and crashes of the past?

I can happily report that some very smart people are trying to answer these very questions. And if early returns are any indication, it looks like they are making progress.

From Offline Banking To Blockchain Banking

A new, New York-based company called Vocean is leading the way when it comes to connecting fixed-income financial instruments to blockchain. A recent white paper issued by the firm lays out the approach that Vocean intends to take, and the benefits to consumers. Essentially, Vocean seeks to create a decentralized lending platform and loan derivatives market that will allow for dynamic collateral management and disintermediated clearing. Using state-of-the-art blockchain technology, Vocean aims to provide assistance to investors managing digital assets, cryptoinvestments, and related financial products in the realm of the "token economy."

In order to understand how Vocean plans to navigate the tricky task of combining traditional financial services products with blockchain, we need to take a look at the role that debt plays in the financial industry. There are many kinds of debt and debt-related financial instruments. They can come in the form of redeemable notes issued by a government, bonds issued by companies, mortgages, personal loans, student loans, and more. (Just use Wikipedia if you want to learn more about the basics of debt and financial instruments.) A debt generally also includes specific, contractual terms regarding the amount and timing of repayments (for example, your minimum credit card payment), and things like principal and interest. Almost all financial products used today find their roots in debt.

Vocean would like to use blockchain to increase the efficiency of the entire financial industry as it relates to the issuing of debt. The CEO of Vocean, Jerry Zhong, is not new to using technology to address financial problems. Zhong was one of the "early birds" back in early 1990s who jumped into the Internet with both feet. He sees the current upcoming wave of blockchain as very similar to the early stages of Internet adoption and sees where we are now as comparable to the period when people were trying to figure out how to push the Internet into broader use. There's no doubt that the Internet succeeded in connecting physical services (financial or otherwise) into online processes. This created efficiencies for everyone. According to visionaries like Zhong, the coming adoption of blockchain is going to migrate everything we do online onto blockchain, allowing us to achieve decentralization and realize new efficiency improvements. We stand at a juncture in which professionals in traditional industries are realizing this. They are preparing for the coming changes blockchain will bring, and they're getting creative with it whenever possible.

Cyptocurrency: The Next Level for Banking Reform

According to Vocean, the current financial industry has three key weak points. However, Vocean believes it will be able to introduce blockchain-based efficiencies that will address all three.

First, traditional banking services suffer from "low efficiency" management of their funds and records. The sheer amount of transactions they must record are huge. All too frequently, banking information is stored in different computer terminals, or on slow computer networks. Because of the information delays this creates, traders at investment banks are less able to make quick and fully informed decisions on behalf of their investors.

Second, financial service firms still need third parties to complete the clearinghouse function. A clearinghouse is a financial institution that facilitates the exchange of payments, securities, or derivatives. Essentially, it functions as a middleman connecting two firms. It also ensures that both firms honor their agreements and fulfill their obligations. You could view a clearinghouse as a kind of early-stage PayPal. PayPal provides not only a platform on which transactions can take place, but it also facilitates the transaction between the buyer and the seller. PayPal usually charges a 3 percent fee for its services, much like a clearinghouse. After the buyer submits a payment, PayPal will hold it temporarily and release it when the buyer confirms the receipt of the merchandise. In the traditional financial marketplace, clearinghouses are necessary to reduce costs and mitigate operational risk.

The third problem Vocean can address is the need for security in cryptocurrency by means of a "custodian." Exchange desks and wallet services have not proven foolproof. Hacking incidents do happen from time to time. The resulting security and safety issues are a barrier for many large institutional investors. As long as they entertain the specter of "losing money because of a hack," they will be reluctant to do business related to blockchain or cryptocurrency. Yet the traditional financial industry has developed effective custodians for investors to help them store and manage their fiat money and traditional assets. JPMorgan Chase, State Street Bank, and Mellon Finance, for example, have been keeping in their custody billions of assets on behalf of other institutions for years. As crypto assets have increased, the need for similar custodian services has become clear. In May of 2018, Coinbase an American Bitcoin exchange and wallet service platform began providing its own version of custodian service. Adam White, the VP of Coinbase, says he is anticipating billions of institutional investment dollars in this connection. And according to the May 2018 issue of Cointelegraph, Nomura Bank, a Japanese financial institution, announced that it would begin providing a "crypto custody solution" for institutional investors. Nomura's venture will be conducted in partnership with digital asset security company Ledger and the investment house Global Advisors. And according to a recent piece in the New York Times, ICE, the parent company of the NYSE, has been developing an online trading platform for Bitcoin SWAP.

Cyptocurrency: The Next Level for Banking Reform

Crypto custodian services present further evidence of forwarding momentum in the evolution of cryptocurrency. As it grows, cryptocurrency will, step by step, be accepted by, and necessitate the ability to interface with, broader financial services. When it comes to these three sticking points, Vocean believes it can provide solutions via blockchain technologies. How are Vocean's solutions going to be different from what's being offered by traditional banking services? Foremost, Jerry Zhong believes that blockchain will greatly increase the efficiency of investing and all related financial services. A big part of this will be the use of smart contracts. Since the smart contract is irreversible, terms can (and will) be executed without human intervention. Things will be automatic. Further, all the data are stored on the public chain, which will be accessible to all parties involved in a transaction and which will considerably lower costs (especially when compared to the traditional price point of managing collateral posted to banks).

Vocean is moving forward by building upon the public chain made possible by Ethereum. Zhong has explained that his ultimate purpose is to maximize outcomes by minimizing the costs and time inputs associated with financial transactions. Vocean believes the infrastructure of Ethereum has been proved solid. The customers targeted by Vocean are financial institutions who put safety and privacy as the two issues at the top of their lists. Are there any trade-offs or challenges? The big one is speed. Currently, Ethereum can process fifteen transactions per second. That might sound like a lot, but Visa can put up about 45,000 transactions per second.

Even so, Vocean believes this hurdle in manageable, and that speed will improve over time. Vocean is also constructing two smart contract systems. One smart contract system will manage the "borrow-lend" function, which connects borrowers, lenders, and mortgage management entities. Through the system, these three parties can execute semisimultaneous trades. The other smart contract system will serve the function of the clearing-houses we discussed above. Due to the complexity of the market, price is in a constant state of fluctuation and adjustment. Vocean is developing a specific smart contract to manage collateral in this environment. When a huge (up or down) price change triggers a margin call, the system will protect the value of assets and serve the best interests of credit holders.

Vocean will also work to enable cross-chain crypto transactions. In traditional financial situations, borrowers and lenders make exchanges across different currencies all the time. Bitcoin and Ether, however, are traded in separate public chains, and sadly, Ethereum does not support cross-chain crypto transactions. Vocean is planning to build an application to enable this service. As I think you can see, Ethereum has become the fundamental infrastructure in much of the blockchain and cryptocurrency world. Despite its prevalence, it still isn't perfect. Blockchain can be seen as a data storage facility that offers a high level of security, but at the cost of low speed. It is not suitable for complicated logic functions, or for repeatable trades of low value. Vocean aims to balance its reliance on Ethereum with other in-chain and off-chain services. In so doing, it hopes to be able to provide the best of both worlds.

There is still a considerable amount of capital waiting outside the crypto door, looking inside to see if it's worth it to come in. There are estimated to be $20 billion in Bitcoins still to enter the market. Vocean is set to be ready when it does. To get the money waiting outside the door comfortable enough to come inside, custodian service providers (usually, certain banks) will need to accomplish the goal of increasing the value of assets. Thus, designing low-risk, fixed-income investments are high on their list. When it comes to investment banks getting into the space, their concern is that they would need a considerable amount of crypto to offset risk and increase liquidity. Often, investment banks solve this issue using "swap and repo" also known as a repurchase agreement. In a typical repurchase agreement, a dealer sells securities to a counterparty with the agreement to buy back the securities at a higher price at a later date. If the dealer borrows money, it is a repo. If the dealer lends money, it is a reverse repo. Once the crypto market becomes consolidated, there will be huge demand for these transactions using cryptocurrency. Vocean is designing a platform to assist custodian banks and investment banks in profiting from these transactions.

As investment banks and hedge funds start getting deeper into crypto assets, the demand for lenders and borrowers will increase. Zhong predicts that within the next twelve months, custodian banks will become a very common sight in the crypto market. Clients who need custodian services such as miners or mining farms will be the holders of large amounts of cryptocurrency. They'll need reputable custodian services to safely take care of their crypto assets. According to a survey published by Reuters, one in five major financial institutions is currently considering trading cryptocurrency by the end of 2019.

Vocean Is Ready For This Market.

Vocean also plans to build an active investing platform (and corresponding online community) with the execution of three key steps. The first step is to build the platform and begin collaborating with custodian banks to migrate the asset. The second step will be to introduce already-existing financial products to a blockchain-based service. And the final step for Vocean will be to build a community of centralized investors to help address any issues that occur with investments. Technically, trading is not going to happen "on Vocean," but off-chain. However, Vocean is building an AI system for lenders and borrowers in which the two will be matched by loan criteria. Such factors as ideal loan term, collateral/loan pair, collateral ratio, interest rate, and liquidation option will be used to connect the ideal lender to the ideal borrower. It will be a little like the algorithm of a good dating site that connects potential partners through their common interests.

Investors in the community will also be rated. Traders' investment performance and credit rating will be documented and posted into blockchain. This system will also analyze their trading behaviors. In addition, the platform will provide training and education-related services for investors to help them learn about risk management in crypto assets.

Blockchain innovations have been coming to us fast and furious. I don't expect the pace of innovation to stop, and I believe that each innovation will make the water feel warmer for traditional investors. But effectively applying blockchain technology to finance will require more than experience on Wall Street or a finance background. True innovators will also need a strong background in technology. In the case of Vocean, a team has been constructed that features leaders with both strong financial experience and deep roots in technology. The key person who is working on Vocean's blockchain platform has been working as a core member of Bloomberg's infrastructure team for over ten years. (And in my opinion, Bloomberg is the Google of Wall Street.) I wanted to spend so much time on Vocean in this chapter because I think it's the best example of what can be accomplished when more and more professionals from traditional industries contribute to blockchain innovations. The experience and expertise they bring will make astounding things possible and will help ensure that blockchain become appetizing to different industries.

The Future Of Blockchain In The Financial Industry.

It's important to remember that it took the Internet over twenty years to really ensconce itself into our daily lives. In the early 2000s, the Internet in China was still very slow, and you could not do much on it. Now, we simply can't live without it! We Chinese are on it almost all the time (except maybe when we're sleeping). Blockchain is experiencing the same adoption period. It was originally created as a tool to allow cryptocurrency to store transaction information. But now, if you look at Ethereum for example, there are over a thousand applications and functions available on it (in addition to storing cryptocurrency transactions).

The effectiveness of blockchain has enabled us to cut out intermediaries, too. For example, when banks issue a mortgage to an individual so that he or she can make a property purchase, those banks need to verify the ownership of the property and also check if the customer has applied for a mortgage before. These requirements introduce real estate brokers into the mix, and they play a major role in the selling and buying of the property. But with blockchain technology, every single piece of property will be documented into blocks of the chain. It will be transparent for everyone. People will be able to go to blockchain to check this information, instead of to a related third party. This will save time and eliminate costs.

Blockchain also has a bright future when it comes to Wall Street. According to Jerry Zhong, blockchain remains popular with many hedge funds, and that popularity is growing. But to become a viable option for replacing the centralized system of storing information (in the way Wall Street would like it to), blockchain needs to address two major issues regulation and safety. The regulatory status of blockchain is still unclear, and the safety measures currently in place are still not adequate for many on Wall Street. Yet I believe these are solvable problems. And with Jerry Zhong at the helm, I think blockchain is going to lead us into the next industrial revolution.

The Top Of The Food Chain And The Birth Of Crypto Exchanges

Here is a simple question: what exactly is a crypto exchange? Essentially, a crypto exchange is a digital marketplace in which traders can buy and sell cryptos using different fiat currencies (or other items of value). It's an online platform that acts as an intermediary between buyers and sellers. A crypto exchange functions similarly to a traditional stock exchange. It matches buyers and sellers, allowing customers to make trades.

The first such exchange was a Bitcoin exchange founded in October of 2009. It was named New Liberty Standard and was located in New York. It was a place where people could exchange Bitcoins for fiat money, or fiat money for Bitcoins. Martti Malmi, an early Bitcoin evangelist, supported New Liberty Standard by investing 5050 Bitcoins as seed money. In return, he received a whopping USD 5.02 via PayPal. When it was launched, New Liberty Standard estimated the value of Bitcoins based on the consumption of electricity per Bitcoin cost. Based on this valuation system, between October and November of 2009, the exchange rate between Bitcoins and US dollars was approximately 1000 to 1.

Back then, Bitcoin was the only cryptocurrency. Yet as more cryptocurrencies have been developed, crypto exchanges have had to evolve to support trading among multiple cryptos. ERC-20 is a technical standard used for smart contracts on the Ethereum blockchain for implementing tokens. ERC stands for Ethereum Request for Comment. Today, ERC-20 drives an increasing amount of tokens into the crypto world through ICOs. ERC-20 was first proposed in November of 2015, and it functioned such that any token that complied with ERC-20 would be compatible with Ethereum wallets. With ERC-20, developers can also build apps (DAPPs), and people who build DAPPs usually issue tokens as "currency" to be used within the DAPP. These tokens are not allowed to be directly traded for fiat money. They have to first be exchanged for Bitcoin or Ethereum. However, the creation of ERC-20 is important to the history of exchanges because of the "currency within a currency" it makes possible. Clearly, the appetite for trading between cryptos is not diminishing.

Before China banned ICOs and crypto exchanges in late 2017, China-based exchanges were a major force in the global crypto market. BTCC, founded in 2011, is generally considered to have been the first crypto exchange in China. The volume of trading on BTCC was immense, among the top three global exchanges. Yet, like many others, BTCC was asked to close in 2017. Current exchanges like Huobi, OKcoin, and Binance were all founded by teams originating in China.

Exchanges are important because they're sort of "on the top of the food chain" of the crypto economy. They're also a place where true entrepreneurs and innovators rub elbows with speculators and scam artists. Their lack of regulation often creates a vacuum in which people can take advantage of one another. In the United States, Japan, and South Korea, all exchanges are registered domestically, which means that they exist under strict government regulation. China was one of the markets that initially adopted the strictest regulations for cryptocurrency. Yet China eventually decided the risk was not worth the reward and shut them down completely.

The Fight Between Centralization And Decentralization

The crypto exchanges that we have been talking about here have mostly been centralized exchanges. Centralized exchange trading provides benefits like the facilitation of liquidity, the assurance of transparency, and the ability to pin trades to the current market price. It is true that there are certain risks associated with exchange trading—such as inner management risks, unethical business practices on the part of the exchange itself, and the potential for asset misappropriation fraud. However, decentralized exchanges can address many of these risks and issues. If you compare centralized exchanges with decentralized exchanges, you'll find big differences between the two.

Centralized exchanges provide services like Know Your Customer, custodian services, and asset clearance. Centralized exchanges also provide sophisticated solutions for clients in terms of asset management. They have flexible approaches when it comes to charging clients. These exchanges will charge users trading fees, initial listing fees related to ICOs, and so forth.

Decentralized exchanges, on the other hand, were once the hottest thing in the crypto market because of their different approach. In June of 2017, Bancor Protocal initiated a crowd-funding ICO to establish a multilayered system of currency wherein one token could be be "reserved" for another. It aimed to set the new standard for cryptocurrency exchanges. (As a decentralized exchange, Bancor Network relies on smart contracts to match trades and execute them automatically.) The ICO raised $153 million worth of Ethereum. (By then, the market price of Ethereum was $273.) It was the most valuable ICO in history at the time. Bancor's ICO also received the endorsement of well-known investors, including Tim Draper, the American venture capitalist. (Even though Bancor has a very successful ICO, it would not be correct to say it has become "the star" of decentralized exchanges. The twenty-four-hour trading volume of Bancor is only $6 million, far behind competitors like Kybernetwork and IDEX.)

Decentralized exchanges like Bancor's satisfy all the demands of investors and traders that centralized exchanges fail to address. Centralized exchanges use a strong ICO filtering system that many find too exclusive. Decentralized exchanges support the trading of any token based on ERC-20. Decentralized exchanges also have a lower market barrier than centralized ones. Some ICOs that are less fortunate in their "launch phases" meaning they don't receive cornerstone investments or cannot afford the cost of being in centralized exchanges find that decentralized exchanges remain an effective way for them to raise capital.

Cyptocurrency: The Next Level for Banking Reform

EtherDelta is an important cautionary tale in this space. It was one of the biggest and most dominant Ethereum decentralized exchanges. About 230 different tokens were actively traded on it. Many ICOs would use it to offer exclusive token sales to investors and institutional investors two days before they were available to the public. Because of this, EtherDelta was a popular starting point for ICOs and at its peak had millions of users.

CEX AND DEX;

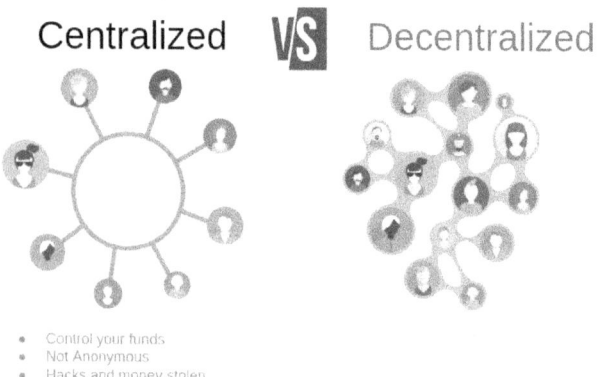

- Control your funds
- Not Anonymous
- Hacks and money stolen
- Server downtime

- Not easy adoption

Whenever a cryptocurrency gets more attention and experiences a corresponding increase in market value the exchanges carrying it draw increasing attention from hackers. Hackers try their best to find any loopholes in the exchanges that will allow them to steal cryptos. (We have talked about the DAO project that ultimately forced Ethereum into two blockchains.) Safety and security were also the issues that brought down EtherDelta. Many users trusted implicitly that a decentralized exchange would be safe from hacking. However, EtherDelta was hacked multiple times. EtherDelta doesn't use a traditional computer server. Instead, it's all backed up on Ethereum blockchain using a smart contract. It is a true DAPP, a distributed app existing in the crypto world. When users trade on EtherDelta, they need to create a wallet that can talk to the smart contract. EtherDelta is what's often called a "wholesome wallet solution." EtherDelta users need to input a public key and a private key when they access their wallets. It is this step that puts users in a spot where they become the target of hackers.

EtherDelta has been hacked three times. Until recently, hackers attacked by entering the safety loopholes in EtherDelta and inputting malicious code that would farm private keys from users' wallets and then steal their tokens. But in December of 2017, hackers directly targeted the exchange's DNS server, which shocked everyone and resulted in losses across the exchange. EtherDelta has now lost the trust of most of its users and is largely considered a "has-been."

The Future Of Exchanges: The Coexistence Of Centralization And Decentralization.

Centralized exchanges and decentralized exchanges are both going to be around for a long time. Centralized exchanges still dominate the market in terms of liquidity and traffic, but decentralized exchanges are sticking around.

Decentralized exchanges built upon Ethereum were once believed to have stronger defense systems, and many felt they could grow in popularity because of their resistance to hacking. However, as cases like EtherDelta proved, nothing is ever truly "unhackable."

The fundamental idea of cryptocurrency (as well as blockchain) is to decentralize, but for the moment, in terms of practical application, centralized exchanges have a stronger economic foundation and a more dominant place in the market.

Business-wise, centralized exchanges have a solid model. They charge users trading fees and charge token sale fees related to ICOs. Leading centralized exchanges are realizing profits in the millions on a daily basis, simply due to the overwhelming volume of the trading they facilitate. (According to Recode, Coinbase, an American Bitcoin exchange, had revenues of over $1 billion in 2017. Binance, now based in Japan, expects a net profit of $500 million to $1 billion in 2018, according to its chief executive officer, Changpeng Zhao. And the volume of cryptocurrency trading is only going to increase in the days ahead.)

Centralized exchanges have the added appeal of being able to cover users' stolen tokens. Decentralized exchanges are not able to do this. On June 19, 2018, one of the world's largest cryptocurrency exchanges, Bithumb, experienced one of the most severe hacking incidents in cryptocurrency history, resulting in losses of $30 million. In the aftermath, Bithumb promised to refund the hacking victims' losses using its own reserve.

Centralized exchanges are constantly spending to improve their security, and to take care of the messes left after a hack. Because the exchanges are so profitable, they have the resources to do this. And their doing so helps maintain the reputation of the entire industry. Because of what they provide and how they work, centralized exchanges are becoming more and more similar to entities like NASDAQ and the New York Stock Exchange. Centralized exchanges have developed well-established trading systems that attract ICOs and investors. They are even beginning to attract "market makers." In the traditional financial industry, market makers can be brokerage houses or independent security dealers who assist investors with the selling and buying of securities. Market makers provide liquidity to the market and make it easy for investors to sell and buy at any moment. Decentralized exchanges support person-to-person trading, but their lack of market makers may become yet another hurdle.

Some Secrets Of Exchanges

The initial listing fee for an ICO on a centralized exchange can be a lot of money. How much exactly? Currently, there is no agreed-upon standard. The cost of listing an ICO on an exchange largely depends on the liquidity and structure of the exchange itself. Exchanges with high liquidity will charge more to list an ICO. The cost will also be related to the "heat" of the ICO. During the peak of the ICO market in 2017, the cost to list an ICO on a centralized exchange crept to between $1 million and $2 million on the top ten exchanges with the highest liquidity levels. Compare that to what stock exchanges charge for an IPO. According to NASDAQ, the initial listing fee of an IPO is usually between $125,000 and $300,000 (excluding the yearly listing fee). Yet for many startups and investors, an ICO is a much easier way to raise capital. Startups benefit from the low cost of money, and early investors like getting in on exciting young technologies before everyone else. Keeping ICOs attractive in the future will be the single factor that most determines if the success of this exchanges continues. Not all exchanges profit through their initial listing fees. Some have instead implemented community voting as part of the selection criteria for new tokens, and they charge a small fee for each vote. (This helps ensure that fake or fraudulent coins not be introduced and also gives the exchange a tidy profit.) Voters pay each time they cast a ballot. More votes means more support for an ICO, and more profit for the exchange.

Bibox, an exchange that I cofounded, uses both an initial listing fee and community voting to select and list ICOs. A few high-quality projects will be listed on the exchange directly after providing legal papers and paying an initial listing fee, but the rest go through the community voting procedure. To stay competitive in this fast-evolving industry, Bibox is constantly improving its community voting mechanism to make the process easier and better. In Bibox's earliest days, community voting was much more simple and direct. Any user could simply open an account on Bibox and start voting. Today, voters pay one token (issued by Bibox) each time they vote. One person can vote 10,000 times if he or she wants to.

Some exchanges have also introduced the "super node" model. To be a super node in the community, a person (or a group of people or institutions) must reserve a certain amount of tokens issued by the exchange. They are also required to have investments with the exchange. But the votes of this super nodes, as you might imagine, can settle an issue once and for all. Initially, supernodes were only seen in crypto investment funds. Now, however, the model has slowly been migrating into traditional venture capital spaces.

The notion of "consensus" is a concept that's bigger than crypto. It can touch all aspects of human society. But when it comes to the financial world, consensus can be dominated by institutional investors or powerful groups. This is a problem, because it's a reversion back to centralization. Community consensus ought to be a way to create balance between elites and the majority. That's why Bibox's next step will be to introduce third-party valuation into the consensus-reaching process. Under our model, one third of voting rights will be given to super nodes, one third will be the community's, and the rest will be reserved for the exchange itself.

Tokens issued by exchanges play a big role in determining community power. Whether it's a super node or an individual investor, voting is always going to be based on how many tokens a group or person holds. In the case of Bibox, each community member is entitled to voting rights equivalent to tokens held. Before voting for an ICO, each voting member needs to reserve a certain amount of tokens.

Cyptocurrency: The Next Level for Banking Reform

Let's looks at MakerDAO. It's a company that aims to create a "decentralized stablecoin" cryptocurrency tied to the US dollar. Their coin is called DAI. It uses a smart contract-based managing system. In their community, the more users hold onto the coin, the more voting rights they will have when it comes to issuing more DAI next year. Ideally, under this model, everyone is supposed to be involved in the community voting process.

There are always new models popping up that we can learn from. Fcoin is another good example, having recently become one of the top ten global exchanges. Fcoin introduced the concept of "trading is mining" in June of 2018, and it has been attracting many investors and traders. This model came about after a loophole was exploited in Fcoin's way of doing business. Fcoin announced it would cease using 30 percent referral fees. The day after the announcement, its trading volume decreased by 5 percent. But with the launch of the "trading is mining" model, it has become more successful than it ever was before! The model of "trading is mining" is innovative and exciting, and others are adopting it. Coinpark, for example, has also moved to a "trading is mining" format. Yet Coinpark goes even further than Fcoin. Newly listed tokens go to Bibox first, and the ones who "survive" the filtering system will then go to Coinpark. It is essentially an exchange for quality tokens! Who can say what innovation will come next?

The Future Of Crypto Exchanges: External Regulation And Self-Regulation

The future of crypto exchanges probably depends on a lot on the industry's appetite for self-discipline. As I noted at the outset, exchanges are commonly known as the "top of the food chain." They control the ebb and flow of trade and play a crucial role in the token economy. Exchanges are not supposed to support insider trading in either the prime market or the secondary market. Because of their influence, any policy or rule an exchange introduces will probably have a powerful influence on the market as a whole. In the early days of crypto, there were many "gray areas" when it came to crypto exchanges. Many investors made a fast buck with unethical business practices. Yet the crypto exchanges expelled the bad elements because they had to. There was no other way to continue to exist. It is my belief that to move forward effectively, the exchanges will have to acknowledge that their journey of self-improvement is far from over.

Due to increasing competition among exchanges, many seem tempted to shirk self-discipline and self-regulation. Accordingly, even in crypto-friendly countries, government regulation is becoming more intense. In January of 2018, the South Korea Blockchain Association attempted to thwart further regulation by launching a self-regulatory program. The Japanese Blockchain Association is working on something similar. It remains to be seen if these efforts will be enough.

Across the board, exchanges needs to increase their self-defense capabilities. Cryptocurrency is continually growing and evolving, and so must the security that protects it. With crypto marching headlong into the mainstream financial market, it would be a shame if it tripped and fell because of unaddressed security needs. According to CipherTrace, in the first two quarters of 2018, $731 million worth of cryptocurrencies were hacked, tripling the total figure for all of 2017. Phishing sites and DDos attacks are continuing to impact the reputations and accountability of exchanges of all sizes and types. Clearly, we are not yet doing enough. Addressing security capabilities will be critical for the long-term sustainability of the industry.

Cryptocurrency is traded between countries and across boundaries of every type. But even so, different countries have different regulations regarding these cryptos. Governments imposes these kind of regulations out of fear, and out of a lack of understanding. To avoid a dark future without crypto, it is up to all of us to make the case that we are not opposed to any regulation. In fact, it must be shown that crypto can be regulated. The best case scenario, of course, is that the industry is able to show that it is trustworthy enough to regulate itself.

The Secondary Market: Low-Lying Land

we've covered basic elements of crypto econom including cryptocurrency, smart contracts, distributed ledger-based DAPPs, ICOs, and tokens. We've also explored how crypto exchanges support direct trading between major cryptocurrencies and fiat money, as well as trading among and between different cryptocurrencies. And we've reviewed how ICOs have established themselves as a powerful new way of raising capital in crypto world. Yet all of above is generally happening in what I like to call "the primary market." And when an ICO is listed in a crypto exchange, it also has to confront investors from the secondary market. The secondary market is kind of similar to the stock market. But because cryptocurrency is still young, when it comes to secondary market influence, we are seeing phenomena that can be quite unusual.

The Secondary Market Of Low Liquidity

There is imbalance between the prime market and secondary market. That's the first thing to understand. The prime market has become standardized and has been so ever since traditional VC came onto the ICO evaluation scene. Many quality ICOs have been received well in the prime market. However, these same ICOs often get the cold shoulder when they're listed on the secondary market. There are many reasons for this. Liquidity reveals how strong a project is in terms of potential cash-out. In a market where there are fewer buyers than sellers, sellers will lower their trading price to attract buyers. In the crypto world, this decreases the value of tokens. The twenty-four-hour trading cycle of the prime market is frenetic and crazy, but the secondary market remains extremely inactive. There are hundreds of tokens being traded in the secondary market, true, but investors do not see any liquidity.

Cyptocurrency: The Next Level for Banking Reform

The reason behind this mainly arises from people trying to make quick money in the secondary market. When ICOs reach the secondary market, the prices are much higher than they were in the prime market. Accordingly, shareholders of an ICO often try to cash out before the prices go down in the secondary market. However, prime market investors making fast money and cashing out leaves a mess for the individual investors in the secondary market who have purchased the tokens at the peak of their price. An ICO is like a stock that needs constant buying and selling to maintain its liquidity and value. When early investors in the ICO cash out their shares, it makes it very challenging to maintain stability.

When a blockchain startup launches an ICO, it's usually still in its early stages. Once it is listed in the market, the startup may find it is not able to keep up with innovations it promised to deliver on paper. What then makes such a situation even worse is when the shareholders try to cash out, which in turn drives the anxiety level of the whole market up. True, some strong projects do continuously improve their service and technology and see their quarterly net profits reliably increasing. However, we cannot assume that this will always, or even typically, be the case.

The design of the early token economy is certainly not perfect. In a traditional financial market, before a company launches an IPO, the CEO and management team design a thoughtful plan detailing how shares will be offered, and price of shares, in a way that ensures the liquidity of the stock after the IPO is launched. But many blockchain projects launch an ICO without sufficient experience (or any experience). This lack of experience usually reveals itself when the secondary market comes in to play. Currently, there are just not enough competent financial teams available to help startups to properly analyze all pertinent aspects of their offerings. As a consequence, many companies overoffer shares to investors when conducting the ICO launch. For example, many only reserve 10 percent of issued tokens, meaning 90 percent of tokens will go flooding into the market, which makes it possible for speculators to manipulate the prices. Once a bad actor controls over 50 percent of the tokens of one ICO, the team on the project will have no control over the tokens or the prices of the tokens in the secondary market. This kind of situation happened a lot in the early days of the cryptocurrency market. Many investors took advantage of insider information to make a quick buck off of people in the secondary market. While the overall situation has improved, the lack of strong regulation still hurts liquidity in the secondary market (as well as some investors in the prime market). Yet, so far, the majority of ICOs are still using the utility token format. They are not traded in markets where security regulations are fully developed. The role the SEC is playing or hints that it may play is increasingly critical. Total transparency would greatly increase market liquidity. As it stands, the violent up and down of token values in the secondary market remains a major issue. (Just look at the market prices at which Bitcoins are valued in different countries.)

According to crypto expert Vincent Molinari, many ICO offers are still no more than schemes a way for a few people to cash in. Yet he believes when regulation is in place, the market value will return to a reasonable level, this schemes will go away, and all good actors will benefit over time. Long-term investment will become the rule and not the exception. Consider that in the prime market of an ICO, it usually takes six months to a year to turn capital into profits. Whereas, in traditional VC, as I noted earlier, it usually takes ten years. As we wait for regulation to be put into place (either from within or without), the token economy is nonetheless constantly evolving on its own. By learning from the past, new ICOs will improve by offering fewer shares so as to have better control of the project and the market prices of issued tokens. In this connection, many investment institutes are already playing important roles in stabilizing the secondary market and increasing confidence in investors.

The cryptocurrency trading provider Altonomy recently launched a crypto "index fund" that includes the top five digital asset trading funds Bitcoin, Ether, Ripple, Bitcoin Cash, and Litecoin. As a digital asset management provider, Altonomy is aiming to help investors enhance their crypto returns. As the market continues to stabilize, we can probably expect to see more funds like this arrive on the scene.

The Unregulated Market Maker

During the process of launching a typical Wall Street IPO, companies often hire market makers to increase liquidity, and also to support the price of the stock. Market makers enable the smooth flow of financial markets. The SEC defines a "market maker" as any firm that stands ready to buy and sell stock on a regular and continuous basis at a publicly quoted price.

In cryptocurrency, most startups will hire market makers to increase the liquidity of their tokens in the first three months of the ICO. Since the end of 2017, there has been a flood of market makers coming into the ICO scene. This is because the secondary market for cryptocurrency is similar to the traditional financial market in terms of operation. Market makers coming into the cryptocurrency space serve the same purpose as when they're working in the traditional stock market. But because of the absence of regulation, market makers in the crypto secondary market are not required to be licensed. Some are still very professional and helpful. But, of course, some are not. Many market makers do little to help increase market liquidity and facilitate trades. Instead, they are only facilitating arbitrage. Accordingly, anyone working in this space should be very careful when dealing with them.

Hot Money In The Secondary Market

Due to the lack of regulation (and/or the lack of enforcement), cryptocurrency often finds its secondary market flooded with speculators and manipulators. Whether you're a quant or a non-quant, it's easy to see that there are many opportunities in cryptocurrency that do not exist in the traditional market. I personally know investors who have made a fortune in crypto using short-term quant strategies. There are several reasons why they've been able to do this.

Cyptocurrency: The Next Level for Banking Reform

First and foremost, many different stock exchanges exist in the secondary market. One token might be traded on multiple exchanges. The prices of one token might be very different from one exchange to another. Many traders invest and profit through the difference in price of the same token on different exchanges.

Second, in the futures market, both Okex and Bitmap support futures trading. This trading can be leveraged a hundredfold. Though the price difference can be very small, if the risk is manageable, the return can be huge. Many people have made fortunes this way.

And finally, the secondary market can be rigged by manipulators. If you put major currencies such as Bitcoin and Ethereum aside, many of the tokens you'll find issued through ICOs are there to be manipulated. These tokens are similar to penny stocks. And everyone wants to believe they've discovered the next Bitcoin and Ethereum.

The problems facing the secondary market in crypto are similar to the problems that were faced by American stock exchanges 100 years ago. When a market lacks certain regulations and oversights, predictable things happen. Pump and dumps are very common in the secondary market of cryptocurrency, just as they were on the US stock exchange so many years ago. Fraudsters spreading false news about new cryptos in a chat room have a great deal in common with con artists who sent false telegrams with information that might impact a stock in 1919.

In any traditional financial market, the practice of market manipulation is illegal. And it should be. The lack of regulation that lets some people make a quick dollar hurts everyone else because it hurts our faith in the system. When contrasted with the traditional stock market, the cryptocurrency market will always have an innate uniqueness. This won't change even when it becomes more regulated. Stock markets are usually open between 9:30 a.m. to 4 p.m. on weekdays, meaning trades only happen during this specific time frame. It allows for high-volume trading and high liquidity, but you can't trade on weekends or at midnight. In contrast, the secondary market of cryptocurrency will always be open twenty-four hours a day.

OTC—Big Players

We've discusses the importance of liquidity and investor confidence in the secondary market. Now I'd like to discuss OTC (Over The Counter) trading, and its importance for the top 1 percent of investors and traders in cryptocurrency world.

OTC is a relatively simple concept. An OTC trade is done directly between two parties without the supervision or facilitation of an exchange, but buyers and sellers still need to find each other to close that trade. In the world of cryptocurrency, OTC is mostly used for fiat-to-cryptocurrencies trades. (Exchange trading is mostly comprised of trades among different tokens and cryptocurrencies.)

Cyptocurrency: The Next Level for Banking Reform

Why does OTC exist in the first place? Well, the financial market is a bit like a domino. When you push one down, it will trigger a chain reaction. In an exchange where information is transparent, a very large movement of cash will trigger sudden price movements in the market which has the potential to impact the person or group of people behind the trade. Many would prefer to go the OTC route and keep things quiet.

OTC traders dealing in amounts over $250,000 are often called "whales." Other customers are often called "small fish." People on exchanges such as Huobi and Binance are often individual traders. This is the visible market that the majority of crypto players are most familiar with. But the liquidity of the visual market is restricted by the number of individuals participating at any moment. It's also restricted by which currencies carry which liquidity. Exchanges are like retail shops on the street, open to everyone. When a whale shows up in the market to purchase a large amount of cryptocurrencies, the whole market goes up. This is usually referred to as "slippage." For big players, OTC is the preferred option precisely because it's not supposed to generate a sudden market up or down. OTC traders can be private traders, brokers, or institutions. Their major function is to provide security during the buy to avoid turbulence on transparent exchanges. The crypto exchange Altonomy serves as an OTC provider and puts its own funds into the platform to secure the liquidity of OTC trades. Increasing liquidity means maintaining a relatively stable and reasonable price for buyers and sellers. Once the price is set, Altonomy will offset the risk in the market. Meanwhile, a price for the trade will be decided. For example, if a buyer is considering purchasing a certain amount of Ethereum, Altonomy will generate a relatively low price that will also have a low influence on the market.

Despite the secretive nature of specific trades, OTC trading has a profound influence over the cryptocurrency market. The liquidity of exchanges is only going to go up as more and more individuals come into the game. OTC also provides a strong support function exterior to the traditional exchanges. For example, the price of Bitcoin and Ethereum is largely dependent on its prices in OTC trading. The volume of OTC trading also reflects the market liquidity and market cap. OTC also influences the confidence of future cryptocurrency trades. The more trades made through OTC, the more confidence is injected into the market. If the amount of cash being invested into the market decreases, so will the confidence in cryptocurrency. According to an OTC trading desk (with whom, full disclosure, my company has a collaboration), the cash flowing into the crypto market in January of 2018 was only two-thirds of what it was in 2017. As a result, the whole market was suffering from poor liquidity, and fewer trades were made during this period.

Currently, in addition, to Bitcoin, OTC trading can be found in traditional venture capital, family office trading, and hedge funds. But due to a lack of regulation, many pension funds, banks, and wealth management companies stay out of the market entirely. However, there's a major OTC desk called Circle, where you'll find very high-profile investors such as Goldman Sachs,

DRW, Genesis, Smart Contract, and Octagon Strategy. According to Reuters, Circle's daily volume of digital assets trades was between $1.5 billion and $2 billion during December of 2017 alone. In addition, I should note that Skype and Google Voice are places where OTC trades can also take place.

The Future Of The Secondary Market

Regulation is going to decide the future of the cryptocurrency secondary market. Money held by traditional financial institutions wants to come in. It is stopped by a lack of sufficient liquidity, yes. But it's also stopped by a lack of regulation. Regulation by the SEC of things like custody services would help traditional investors decide to what degree digital assets may be safely invested into the market. According to Coinbase, about $200 million worth of digital assets are currently "watching the SEC" and waiting to be invested. Once an effective solution to custody services appears, all those digital assets will join the market, which will increase market liquidity wonderfully.

An SEC decision to regulate crypto trading products will also impact the influence of institutional investors. So far, the SEC and CFTC (Commodity Futures Trading Commission) have shown themselves to be very fond of derivatives. Yet limited tradable cryptocurrencies are not giving a lot of incentive for old money to come into the market. In July of 2018, a Chicago-based exchange handed in an application for a Bitcoin ETF to the SEC. Previously, Gemini and Winklevoss had tried to apply for an ETF with the SEC. (We'll have to wait and see if this one takes.) Having more financial derivatives available will increase liquidity in the secondary market. According to a Reuters report from March of 2018, the British exchange house Coinfloor will soon begin selling Bitcoin futures. Their product targets hedge funds, sophisticated individual traders, and Bitcoin miners.

So far, US regulators haven't been interested in creating specific regulations for crypto exchanges. Accordingly, the crypto market lacks the sophisticated financial products needed to attract big players. This will be a barrier not just for the secondary market, but for the whole crypto industry in the days ahead.

Leading Currencies In The Field

It was tempting to write an investigations book about Bitcoin since, at the time of writing, it is the brand synonymous with the word cryptocurrency in the public mind. However, as I spent more time with Monero, Litecoin, Ethereum, and others, I realized that although they were all subtly or sometimes significantly different and set out to provide certain abilities to their users, for an investigator, they all worked in the same fundamental way. When you consider that technology is a hard taskmaster and that online services hit the proverbial fan almost as fast as they spend their venture capital money (MySpace anyone?), will Bitcoin still be valuable and newsworthy in two years, or even a year? Could Ethereum be the next Facebook of the currency world and become the default choice for transactions and contracts of all types? Only the future will answer that question, but the methods of investigating crime involving a cryptocurrency will remain basically the same. So, although Part II of this book deals with investigations that are focused on tools for Bitcoin with its spin-offs and alt-coins, and Ethereum, this is only because tools are available for them. Should Monero takes the limelight in a few years' time, undoubtedly an investigator will be able to find similar tools to help them investigate effectively.

In late 2017, investopedia.com, the world's largest financial educational website, named Litecoin, Ethereum, Zcash, Dash, Ripple, and Monero as the best investable cryptocurrencies aside from Bitcoin, but that should not necessarily drive research by an investigator. Some of the new breeds of currency lend themselves to criminal uses. For example, Zcash offers "shielded" transactions where the sender's and receiver's details are hidden, and Dash provides increased anonymity over Bitcoin. It is more likely that these features, rather than Bitcoins' burgeoning value, would attract someone with the need to hide his or her transactions for nefarious purposes.

I ought to be clear that I am in no way accusing these companies of deliberately attracting a certain type of client, any more than Tor (which was partly developed and funded by the U.S. government), and designed to hide terrorists and pedophiles. However, if you, as an investigator, are aware of the specific security and anonymity features of a particular currency, you may be more prepared to research and ultimately exploit them during an investigation.

Due to these issues, I will decline from the obvious inclusion of a list of available cryptocurrencies, since by the time you read this, there may be a new pretender in town being used by our suspects. Instead, this book will try to both be specific as to investigation methods you can use now and look at the generic principles behind this type of analysis. The website Coinmarketcap.com maintains a constantly updating list of the primary cryptocurrencies, almost 900 were listed at the time of writing. If you are interested in launching your own cryptocurrency and becoming wildly wealthy, you will find an excellent tutorial at www.ethereum.org/token. (And once you are a billionaire, please remember who gave you the tip and at least invite me onto your boat!)

Is Blockchain Technology Just for Cryptocurrencies?

Although we look in detail at what a blockchain is, suffice it to say that it is simply a list of transactions, distributed to many nodes on a network, grouped into clusters called blocks, and using a physical analogy stacked on top of one another like a Lego Brick Tower.

The concept of a virtually anonymous, distributed ledger, the contract-led blockchain-based system certainly has some significant possibilities, but believing what you read in the press and in a company's marketing materials would be a major mistake. In 2018, you need to include two terms in your prospectus to float your company on the stock market or add to your brochure to sell your latest product: artificial intelligence (AI) and blockchain! In fact, throwing a bit of "cloud" in there could not hurt either. I saw the marketing headline "The First A.I. Big Data Marketing Cloud for Blockchain" on a software website recently. It seems that any system that adds up 2 + 2 or includes an "if . . . then" decision tree is now considered AI that may take over the planet at any moment. It's not and it won't, even if it's got a lot of "big data in the cloud"!

It is the same issue with the blockchain: Business analysts have watched the extraordinary rise in the value of Bitcoin, read an article on the technology it is based on, and then added the word to any system that needs to sound a bit more hip and cool (although I am well aware that the words "hip" and "cool" themselves are no longer considered "hip" or even "cool").

A quick search of the Internet, reveals insurance companies that will put your insurance agreement on the blockchain, delivery companies that will use smart contracts to deliver your parcel, auction sites that use the blockchain to reduce fraud, and security companies that promise the blockchain will prevent you from ever being hacked again. Sound far-fetched? Most are. But consider the following auction-house example.

Several years ago, I bought an old book at auction or at least I thought I had bought it since I was the final bidder. However, the auction house told me later that it did not have a record of my final bid, and since the previous bid had not reached the reserve, the book would be put up for sale again. Because the auction software was hosted in a single location and the auction house controlled it, I had no recourse or way of proving otherwise. However,

I had taken a screenshot of my browser with my high bid and my successful purchase message. The auction house then told me that it had "lost the book." After a few choice words and threats of legal action from me, it "found" the book and honored the bid. It was clear that the auction house wanted more from the auction and simply wanted a chance to sell again with a better audience. How would a blockchain-based system have improved this situation?

A blockchain auction system could work as follows: Every bidder is a node on the blockchain. A product to be auctioned is set up as a token with a contract of sale connected to it, based, for example, on the Ethereum network. Each bid made is a transaction between the auction and the highest bidder with the "token" moving seamlessly from high bidder to high bidder. Whoever is the final bidder when the real or virtual gavel comes down is left as the owner of the token. Everyone on the blockchain can see the final transaction, and the contract is set. I own the item because I own the token, and it's proven by every node on the network. The sales contract can also form part of the blockchain contract, minimizing paperwork. (If anyone sets this system up and makes a million, please once again remember me when you are out on your yacht.)

How does this affect the investigator? Blockchain transactions on Bitcoin are one aspect of the technology and require a skill set that you will learn about in this book. However, in the future expect to find blockchain-based systems with transaction-centered contracts, in a wide variety of business sectors. An analyst will need to have the skills to learn how a blockchain functions, and be able to decode contracts, and follow the flow of contract transactions. I will cover contracts in a little more detail later in the book, but if you choose to carry out further research on the smart contract-based platforms such as Ethereum, it would not be a waste of time.

CHAPTER 5

Key Actors in Digital Technology

Although digital and non-fiat forms of currencies have been utilized for decades, nevertheless, the current emanation is substantively far superior and complex. The players in the latest innovative financial evolution are as follows:

- *Inventors (creators).* The major figure who initially created the revolution of DLT is the mysterious figure(s) of Satoshi Nakamoto, who is or are responsible for the creation of Bitcoin which used as its basis a form of blockchain technology, discussed in greater detail hereinafter. Alternative versions of blockchain then evolved separate from Bitcoin so that an almost infinite multitude of players could utilize the positive benefits of DLT (e.g., government agencies, financial institutions, private businesses, professional firms, and individuals) due to its alleged total imperviousness from hacking and thus affording total privacy. Among the emanations evolving from blockchain are smart contracts; security by "proof of stake" (groups called "miners" are able to use computing power for decision-making and have "proof of work"); and "blockchain scaling" (acceleration of blockchain transactions). Another major inventor is Vitalik Buterin, who created the Ethereum blockchain, which differs from Bitcoin (discussed at greater length below) in transaction time, the amount of Ether distributed, the method of costing transactions and other differences. The Walt Disney Company created Dragonchain which is another form of blockchain and is also a further evolution of Disney's prior animatronics and digital animation creations.

- ***Issuers or administrators.*** Following the dizzying success of Bitcoin, there are a multitude of individuals and companies creating and sponsoring a large variety of virtual currencies and other innovations, maintaining ledgers, and redeeming virtual currency. Their activities will inevitably transform how the financial and social world operates.

- ***Miners.*** Miners generates new virtual currency by utilizing special computer hardware, usually with ASIC-centric machines that solve cryptographic (mathematical) problems in return for which bitcoin, Ether, or other forms of cryptocurrency tokens or awards may be issued in return. The word "miners" is derived from traditional miners who dug mines in search of valuable minerals such as diamonds. Modern "miners" validate, often as a group, a set of transactions called a "block."

- ***Processing service providers.*** These are firms that provide the means of transferring virtual currencies from one user to another. There are numerous companies formed and are being created to provide these services (e.g., DC POS, Coinfy, CoinCorner, Coinbase).
- ***Users.*** There are an almost infinite number of users of the technology with applications being added daily and exponentially as the technology takes hold. Among the major areas of uses are financial services including international payments; securities trades; improvement of capital markets; use of smart contracts; improvement of online identity management; regulatory compliance; protection against money laundering and theft of assets; healthcare services given the need for privacy protection of patients' data and records; real estate transactions; record management; cybersecurity; accounting; and numerous other uses. In addition, there are the people connected to these areas.
- ***Wallet.*** A virtual currency "wallet" is a secure medium that is used to store, send, and receive digital currencies such as Bitcoin. Almost all coins issued require the use of the particular wallet to store the designated cryptocurrency. The wallet is actually a private key containing a secure digital code known only by the person possessing the crypto- currency together with the public key used to send and receive coins. Individuals and firms engaged in mining are not completely risk free as

evidenced by the theft of some 4736 BTC (bitcoins) on December 6, 2017 valued at $78.3 million from the cryptocurrency mining marketplace, NiceHash, that was founded in 2014. The methodology used to accomplish the theft has not been revealed and was being investigated by the company and governmental authorities.

- *Wallet provider.* A wallet provider is an entity that uses software applications or other means to enable the user to store, hold, and transfer virtual currencies as well as provide the means of maintaining a customer's balance online or offline, and security.
- *Exchanges.* Exchanges are individuals or companies, almost always businesses, who operate analogously to stock exchanges by exchanging convertible virtual currency for fiat money or for other virtual currencies, precious metals, and other comparable assets and vice versa. Bitcoin has become mainstream with the announcement that Chicago's two largest financial exchanges, the Chicago Mercantile Exchange (CME) and the Chicago Board Options Exchange (CBOE) have made available Bitcoin futures that investors can engage in by shorting or otherwise, thereby giving legitimacy to this cryptocurrency trades. On December 10, 2017, trading on Bitcoin was inaugurated by CBOE and trading had to be shut down due to the frenzy which caused the price of Bitcoin to surge by 26 percent. The CME launch was to take place on December 18, 2017 and

proceeded to do so only to witness the extreme volatility of the futures.

- ***Trading platforms.*** A trading platform is the means whereby currencies are exchanged. The most well-known exchange platform for the exchange of foreign currencies is FOREX, which enables parties to exchange currencies of different countries often coupled with a short- term gain for a fee. The ascendance of virtual currencies added a new wrinkle to the conversion inasmuch as trading may involve a closed virtual currency between two parties without the intervention of a third party. Nevertheless, there are numerous platforms that have arisen to engage in electronic trading of virtual currencies, particularly by parties who wish or may only be able to afford a percentage ownership of the cryptocurrencies made available for purchase. They permit the exchange of fiat currencies for digital currencies. The exchanges may be private or open to the public. The exchanges vary in fees, verification requirements, exchange rates, and other features. Among the exchanges are Coinbase, Binance, CoinMama, Bittrex, CEX.IO, and Bitfinex. Investors are cautioned to be wary about platform trading especially, according to the Federal Bureau of Investigation (FBI), with respect to schemes operated by that who falsely represent that their platforms afford above-average market returns at below-market risk through the trading of bank instruments.

- Numerous other actors. These may include merchants, brokers and dealers, software developers, and various other potential actors engaged in the latest innovative advances in virtual currencies.

Benefits And Risks Of Digital Currencies

Benefits of Digital Currencies

As with almost all technological innovations, there are benefits and risks associated with the latest advances. Benefits include:

- Verification of identity;
- Significant reduction in costs due to the removal of intermediaries such as banks in the payment processes;
- Speed of money transfers by the elimination of clearing houses;
- Facilitation of micro-payments for low-cost online goods and services;
- Reduction of exposure risks that may occur when transacting bearer instruments;
- Use by those unable to use banking and credit facilities owing to lack of credit (e.g. having refugee status or lacking a credit history); and
- Recording of transactions including deeds and other indicia of property ownership.

The uses which may have both positive and negative outcomes are:

- A store of value—they are comparable to precious metals in that they do not ordinarily pay dividends or interest unlike metals are assets that may be divisible and portable;
- Trading—virtual currencies may be purchased, sold, and act as security. As with other assets they may result in capital gains or losses but, at least at this juncture, they are much more volatile causing height- ened speculation;
- Payments and transactions—may be used where accepted as payment for real and personal property or fees; and
- Transfer of money—may be utilized at a lower cost internationally to transfer remittances or for similar purposes.

Risks of Digital Currencies

The negative aspects of digital currencies include:

- Lack of acceptance by banks and the protection afforded by them and by merchants;
- Loss of interest on deposits;
- Security concerns such as use by terrorists, drug dealers, money launderers, and other criminal elements;
- Currency volatility;
- Payment beneficiary identification—loss of identity, for example, through death or mental incompetence may cause loss of holdings and transactions;
- Limited user base;

- Uncertainty concerning future regulation and tax treatment;
- Cyber-threats such as hacking, theft, and loss;
- Cross-national nature makes prosecutions very difficult;
- Lack of governmental backstops;
- Lack of backing by other secure assets; and
- Lack of intrinsic value.

U.S. Government Agencies' Risks Advisories

Commodity Futures Trading Commission (CFTC)

The Commodity Futures Trading Commission (CFTC) categorized risks of virtual currencies as:

- Operational risks—virtual currencies, having many different platforms, are not subject to supervision that otherwise applies to regulated exchanges; these platforms may be missing critical safeguards and customer protection;
- Cybersecurity risks—some platforms may commingle customer assets which may affect whether or how one can withdraw the currency; and some may be vulnerable to hacks resulting in theft of virtual currency or loss of customer assets;
- Speculative risks—virtual currency is subject to substantial volatility and price swings often due to inadequate trading volume; promises of

guaranteed returns may be part of fraudulent schemes; and

- Fraud and manipulation risk—depending on the platforms, they may be vulnerable to hacks resulting in theft of virtual currency and loss of assets, Ponzi schemes, and fraudulent "bucket shop" schemes.

An example of the risks is the theft of $30, 950, 010 USDT (a cryptocurrency pegged to the U.S. dollar) that was removed from the Tether Treasury wallet on November 19, 2017 and transferred to an unknown Bitcoin address. The company, in announcing the theft, stated that it was in the process of recovering the stolen funds and further warned potential purchasers of the funds that none would be honored.

Consumer Financial Protection Bureau (CFPB)

The Consumer Financial Protection Bureau (CFPB) has also posted consumer advisories noting risks as stated above by the CFTC and adding problems associated with bitcoins. Among the added risks were: (1) persons alleging they were exchange representatives to whose accounts moneys were transferred to purchase bitcoins but the exchanges never transpired; and (2) Bitcoin kiosks that are connected to the Internet to permit the exchange of cash for bitcoins appear to be ATMs but do not function as traditional ATMs in that they are not connected to a bank, lack the safeguards of bank ATMs, often charge large transaction fees as high as 7 percent, may well have high exchange rates, and when the insertion of a wrong 64-character public key can result in funds being sent to another person; and that the loss of the private key may cause a total loss of the bitcoins. Initially, the Bureau had few complaints pertaining to virtual currency transactions (six in 2016) but in 2017 and after there have been hundreds of complaints from the inability to access funds within the time period promised, transaction or service problems, to fraud.

Although Bitcoin and other forms of digital currencies have been associated with money laundering and unlawful drug transactions owing to the anonymity provided by bitcoins, nevertheless, it has been suggested that these risks are overestimated. The ownership of virtual currency is public thereby permitting substantial analysis of the transactions. Bitcoins have come out from undercover to be used by large companies internationally. A possible contrary view was voiced by the new chairman of the Federal Reserve, Jerome Powell, who warned that central banks engaging in issuing digital currencies are vulnerable to cyberattacks, criminal activities, and privacy concerns. He stated further that there are tradeoffs between strengthening security and enabling illegal activity. Advance cryptography, while reducing vulnerability to cyberattacks, also facilitates unlawful activity.

Government Services Administration (GSA)

The GSA and other federal agencies are exploring the use of DLTs like blockchain for financial management, procurement, IT asset and supply chain management, smart contracts, intellectual property, etc. through its Emerging Citizen Technology program. The program launched the U.S. Federal Blockchain platform for federal agencies and U.S. businesses interested in exploring DLT and its implementation within government. It hosted the first U.S. Federal Blockchain Forum on July 18, 2017, uniting more than 100 federal managers from dozens of unique agencies to discuss use cases, limitations, and solutions.

Securities and Exchange Commission (SEC)

The Securities and Exchange Commission (SEC) has issued a series of investor bulletins warning of the risks associated with initial coin offerings (ICOs) and other digital related offerings. Its Office of Investor Education and Advocacy issued a report on July 25, 2017 cautioning issuers and investors that virtual coins or tokens offered may be securities depending on the facts and circumstances of each ICO and may have to comply with registration requirements under the securities laws. It also cautioned investors to be wary of claims that an offering is exempt from registration, particularly if investors are not accredited or are described as crowdfunders. Investors are advised to ask what the money invested will be used for and the rights the virtual coin or token provide. Investors are particularly warned about persons using innovative technology to commit fraud or theft. The lack of a central authority and the international scope of offerings may preclude governmental intervention and assistance. Issuers are cautioned about compliance with applicable federal and state registration requirements.

In a follow-up alert, the SEC's Office of Investor Education and Advocacy repeated earlier warnings to investors due to the increasing use of ICOs by developers, businesses, and individuals who may use the offerings for publicity purposes to enhance the price of a company's stock.

The SEC advises it may suspend trading under circumstances where there is a lack of current accurate information about the company; when questions arise about the accuracy of publicly available information; and when there are concerns about the trading in the stock, particularly by insiders who may engage in market manipulation such as by "pump-and-dump" schemes. Investors additionally were given tips before making investments including research about the company; caution regarding stock promotions; possible microcap fraud; online blogs; promotional and press releases; frequent changes in a company's name, management, and type of business; and other cautionary guidelines.

Immigration and Customs Enforcement (ICE)

Immigration and Customs Enforcement (ICE) is particularly concerned with the unlawful use of virtual currency at an international level. Its HSI (Homeland Security Investigations) Illicit Finance and Proceeds of Crime Unit (IFPCU) operates in conjunction with members of the compliant virtual exchange industry and with the financial industry to combat the movement of illicit funds through the financial services industry. Among its activities is the expansion of its knowledge base by overcoming technological obstacles its agents encounter involving the emerging technologies such as blockchain; investigator training and procurement of equipment to enable investigators to combat illicit online activity; and collaboration with industry leaders to acquire the latest innovative forensic tools to analyze and identify information through the blockchain.

Federal Reserve Board (FED)

The FED does have an interest in the digital economy in as much as the payment, clearing, and settlement (PCS) processes involve some 600 million transactions per day. Accordingly, as stated in a study of DLT, it has expressed a keen interest in the development of innovations that affect the structural design and functioning of the financial markets.

European Union Agency for Network and Information Security (ENISA)

The European Union Agency Network and Information Security (ENISA), which is the center for cybersecurity in Europe headquartered in Greece, repeated many of the concerns stated above and added or modified them, as follows:

1. key and wallet management the need to protect one's private key which a malicious user may attempt to discover or reproduce;

2. cryptography risks the need to follow stringent key management policies and procedures to avoid software programs used to generate keys that are weak and vulnerable to attack;
3. attacks on consensus protocol the concern about being vulnerable to a "consensus hijack" or a "51 percent attack" where a malicious party may try to obtain more than 50 percent of the computing power of the entire network and possibly trigger double-spending attacks;
4. distributed denial of service the use of large numbers of spam transactions in the cryptocurrency network by multiple users that may cause denial of services (this actually occurred in March 2016);
5. smart contract management the substitution of code for legal language increases the complexity of the contract and requires skill usage or else is open to human error;
6. illegal use terrorist and/or criminal usage;
7. privacy—the E.U. General Data Protection Regulation60 may be violated by the public nature and perma- nency of the ledger because it requires deletion of personal data when no longer necessary; and
8. future challenges—the technology, especially that of quantum computing, may impede the security of algorithms and protocols.

Nobel Laureates' Concerns

Two Nobel Laureates in Economics expressed their apprehensions concerning virtual currencies, particularly, Bitcoin. Professor Robert J. Shiller of Yale University noted at the World Economic Forum (WEF) that while Bitcoin is a clever idea, it will not be a permanent part of our lives. Its underlying technology, blockchain, will have other applications. At the WEF there appeared to be a consensus that fiat money (cash) is going out of style. 62 Shiller said at another conference in Vilnius, Lithuania in December 2017, "Bitcoin, it's just absolutely exciting." He noted that the concept of Bitcoin as anti-government and anti-regulation is a wonderful story, "if it were only true." Another Nobel Laureate, Joseph Stiglitz, of Columbia University, expressed the view that Bitcoin should be outlawed inasmuch as it does not serve any socially useful function.

We've examined the technology underlying Bitcoin and other cryptocurrencies and examine some that have created a revolution in the way, where virtual currencies are currently exchanged and their increasing use in the near future.

Banks And Blockchain Technology

After, perhaps with justification, expressing fear that cryptocurrencies and blockchain technology will replace many bank functions and profit centers, it appears that banks are adapting to the innovations that inevitably occur. Among the banks that have indicated their interest in Bitcoin and DLT are two French banks, BNP Paribas and Société Générale, the U.S. Citibank, the Swiss investment bank UBS, Barclays and Standard Charter Bank, both of the U.K., Goldman Sachs, and the Spanish Banco Santander. All of these banks operate internationally and have determined that the many advantages of blockchain technology would reduce their costs significantly as well as offering increased security against hacking, among other advantages.

Types Of Cryptocurrencies

Bitcoin

The most commonly known cryptocurrency that has received global attention is Bitcoin. Although Bitcoin has a vast amount of publicity and is the largest of the cryptocurrencies, nevertheless, there are well over 1000 other currencies in existence that offer competing and varying alternative products, and offer services that differ from Bitcoin's. Among them are ZCash, Ethereum, Ripple, Litecoin, Dash, Manero, Hyperledger Fabric, Intel Sawtooth, and Corda.

How Bitcoin Works

Bitcoin is the creation of one or more persons using the pseudonym Satoshi Nakamoto. As there was wild speculation over the identity of "Deep Throat," the individual who exposed the Nixon Era Watergate scandal, later identified as Associate Director of the FBI, Mark Felt, comparable specualtion centers on the identity of Satoshi Nakamoto. Among others it has been rumored that the person is Nick Szabo who first used the expression "smart contract" based on his polymath and legal background, and his lectures on Bitcoin, blockchain, and Ethereum and their supposed attribution to the writings of Friedrich Hayek and Ayn Rand famed for their antipathy to government interference in economic and social life. Bitcoin and other cryptocurrencies are gradually being accepted as virtual legal tender for products and services. It had been reported that a prospective buyer could have purchased a new apartment in Dubai for 30 or 50 BTC (bitcoins) for a studio or one-bedroom apartment respectively (50 BTC was approximately $242,000 in early September 2017). Bitcoin is a decentralized virtual currency whose protocol allows for the storage of bitcoins in a "digital wallet" which are identified by the user's public key that may be transferred from one person to another anonymously without a central authority or other third party such as a bank to oversee or interfere with the transaction. Its value is based on whatever the customers determine and not by the input of external forces such as central banks, financial institutions, or governmental authorities. Bitcoin is not redeemable for another commodity, does not have a physical form, and has no government backing including the $250,000 insurance offered to depositors per bank account in U.S. insured banks and similarly in other countries.

Transactions in Bitcoin are accomplished by use of the Internet and are based on the principles of cryptography. Each Bitcoin and each user is encrypted with a unique identity. The time and amount of each transaction together with its Bitcoin addresses are permanently recorded on the decentralized blockchain ledger which is visible to all computers using the network but reveals no personal information about the parties. Each Bitcoin is divisible to eight decimal places thereby permitting extensive use. The transaction is irrevocable and the use of cryptography ensures against wrongful intrusion. In order for a user to transfers bitcoins to the receiver, the latter provides his or her Bitcoin address and the sending user authorizes the transaction by the use of a private key, which is a random sequence of letters and numbers and which unlocks the digital wallet. Asset up by the founder, a Bitcoin is issued every 10 minutes and this will continue until the total supply of 21 million bitcoins has been disseminated. Approximately, 12 million bitcoins having been issued to date (beginning of 2018). This is why, in part, there was frenzied financial activity around Bitcoin because there is a limited supply whose value is based on the supply and demand for bitcoins.

Mining

There are three ways to obtain bitcoins, namely:

1. by using one of the legally registered exchanges;
2. by mining new bitcoins; and
3. by the exchange of goods and services for bitcoins. Mining, defined as the process of adding transaction records (new blocks), that have been verified, to Bitcoin's public ledger of past transactions known as blockchain, is a concept unique to cryptography in which persons either alone or with other individuals located anywhere globally are encouraged to solve computational (mathematical) problems for which a reward (a

"block reward") of newly minted bitcoins and transaction fees are given for the successful endeavor. The reward began at 50 BTC in 2009 which decreases by one-half (now 25 BTC) for every 210,000 blocks mined. The block rewards will end once a total of 21 million bitcoins has been released. The public ledger is important because it prevents forgery or counterfeiting and eliminates the need for a third party to oversee the transaction.

The proof-of-work relates to miners who find a random number known as nonce which when inserted into the current block makes the hash fall below the current target. This is then sent around the network whereby other miners check the proof-of-work by hashing the block and checking the result. Mining is very difficult to accomplish due to the requirement that the SHA-256 hash of a block's header must be lower than or equal to the target. It requires that the hash commences with a certain number of zeros requiring many attempts to accomplish. The difficulty is apparently intentional to prevent inflation. As more miners attempt to join, the difficulty of the rate of block generation increases as well as the difficulty to compensate, in order to reduce the rate of block creation. The adjustments occur every 2016 blocks or approximately every two weeks. It has been calculated that to find a new block requires a degree of power than could run small countries. Mining can be successfully accomplished by either possessing equipment enabling the user to attempt the solution or join with others in sharing power needs. Use of CPU

(Central Processing Unit) mining is inefficient because it uses a general purpose processor whereas, use of a GPU (Graphics Processing Unit) is greatly preferred because this is a special processing unit that gives more hashing power and is, thus, far more optimal for mining. Currently coders have turned to ASICs (Application Specific Integrated Circuits) for mining, which is much faster, designed for a specific purpose, and takes place in thermally-regulated data centers having access to low-cost electricity. Another alternative is FPGA (Field Programmable Gate Array), an integrated circuit that can be programmed by the user) mining which was an improvement over CPU mining but is now obsolete due to the superior processing of ASICs. Because of the significant cost of electrical power needed, a possible alternative is to join people in countries with cheap power (e.g., Iceland). Chinese power would also have been a cheap alternative source but the government has banned its use for mining together with a ban on cryptocurrencies. Some miners have looked to cheaper U.S. electrical power sources such as Chelan County, Washington. Whether improvements and innovations in solar power, cold fusion, or other sources will replace current power sources remains for the future.

Although blockchain use and the underlying cryptography preserve the anonymity of the parties to the transaction, as stated below, there are means by which governments can ascertain the identities of the users such as tracking withdrawals and deposits of large sums of fiat money resulting from the transactions; subpoenas of computer and smartphone records; whistleblowing; and other backdoor techniques. A number of prosecutions and litigation are discussed.

A classic issue that inevitably arises in finance is whether a spectacular rise in the price of shares, the price of homes, and other assets will lead to an equally spectacular crash. The price of Bitcoin has risen so dramatically that a comparison to "tulipmania" is inevitably made. The most recent example of a price bubble occurred a decade ago when the U.S. housing market witnessed an extraordinary rise in house prices in certain parts of the country only to then fall dramatically. At a meeting of the SEC Investor Advisory Committee on October 12, 2017, this issue, among others, was raised in connection with Bitcoin and typically committee members could only speculate whether the run-up in its price will follow along similar lines to such historical events. Ultimately, after rising to an almost unconscionable price level approaching $20,000, there was a drop of some percent in value followed by a less spectacular recovery. There are innumerable naysayers that predict a major downturn for 2018. One commentator, when adroitly summarizing Bitcoin mania, divided investors (customers) into "devotees" who purchase Bitcoin as a rebellion against government controlled currency by substituting the decentralized anonymous currency and "sheep" who follow the devotees' lead on seeing how the price has risen so dramatically. Most economists and financiers agree that when the average person begins investing in a particular asset class whose value has risen dramatically, whether it be stocks, real estate, or other assets, it is then inevitable that a significant drop will take place.

Cyptocurrency: The Next Level for Banking Reform

Diagram of How Bitcoin Is Transacted.

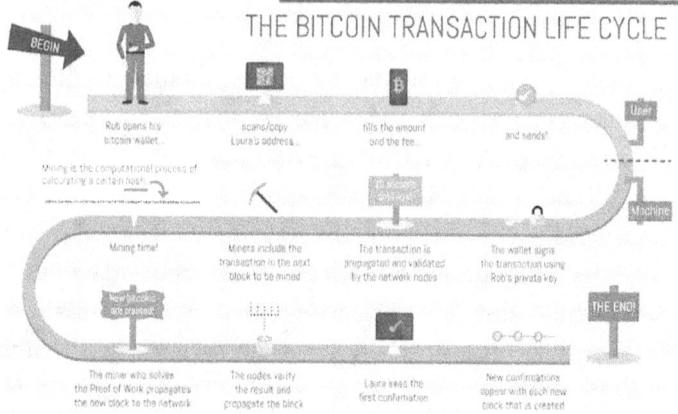

Ethereum

Whereas Bitcoin is digital money or currency that can be exchanged without third-party involvement, such as a bank, and is not subject to banking regulations, Ethereum is also a form of cryptocurrency that uses blockchain as its underlying technology but which possesses much broader uses, allowing other decentralized applications to be erected upon it such as smart contracts. It was created by a 19-year-old programmer from Toronto, Vitalik Buterin, who was highly critical of the limited use of Bitcoin and sought means to enlarge the capability of blockchain to encompass numerous additional features. As a co-founder of Ethereum with three other members, he worked in conjunction with a major proponent, Gavin Wood, who published an article detailing the mathematical and scientific aspects of Ethereum. Wood stated that Ethereum is "a transaction-based state machine" that may encompass a broad spectrum of account balances, reputations, trust arrangements, and almost anything that can emanate from a computer. "Ethereum is a project which attempts to build the generalised technology; technology on which all transaction based state machine concepts may be built. Moreover, it aims to provide to the end-developer a tightly integrated end-to-end system for building software on a hitherto unexplored compute paradigm in the mainstream: a trustful object messaging compute framework."

Ethereum possesses a support system known as the Enterprise Ethereum Alliance which, according to its website, connects Fortune 500 enterprises, startups, academics, and technology vendors to manage highly complex applications expeditiously. Both Bitcoin and Ethereum are revolutionary digital applications but, as one author stated, "Whereas Bitcoin is disrupting currency, Ethereum is disrupting equity." A future application, as envisioned by another author, is the elimination of third parties, including attorneys and escrow agents, in real estate transactions whereby home ownership and purchase moneys can be transferred using smart contracts by means of a piece of code that automatically accomplishes the transfer. Removing third parties from many forms of financial transactions such as Uber, Airbnb, eBay, etc., results in lower costs for participants, as well as speed, control, limitation of collusion, and other benefits.

Comparison of Bitcoin and Ethereum

Whereas Bitcoin was the first major effort to encompass blockchain attributes, nevertheless, it is limited in scope and size. Ethereum thus fills a need that Bitcoin cannot. A comparison of some of their attributes is follows:

- Bitcoin and Ethereum are decentralized (no third party is in control), are open-sources, and offer a secure anonymous access that cannot be compromised.
- Bitcoin is a payment system while Ethereum is a decentralized platform that has far more extensive applications and one that runs smart contracts and allows numerous other applications.
- Bitcoin's block time is about 10 minutes whereas Ethereum's average block time is around 14 seconds (14.38 seconds on December 26, 2017).
- The "rewards" differ Bitcoin offers a "block reward" of BTC (unit of currency or amount) to miners who create a block. This was originally 50 BTC per 10 minutes but which halves over time (and is presently 25 BTC). Ethereum's reward consists of 5 Ether (the "fuel" for operating the Ethereum platform) which remains the same and does not diminish over time plus 1/32th per Uncle block. (Uncles are stale blocks with parents that are a maximum of six blocks back from the present block.)
- The underlying protocol differs in that Bitcoin is written in C++ computer code while Ethereum uses Turing complete internal code.

- Bitcoin mining is by ASIC, a specific integrated circuit that was customized for Bitcoin's particular use; whereas Ethereum is by GPUs (graphics processing units), found in smart phones and personal computers), originally used for computer graphic computations and are specialized electronic circuits for the creation of images.
- Bitcoin's initial distribution was by mining, while Ethereum did so by ICOs.
- Bitcoin's hash rate is 1.8 Exahash (extraordinary processing of transactions proof of work) while Ethereum is 3 TeraHash (a measure of mining performance).
- Bitcoin's cost is based on competing with one another while Ethereum's cost is based on the amount of "gas" used for each computational step and set between the miners and the users.
- Bitcoin was the creation of Satoshi Nakamoto, an unknown person or persons, while Ethereum was created by Vitalik Buterin and the expansion of Ethereum was financed by crowdfunding.

Other Variations of Cryptocurrencies

Litecoin

Litecoin was created by Charlie Lee on October 7, 2011. His goal was to create "a lighter type" of Bitcoin, alleging it is silver compared to Bitcoin's gold. It is open-sourced on GitHub and its aim is to provide a cheaper and more everyday-purposed currency. According to its website, Litecoin's market capitalization (when downloaded on December 29, 2017) was over a half billion dollars or about 1/11th that of Bitcoin's; its coin limit is 84 billion vs. 21 billion for Bitcoin; its algorithm is Scrypt (a memory hard key-derivation function) vs. SHA-256 for Bitcoin; its block reward is halved every 840,000 blocks vs. every 210,000 for Bitcoin; its block time is one-fourth that of Bitcoin's (2½ minutes vs 10 minutes); and its block explorer is block-explorer.com vs. blockchain.infor. Like Bitcoin, its value has risen extraordinarily, and investors may question whether it is one of the numerous tech shares and currencies that are evidence of a major bubble. Its main advantage is less energy use, allowing a greater number of miners to partake.

IOTA

IOTA's website alleges that it is scalable, decentralized, modular, and without fees. It claims that it enables companies to explore new Business- to-Business (B2B) models through its service to be traded in an open market, in real time, and without cost. By means of its "Autonomous Machine Economy" it is able to settle transactions without fees or use of blocks that enables devices to trade exact amounts of resources on demand and store data from sensors and dataloggers securely and verifiable on the ledger. In a White Paper by Serguei Popov, the mathematical foundations of IOTA are discussed. In it, he states the main feature of this cryptocurrency is the "tangle," which is a directed acyclic graph for storing transactions. It purports to be the next evolutionary step in blockchain that offers features to establish a machine-to-machine micro-payment system.

It is the "Internet of things." Its credibility lies in the fact that it has partnered with Microsoft and one of the "Big 4" accounting firms (PricewaterhouseCoopers) and has been heavily invested in by other major companies. With a market cap of $14 billion, it is the sixth largest cryptocurrency globally.

Golem

Golem also alleges that it is scalable, decentralized, secure, open to development, without a single point of failure, and capable of connecting millions of nodes using a P2P (Peer-to-Peer) architecture. According to its website, developers are able to deploy their own integration on Golem and implement an appropriate monetization mechanism through personal laptops and data centers. Users can earn money by "renting" out their computing power or by developing and selling software. Golem utilizes an Ethereum-based transaction system that clears payments between providers, requesters, and software developers. Its application and transaction framework enable anyone to deploy and distribute applications on the site's network. Called the Airbnb of cryptocurrencies, it is the tenth most valuable cryptocurrency with a market capitalization of approximately $113 million, which, like other like cryptocurrencies, has risen in value dramatically.

Request Network

In the Request White Paper, it alleges that Request is a decentralized network that permits anyone to ask for a payment (a Request Invoice) that can be accomplished in a secured way. The information is stored in a decentralized authentic ledger which is universal, i.e., is designed to support all global transactions regardless of the type of currency, legislation, or language. It is allegedly cheaper and more secure than existing payment mechanisms allowing a wide range of automation possibilities. It seeks to become the backbone of world trade and is at the origin of exchanges integrating a computerized trade code, and acts as the management of a multitude of payment terms. It is another layer on top of Ethereum which permits requests for payments that satisfy existing legal frameworks. Its advantages, according to its White Paper, is security that is without risk of interception, unlike banks; its simplicity with one-click operation to pay without the possibility of manual input error; and lower cost in comparison with third parties such as Paypal, Bitpay, or Stripe which charge between 1 and 7 percent for their services. Its market cap at the time of its ICO was $59 million. Some of the intended uses and future consequences include the automation of accounting processes such as payments and Value Added Tax (VAT) refunds, auditing through use of blockchain to simplify compliance, and simplification of commercial tools for easy access to tools such as those used for escrow payments or factoring.

Dash

As with other cryptocurrencies, Dash is an open-sourced and P2P cryptocurrency. Its mission, according to its website, is to make digital cash easy to use and accessible to all users including those with limited technological backgrounds. It alleges that anyone will be able to set up an account on blockchain, add contacts, and pay for purchases from websites or mobile apps with one-click process. The value of a Dash coin had risen from $10 to $1531 by December 21, 2017.57 Initially called XCoin and later, Darkcoin, its dominant feature is the enabling of users to engage in payments for goods and services with merchants who have adopted its use in a much more expedited manner than other cryptocurrencies.

Ripple

At the time of writing (February 17, 2018), Ripple was the second largest cryptocurrency by market cap at almost $47 billion (was $86 billion in late December, 2017) having surpassed Ethereum. Started in September 2013, by its creator, Jed McCaleb, it is a payment network that is currently being used by many banks such as the Bank of America, Santander, American Express, and UBS. Its code is not open-sourced but rather is privately owned by Ripple. Unlike Bitcoin which is decentralized i.e., users obtain units by mining Ripple is centralized meaning that only it may issue units as it so chooses, and this is done by the Ripple Foundation which has created 100 billion units (XRP). According to its website, it is scalable, secure, and interoperates different networks. Its software solution, xCurrent, enables banks to instantly settle cross-border payments with end-to-end tracking. Banks message each other in real-time confirming payment details before initiating the transaction and then confirm delivery after settlement. It minimizes costs and capital requirements for liquidity. It uses a standard interface, xVia's simple API (Application Programming Interface) that requires no software installation and enables users to seamlessly send payments globally with transparency of payment status.60 As of the end of December 2017, a co-creator, Chris Larsen, the largest holder of Ripple tokens, rivaled Jeff Zuckerberg for financial supremacy based on Ripple's growth of 30,000 percent in a year.

Monero

Monero is a leading cryptocurrency that claims it is "secure, private, and untraceable." Open-sourced, the Monero website alleges it is decentralized, accessible to all and so permitting users to be their own bank, allowing them to maintain accounts and transactions anonymously, be secure owing to the use of ring signatures and other means to prevent third parties from prying, and fungible in that it cannot be blacklisted by vendors or exchanges. Allegedly, it has been used by darknet markets as well as people with legitimate interests.

Digital Tokens (Cryptotokens)

Digital tokens are the basis for the latest get-rich-quickly mania. They are used by startup companies to raise capital for technology being developed by coders. As with bitcoins, their value is what the investors give to them. To date, many billions of dollars have been invested in tokens' ICOs for startup companies wherein the purchasers of the tokens contribute capital to these digital enterprises in the hope that the tokens will substantially rise in value and the digital products emanating from their investments will result in monetary gain. Although venture capitalists have invested in these ICOs, unlike in the past when new startup companies often relied on them to fund their proposed ventures, these tokens may be purchased by ordinary investors in much smaller amounts that collectively not only rival sums invested by venture capitalists but now greatly exceed those sums. Many ICOs limits the tokens that can be purchased in the hope of encouraging investors who will contribute more than monetary sums but assist in the development of their products. They generally limit their offerings to non-U.S. purchasers due to fears that the SEC and U.S. tax authorities may intervene. The ICOs often have check boxes whereby the purchasers of tokens state they are not U.S. residents or green card holders.

Tokens represent an asset, such as property or utility or act as securities. They are fungible and may offer income or rewards. The best known is Ethereum which offers tokens whereas Bitcoin offers coins. They are generally tradable and usually reside on top of the blockchain thereby making it unnecessary to modify the existing protocol or blockchain. They are created in an ICO and may be considered as security requiring registration and conformity to other laws and regulations as illustrated in the DAO litigation discussed hereinafter.

Types of Tokens

Although ICOs have raised only a small percentage of capital (2 percent) compared to overall sums raised by IPOs globally, nevertheless, they have expanded exponentially going from a small sum in 2015, to approximately $96.3 million in 2016, to $4 billion in 2017, and to an expected 180 new offerings in 2018.67 The market cap for the 1453 cryptocurrencies as of January 19, 2018 was $583 billion with a Bitcoin dominance of 33.8 percent. Traditionally, IPOs were relegated to sophisticated hedge fund investors, venture capitalists, and others having substantial capital to invest in exchange for a percentage share in the company's equity (shares of stock). ICOs differs from IPOs by offering products or services. They are becoming mainstream where even those persons with meagre incomes and capital are engaged in the purchase of interests in newly emerging startups. For example, this author when discussing Bitcoin and other cryptocurrencies with an undergraduate class, was astonished to hear a number of students stating that they have invested in companies offering cryptocurrencies, which has never occurred in several decades of lecturing. Investments were made by the offering of tokens through the blockchain-based offerings that enabled the creation of new currency offerings and the raising of capital almost literally overnight, avoiding the regulatory time-consuming roadblocks of traditional offerings.

There are several types of tokens that can be purchased: from utility tokens. They are from, to equity and debt security tokens, and other cryptocurrencies, each offering a type of benefit to the purchaser in a multitude of products and/or services. They often arise from crowdfunding (discussed in the chapter on "Crowdfunding and the Taxation of Virtual Currencies"). They are transferable to others in a secondary market and are unlike traditional venture capital investments and IPOs which are subject to time constraints under the 1933 and 1934 Securities Acts. The ICOs pre-sell coin tokens to potential investors in accordance with a concept generally laid out by the firm in a White Paper that contains both conceptual and mathematical algorithm jargon. The discussion generally states the mission, timeline, target budget, and the manner of coin sales to take place. Examples is Ethereum's cryptocurrency tokens, Golem's tokens received by selling computing capacity, Anryze's use of tokens to decode audio files, and stock tokens sold on exchanges.

An excellent example of a White Paper discussing token sales is that of the Ethereum and TrueBit founders and chief architects, who discuss Ethereum's token offerings. They state that typically buyers desiring to purchase Ethereum's ERC20 tokens over the Ethereum network do so in exchange for Ethereum's own currency. Unlike equity sales in IPOs, these tokens have no known initial market valuation and buyers must rely on projections and possibilities. Ethereum has made capped offerings, i.e., capped at a determined maximum or minimum number of tokens for sale, and uncapped offerings whereby the sales are potentially unlimited. Other types of token sales can involve hidden caps and reverse Dutch auctions. (A Dutch auction is when an initial high offering sum is gradually lowered until a sufficient number of buyers agree to purchase.)

Forks

Complicating the various types of digital currencies are alternatives to Bitcoin and its underlying blockchain technology known as altcoins, coins or forks which in turn may be subdivided into hard forks and soft forks such as Litecoin, Namecoin, and Dogecoin each of which has its own variant of the underlying blockchain technology. A fork in connection with cryptocurrency occurs when alternative versions of the particular currency are created. The problem is that there are different versions of the currency (e.g., Bitcoin split into Bitcoin and Bitcoin Cash) and the issue of compatibility arises. By being open-source, modifications can be made ostensibly by any user. The fork may arise either by the particular blockchain used, as in Bitcoin, which may then be split into alternative but compatible versions, or where a new version of the technology arises that alleges it is either better or seeks to apply it to other uses (Litecoin, IOTA, Ripple, etc.). A hard fork occurs when the cryptocurrency is split into two different cryptocurrencies, generally due to the inability of non-upgraded nodes (persons in possession of a copy of a blockchain) to vali- date blocks created by newer upgraded nodes, while a soft fork refers to a divergence in an updated version of the blockchain that modifies the earlier version but remains compatible. A number of coins use the SHA-256 algorithm that also underlies Bitcoin while many other use script algorithm, and hybrid and CPU alternative cryptocurrencies.

Altcoins

Altcoins are alternative cryptocurrencies not compatible with Bitcoin but emulate it generally by using the same hashing algorithm as Bitcoin, i.e., SHA-256. They are P2P, using a mining process to generate new blocks based on blockchain technology. They may be considered "hard forks" to Bitcoin and it is often claimed that they are an improvement over it by performing different functions or constitute an improvement of some component of Bitcoin. There are several hundred altcoins that have emerged as alternatives ("forking the code") and a number of ICOs that will be offered in the near future. Exemplified by Ethereum, Dogecoin, Feathercoin, and Peercoin, they attempt to offer cheaper alternatives to Bitcoin using less computer power to generate blocks. A major altcoin is Litecoin with its different hashing algorithm and higher currency units. It alleges, as stated previously, that it is "silver to Bitcoin's gold."[74] Other alternative altcoins include Namecoin (a domain registration system), Dogecoin, Manero, and Peercoin, A well-known online store which sells a large variety of consumer goods, Overstock, stated on August 8, 2017, that it would accept payment by altcoins such as Ethereum, Litecoin, Dash, and every other major currency as payment from its customers. Its CEO, Patrick Byrne, who is also an economist, said to a

Fortune magazine interviewer that it would accept 40 or 45 digital currencies at any given time.

Meta Coins

Meta coins are protocols built on an existing cryptocurrency platform. A prime example is that of Counterparty, which is a P2P financial platform using its own currency XCP, and shares the same benefit in not needing a trusted third party: its goal is to "democratize finance in the same way the Internet itself democratized the creation and sharing of information." It is built on the Bitcoin platform that permits users to engage the financial sector in an inexpensive way, sharing the same features of being user friendly, open, safe, and secure. It can make bets, construct smart contracts, create and sell one's own tickets for particular functions, broadcast information, and perform a multitude of other financially related tasks.

Sidecoin

Sidecoin is a fork of Bitcoin which, according to a Side Bitcoin White Paper, "is a mechanism that allows a snapshot to be taken of Bitcoin's blockchain." The developers stated that they compiled a list of unspent transaction outputs which they then utilized with corresponding balances to bootstrap a new blockchain. The developers took a snapshot of available public addresses in the Bitcoin network by downloading the Bitcoin blockchain with their public keys and converted the hash 160s into commonly used Bitcoin addresses, then "parsed" the balances in the Bitcoin blockchain. Its alleged use of the sidechain is to enable those who wish to make an altcoin and dramatically increase community adoption.

Sidechain

A sidechain is the use of a separate blockchain but one wherein the user may revert back to the original blockchain (main chain). When used in Bitcoin, the user sends bitcoins to a special address on the Bitcoin blockchain that is set off from the original blockchain. Ethereum has a private Ethereum-based network that permits its ether to be sent to a private blockchain away from the public Ethereum main chain. Having briefly explored the nature of digital currencies, we will now examine, in the chapter on "Legal Issues of Digital Technology", the legal issues and how the legal systems, both domestically, and internationally, deal with the new technology. Typically, the law moves slowly when confronted with new developments as illustrated by the issues raised by the Internet's development. Judges and legislatures often attempt to apply existing legal doctrines to solve problems that require the same degree of innovative legal strategies as the new developments, much like trying to apply traditional legal principles to innovations. As seen later, legislatures everywhere are attempting to move beyond their normal snail like pace to meet the challenges, especially after the extraordinary price rise of Bitcoin which almost all commentators agreed would face an inevitable collapse, as experienced in recent years by other bubbles in the financial sector. Whenever there are innovations that seriously affect financial markets, governmental authorities will inevitably intervene in an endeavor to prevent fraud and other malfeasance. We will review how government is becoming concerned, as illustrated by its attempts to curb abuses or strongly advise customers of the dangers inherent in the ultra-new technologies.

CHAPTER

Issues of Digital Technology

Legal issues arising from blockchain technology and other advancements in the digital arena are reminiscent and comparable to the rise of the Internet some two decades ago. Among the difficulties presented in the civil and criminal arenas are the adjustments required by legislators, regulators, and judges to address new challenges posed by innovative technologies. The following areas are some that have to be determined.

Jurisdiction

Jurisdiction is based on the concept of boundaries; it is the power of a particular court to exercise its authority in a given case. In the United States, there are multiple levels of jurisdictional issues that may arise, depending on the nature of the parties, i.e., where they reside and where the controversy arose or is based on, and disputes called subject-matter that concern the laws and regulations therein. In the United States, there are 51 government entities that exercise jurisdiction within their domain, namely, the federal government, based in Washington, D.C., and the 50 states. Each of the governmental entities possesses a judicial system unique unto itself and each exercises jurisdiction or power over its inhabitants according to the laws and regulations promulgated therein. Federal subject-matter jurisdiction is based upon Article 3, & 2 of the U.S. Constitution, which states: "The judicial Power shall extend to all Cases, in Law and Equity, arising under this Constitution, the Laws of the United States, and Treaties made…to Controversies between two or more States; between a State and Citizens of another State; between Citizens of different States;…and between a State, or the Citizens thereof, and foreign States, Citizens or Subjects."

Federal jurisdiction is very broad, extending to all laws passed by Congress, issues related to federal questions, to cases involving ambassadors and other foreign diplomatic personnel, to disputes between states, and matters arising out of the U.S. Constitution. Its jurisdiction may be exclusive, meaning that only federal courts may hear the cases or controversies, or concurrent, whereby jurisdiction is shared with state courts according to the laws and regulations enacted therein. Generally, when a federal statute is enacted, it will provide for whether it is to be enforced exclusively or permissively with the states. Exclusive jurisdiction would include subject areas such as bankruptcy, federal crimes, and international treaties. Federal courts may share jurisdiction in cases where a citizen of one state sues a citizen of another state. Jurisdiction may exist in state courts wherein the cause of action has its main locus or may be exercised in the federal court provided the controversy is for more than $75,000. States also have both exclusive and concurrent jurisdiction with the federal government and also with other states depending on the nature of the litigation. If the controversy is between citizens of different states and the sum in question is for $75,000 or less than the litigation is reserved to the states.

Jurisdiction may also be based by service of a summons upon the party being sued either within the state (in personam jurisdiction) or by service outside the state (long-arm jurisdiction) provided certain due process constitutional requirements are met. Other bases for jurisdiction may be obtained in rem, that is, by be the assertion of authority over property located therein and also attachment jurisdiction that permits the seizure of instate property belong to out-of-state persons.

Comparable to cyberlaw concerns, courts will need to address the locus of activities and whether a particular court may entertain a lawsuit arising out of alleged contractual or tortious breach inasmuch as blockchain usage may take place at any site globally The issue and determination are more complex than cyberlaw cases where, in most cases, the parties and their locations are known. In the virtual arena the parties act anonymously. Nevertheless, the location of federal and state courts have evolved a variety of concepts having at their bases due process obligations under the 5th and 14th Amendments of the U.S. Constitution as exemplified by the "minimum contacts" requirements as set forth in International Shoe Co. v. Washington and Asahi Metal Industry Co. v. Superior Court. Federal courts have adopted a "sliding scale" based on active or passive use of the Internet to determine whether they will entertain jurisdiction as illustrated in Zippo Mfr. Co. v. Zippo Dot Com, Inc It would appear that these precedents will be applicable to litigation arising from digital currency-based disputes.

Due to the anonymity of blockchain users, enforcement authorities are at a loss as to how to oversee and enforce legal obligations to protect investors and other parties to particular transactions. Jurisdiction can be asserted successfully over firms acting as brokers or exchanges provided their activities are within the national boundaries of the courts, or even worldwide if multi-national co-operative agreements are secured. The global nature of these transactions and the vast array of statutory, regulatory, and customs of particular national and local authorities render enforcement often improbable. For example, owing to twentieth century historical conflicts, the European Union (EU) is exceptionally concerned with privacy matters, as evidenced by the new EU Data Protection Regulation. The fear is that wrongdoers may be exempt from lawful regulatory regimes.

Scholars have offered a variety of possible solutions to the conundrum. Among them include the suggestion that there be "an open source platform ecosystem of smart contracting dispute resolution" whereby parties to the contract can opt into particular dispute resolution mechanisms. They would be platform-based ecosystems for dispute resolution of "cryptotransactions" that would facilitate anonymity but also permit users to choose which judges or arbitrators are to decide conflicts among the parties. The Aragon Jurisdiction Network offers a possible alternative decentralized dispute mechanism by defining a set of contracts open to arbitral resolution wherein an individual having a dispute post a bond with the Network, which will be returned only if the party is successful but forfeited if unsuccessful. Thereafter, a panel of five judges will review the rules and materials forming the basis of the claim dispute and make a decision, which may either be accepted by the applicant or disputed, at which time a larger bond is to be posted. Ultimately, the case can be elevated to the Network's nine-member Supreme Court which makes the final decision that may not be appealed. Unlike the traditional norm of judicial decision-making, prior judges of the Network are rewarded or penalized for their proper or wrongful determination.

SEC v. Shavers

There is a paucity of cases that concern the issue of jurisdiction particularly relating to bitcoins. An important early case where the court discussed whether it possessed jurisdiction in a Bitcoin-related litigation was SEC v. Shavers. In its decision, the court determined that jurisdictional requirements had been met which resulted in a decision granting summary judgment to the Securities and Exchange Commission (SEC) that decreed the disgorgement of $40 million from the defendants, Trenton T. Shavers and his unincorporated affiliated entity, and a fine of $150,000. Shavers and his unincorporated online entity, in essence, operated a Ponzi type scheme where investors were told that he was in the business of selling Bitcoin to local people and offered investors up to 1 percent interest daily until the funds were either withdrawn or the host's dealings were no longer profitable. Shavers obtained 700,467 bitcoins from investors valued at $4.592,806. The investors lost 263,104 bitcoins, equivalent to $1,834,303 (at the then value) when invested.

With respect to jurisdiction, the court determined that the Bitcoin constituted investments over the Internet operating under the Internet name of "pirateat40"; that solicitation was made in online chat rooms and on the Bitcoin Forum, an online forum with a promise of a 7 percent return weekly; that Shavers used new bitcoins received from investors to pay purported returns on outstanding investments; and that he diverted investors' bitcoins to his personal use. Shavers was, at all times, a Texas resident soliciting investors to invest in the Bitcoin-related investment scheme and Bitcoin is an electronic form of currency not backed by any real assets and without specie. Contrary to Shavers' contention that bitcoins were not money and thus not securities, the court determined that the investments were securities holdings and that they were investment contracts having met the three-fold requirements of a security under the SEC v.

Howey case, namely;

1. an investment of money,
2. in a common enterprise,
3. with the expectation that profits will be derived from the efforts of the promoter or a third party. The court concluded that the scheme was a Ponzi

scheme constituting a fraud on investors all in violation of 5 and 17

(a) of the Securities Act of 1933 and §10
(b) of the Securities Exchange Act of 1934 and Rule 10b-5 there under.

Thus, they determined that it had subject-matter jurisdiction under 20 and 22 of the 1933 Act and 21 and 27 of the 1934 Act.

Gordon v. Dailey

In a New Jersey federal case, Gordon v. Dailey the court also determined it possessed jurisdiction in a civil case wherein the plaintiffs complained that the defendants' sale of securities violated the provisions of the Securities Act of 1933 and the Securities Exchange Act of 1934 based upon diversity of citizenship and the sum complained exceeded the required jurisdictional sum of $75,000, to wit, over $1 million in Bitcoin value. The complaint, in essence, stated that the defendants offered 100,000 bonds to the public that were tiered in value to be purchased in Bitcoin. All dividends received for mining Bitcoin would be paid in Bitcoin, although no guarantee of value was made respecting the said offering. The complaint further alleged that the IPO offering of Bitcoin securities was never registered as required by the said securities statutes.

Virtual Currencies as Money

Virtual currencies, and in their major incarnation as Bitcoin, are not fiat money, and possess no backing from

Cyptocurrency: The Next Level for Banking Reform

the Federal Reserve, but the issue remains whether they are considered to be moneys exchanged from one party to another by digital means. The IRS considers them as property and taxable when exchanged at a profit (see the chapter on "Crowdfunding and the Taxation of Virtual Currencies"). Although governmental entities may deny virtual currencies as "money" for tax purposes, nevertheless, they may hold that status in the minds of their holders. They are considered as monetary assets that are used for the payment of goods and services, which begs the question at the outset of the fundamental meaning of the word "money."

The confusion is reflected in scholarly articles wherein authors cite the basis for holding virtual currency, particularly Bitcoin, as either "money" or "property." The argument for its status as "money" is illustrated by the purpose of Bitcoin to act as an alternative currency that avoids the need for third parties such as governments, central banks, and "shadow" (non-bank) banks. It is used currently in some quarters as a medium of exchange, albeit not universally, but is increasingly common as merchants become accustomed to the new technologies and willing to accept non-fiat money. The advantages are the avoidance of credit card fees of generally 2–4 percent to the merchant, and monthly interest to the consumer, which enables the former to discount merchandise. The obvious problems that arise are the volatility of the virtual currency and how to deal with returns. Some merchants resolve the issue of returns by offering credit on store-based credit cards. In addition to acting as a possible medium of exchange, the virtual currency may act as a store of value, i.e., an asset to be retained pending an expected rise in value.

Virtual currency as "property" is illustrated by federal and state laws that treat Bitcoin and other virtual currencies as intangible property. It is so designated by the IRS, by FinCEN, by the CFTC as a commodity under the CEA; under bankruptcy laws; as part of equitable distribution or division under divorce laws; by the New York "BitLicense Requirement"; under trust and estates laws that concern inheritance; under the Uniform Commercial Code Article 9 as a security interest in personal property; and under other diverse statutes and regulations. Confusion thus remains and future regulatory agencies will have to decipher it.

Smart Contracts

Smart contracts are virtual contracts using and are atop the Ethereum platform, which are entered into without human intervention. They are based on a sequence of coded events that automatically verify and execute the agreed terms of the contract. The terms therein are recorded in a computer rather than hard-copy legal language. The concept of a "smart contract" was conceived by Nick Szabo, cited previously, who is a polymath, computer scientist, and legal scholar who was interested in the interrelationship between contracts and digital technology. The system involves a decentralized platform run on a custom-built blockchain that has smart contracts and which Ethereum alleges is run "exactly as programmed without any possibility of downtime, censorship, fraud or third party interference." There are no intermediaries such as clearing houses inasmuch as they are linked to DLT.

Among the benefits of a smart contract is its coding that is less ambiguous than verbal language, verifiable, self-executing, and integrates with IT systems. However, it also has negative aspects such as the lack of knowledge concerning its methodologies, privacy and transparency concerns, and the need for continuous updates.19 Thus, the federal government is exploring the use of smart contracts internally which offer considerable savings, time, and ostensible freedom from hacking. The government has awarded $1.3 million in blockchain contracts in 2017 and will likely substantially increase its investment in the technology, particularly to streamline record-keeping and promote transparency and accountability. States, such as Arizona, Illinois, Maine, and Vermont, are beginning to adapt blockchain for permanency in record-keeping and security.

Unlike the traditional contract whereby a party may commence litigation to enforce it, including seeking damages for non-fulfillment or requesting a court to exercise its equitable powers in granting specific performance, a smart contract by definition has already been executed and a party suing essentially requests a court to undo what has already been accomplished. It is the performance of the contract that signifies its acceptance. Once the agreement has been encoded, a party may not undo it unless the agreement so permits. There are judicially permitted exceptions for illegality, lack of capacity, and other such defenses, but smart contracts adapted to particular needs, such as the purchase of real estate, pre-nuptial agreements, construction, and other financial areas, are likely to be the future trend making traditional contractual arrangements less common.

Smart contracts will require law firms to adapt to the new technologies. Among the personnel required to make the transformation in larger firms are attorneys knowledgeable about contracts, software developers who assist in providing the technical expertise of transformation using blockchain, and software coders and programmers who will code the various terms of the contract. Law schools, in conjunction with information systems professionals, will have to train future attorneys in making the transition. There will be new terms such as "dynamic transaction" and "smart contract mediator." The smart title company of the future will see the elimination of current title searches and recording processes, and other changes which will reduce costs and time, and lessen the possibility of fraudulent activity. The need for title searchers and title companies themselves may be eliminated together with third parties who participate in the process of conveying title from one party to another.

There are consumer protection risks due to the complex nature of the technology for ordinary consumers who may not understand the terms to which they are agreeing. Other fears include financial instability brought about by the non-reversible nature of the contracts which could enforce adverse terms automatically through the financial system. Additional practical issues include the admissibility of the contracts under existing rules of evidence; the application of burden of proof to the accuracy and authenticity of the agreements; who is accountable for an alleged breach; the application of rules of evidence such as the parol evidence rule and the dead man's statute; legal defenses such as minority, fraud, mutual mistake, identity of the parties; and bringing both attorneys and judges up to speed in understanding their technology-based nature.

Intellectual Property

Are the many forms of virtual currency and the underlying technology protected by intellectual property (IP) in the form of patents, copyrights, trademarks, and/or trade secrets? It would appear that they may come within the parameters of protection, at least within the United States. The basic definitions are as follows. A patent is a grant of property rights by the U.S. Patent and Trademark Office to whoever invents or discovers any new and useful process, machine, manufacture, or composition of matter, or any new and useful improvement thereof. Its protection is dependent on whether it is a utility patent, which is good for 20 years from date of filing, or a design patent which has 14-year protection. A copyright is a form of protection provided to authors of original works of authorship such as literary, dramatic, musical, artistic, and other such forms, and is protected for the life of the author plus 70 years. A trade- mark is any word, name, symbol, or device, or any combination thereof, that is used, or intended to be used, in commerce to identify and distinguish the goods or services of the holder thereof and is protected for an initial 10-year period and renewable indefinitely for additional 10-year timeframes. A trade secret is any information that provides economic value that is not in the public domain and that has been a reasonably kept secret. It protects formulas, patterns, compilations, programs, devices, methods, techniques, or processes as long as they remain secret.

Ordinarily, when discussing IP, we discuss whether a particular invention, idea, or symbol qualifies for statutory protection, but blockchain technology is an innovative benefit in that it may act as registry for IP rights permitting users to file and catalog their creations. It can act as evidential proof of ownership of copyright-protected original works in contested proceedings not only in the United States but also worldwide. The use of blockchain prevents vulnerability of the works by other persons alleging ownership because it is stored on a main centralized register that is part of a connected, publicly distributed, system of registers. Currently, there are platforms already making use of the technology such as Binded, formerly known as Blockai, which is a copyright service using Bitcoin blockchain to create legally binding records. Although its use is free, the site offers to register the copyright with the U.S. Copyright Office for the cost of the filing fee using one-click process. There are numerous other websites offering comparable services that, for example, include securing trade secrets, establishing prior art in patent cases, and enhancing contracts by alleged "decentralized, uncensorable, permissionless, resilient" platforms.

Blockchain technology may be used for smart contracts in relation to IP whereby persons wishing to use copyrighted works could secure permission from owners by making micropayments directly, thereby avoiding significant transactional fees that often accompany such usage. Licenses in IP could be made self-executing, especially in the music industry, so that the owners would possess greater control over their works in addition to having unassailable proof of their creative works. The fashion industry is particularly vulnerable to misuse with theft of designs and other IP protected works, often by larger, well-financed enterprises which have the resources to defend against litigation by less well-financed enterprises. Blockchain has made proof of misuse much easier to establish with less costly outlays for proof in litigation. It is invaluable for its record-keeping capabilities, registration, ability to detect forgeries, fake goods, gray goods (goods sold in violation of contractual obligations, generally, beyond the intended national borders for resale), evidence of first use, payments, and other uses.

Governments faced with newly innovative financial products or services are understandably unable to react until a learning process has taken place and abuses begin to emerge. In the chapter on "Federal Regulation of Virtual Currencies", we will examine the federal regulation of virtual currencies and the agencies that are presently engaged in overseeing those aspects that come within their domain.

Federal Regulation of Virtual Currencies

National and local governments, both in the United States and abroad, are attempting to understand and regulate these virtual currencies which raise issues affecting investors and consumers using them. Among the issues are potential fraud, use by drug dealers and other criminal elements for money laundering, etc. due to the current near impossibility of tracing, tax aspects, the displacement of national currencies, and other concerns. It has been reported that ostracized governments, due to the sanctions imposed upon them, including bank restrictions, have amassed large sums of Bitcoin and other currencies which serve as hard currencies for their endeavors.1 Due to its open-source software as a decentralized model, North Korea, in order to overcome United Nations, U.S., and other governmental restrictions, has engaged in Bitcoin mining to add to Bitcoin's blockchain in an endeavor to raise funds that have been blocked for its missile and nuclear programs. North Korea began its mining on May 17, 2017, continuing in its efforts exponentially to avoid restrictions and have access to global capital.

Bitcoins were earlier adopted by criminal elements because of the anonymity and inherent difficulty of determining whether law enforcement had the power to regulate activities that most often were borderless. Some commentators have asserted that the only or most noteworthy value of Bitcoin is its "underlying value as a medium of exchange by lawbreakers." The surge in the value of Bitcoin may be attributable, in substantial part, because of its use by drug kingpins, terrorists, white-collar criminals, and Russian cybercriminals. Bitcoin and other cryptocurrencies have also gained the attention of Islamic terrorists as a means of receiving financial contributions from sympathizers while preserving their anonymity. In a detailed study of terrorist use of virtual currencies, it was found that ISIS (Islamic State in Iraq and Syria) members have made use of virtual currencies to fund their operations but, unlike other criminal enterprises, are limited particularly to countries where the infrastructure supports the exchange of virtual currencies. The advantage of such use, of course, is the global nature of currency exchange in an anonymous manner. The authors suggest a series of policy recommendations:

1. a better understanding of the evolving threat of virtual currencies financing terrorism;
2. prioritizing terrorist financing as a matter of public policy and law enforcement significance; and
3. prioritizing terrorist financing as a compliance matter within private institutions.6 Nevertheless, it appears that cash still remains the major source of terrorist financing owing to the lack of technological infrastructure especially where such terrorism is dominant in underdeveloped regions such as northern Nigeria and Yemen.

On the other hand, it appears that governmental agencies are beginning to crack the wall of anonymity by partnering with companies able to analyze data, often from anonymous sources using Bitcoin, that draws inferences from persons using the blockchain technology and its products. One company, Chainalysis, is working with the U.S. and foreign governments to track the flow of funds, aided by the discovery of Bitcoin addresses found in a suspect's possession which then may be used to secure court orders for further discovery. Researchers at the University of Luxembourg, using relatively inexpensive equipment, allege that they are able to ascertain the identity of between 11 percent and 60 percent of all Bitcoin transactions. The method used is by "abusing" the firewalls protecting anonymity and de-anonymizing the network protecting the identity of those using the network to conceal their transactions.

A number of U.S. and international governmental agencies have begun to focus major financial resources to assure compliance with existing laws and regulations and to ascertain and punish criminal behavior. The U.S. federal and state agencies concerned with cryptocurrencies are discussed below. A critical question that has arisen for regulatory purposes is whether virtual currency is currency or property and whether the offerings are securities. The U.S. government, as previously, stated, has determined that virtual currencies such as Bitcoin are deemed to be property rather than currencies. The tax treatment of virtual currency efforts discussed in the chapter on "Crowdfunding and Taxation of Virtual Currencies."

U.S. Government Agencies Concerned With Virtual Currencies

Securities and Exchange Commission (SEC)

The SEC is the primary regulator of the securities market including securities exchanges, securities brokers and dealers, investment advisers, and mutual funds, for the protection of investors and the general public against fraud. The basic question is whether it deems cryptocurrencies as "securities," thus granting it jurisdiction to regulate. The seminal case of SEC v. Howey, cited previously, is the basis for the assertion of authority by the SEC.

The SEC, which has been unusually reticent concerning the regulation of Initial Coin Offerings (ICOs), has begun to weigh in with comments and investigations as to their character and the need for oversight. It noted that some promoters of ICOs have told potential investors that they may expect a sizeable return on their investments or participate in a share of returns from capital raised from the sales of coins to fund development of a digital platform, software, or projects. In so doing, they may fall under the Howey definition of a security and thus be subject to possible regulation by the SEC by

1. its investment in a common enterprise,
2. through the efforts of others,
3. with the expectation of earning a profit.

Enforcement of securities laws has to date been undertaken by the newly formed Cyber Unit of the SEC's

Enforcement Division. The Unit was created to focus on cyber-related misconduct including market manipulation, hacking, use of the dark web for unlawful conduct, violations involving DLT and ICOs, and other cyber-related threats to investors and to the general public. Much of the confusion may also be attributable to the exemption from securities registration given to crowdfunding efforts discussed in the chapter on "Crowdfunding and Taxation of Virtual Currencies." Unlike typical IPOs that raise capital by the sale of shares of stock, ICOs may offer tokens that have a variety of other incentives such as social causes, games, or the receipt of present or future products or services. There are a number of excellent analyses of whether tokens distributed on virtual currency websites are securities offerings subject to SEC registration requirements or are exempt from the said regulations. Distinguishing between legitimate and illusory offers may bring about SEC enforcement based on the Securities Exchange Act of 1934 for fraud. Examples of prosecutions are the PlexCoin ICO and the Munchee ICO discussed below.

SEC First Enforcement Action: REcoin

On September 29, 2017, the SEC filed a complaint seeking a temporary stay and final injunction, disgorgement of profits, and other relief against REcoin Group Foundation, DRC World, Inc., and Maksim Zaslavskiy. The complaint alleged that Zaslavskiy, who was president of the two companies, had raised $300,000 in ICOs from investors through misrepresentations and deceptive acts relating to alleged investments in tokens or coins offered by the companies. The SEC claimed that the tokens or coins were unlawful offerings of securities for which no registration statement was filed as required by law. The purpose of each ICO, according to the complaint, was to convert "fiat currency" or "digital currency" obtained into "tokenized" currency backed by investment in assets, to wit, real estate for REcoin, and diamonds for its Diamond Reserve Club.

The defendants' posting characterized the offering as "The First Ever Cryptocurrency Backed by Real Estate." It was expected that the investments would generate returns from their appreciation in value and the appreciation in value of the tokens by reason of increased demand. It was alleged that the false and misleading statements included claims made by Zaslavskiy that investors were in fact purchasing tokens or coins; that defendants raised over $2 million, later raised to $4 million, from REcoin; that REcoin had a team of lawyers, professionals, brokers, and accountants that would invest the proceeds into real estate, and that Diamond had experts to select the best diamonds; that REcoin had to shut down because the government compelled it to do so; and that investors could expect to reap rewards of 10–15 percent on their investments. The statements were allegedly untrue. The complaint further stated that defendants also attempted to evade registration requirements by refashioning the sale as memberships in a club which had the same attributes of securities that required registration under both the Securities Act of 1933 and the Securities Exchange Act of 1934 and regulations issued thereunder.

It is becoming increasingly evident that ICOs, which, unlike IPOs, were perceived by investors to be unregulated, are now facing governmental scrutiny. It is estimated that the ICO market will have received some $1 billion to $1.5 billion from investors by the close of 2017. The confusion attendant to virtual currencies initially led to a lack of regulatory intervention but whether perceived as currency or as securities or other forms of monetary mechanisms, the potential and actual loss of investments to unscrupulous entrepreneurs has now caught the attention of federal and state regulatory authorities. The chairperson of the SEC identified ICOs as a priority for enforcement. The characterization by companies engaged in ICOs pertaining to sales of tokens or coins will be left to Congressional authorization and judicial interpretations. Issuers of offerings of utility tokens will have to carefully scrutinize compliance regulations, both of the SEC and of the CFTC that oversees futures offerings. State law observance, especially as to banking and payments requirements, also adds to the confusing current state of ICOs.

The DAO Conundrum

The SEC investigated a new cryptocurrency offering to determine whether the Decentralized Autonomous Organization (DAO) violated U.S. securities laws through its sales of DAO Tokens to investors to be used to fund projects. The DAO is an organization created by German nationals that arose from the crowdfunding exception to the Securities Act of 1933 which implemented the requirements of Title III of the

Cyptocurrency: The Next Level for Banking Reform

Jumpstart Our Business Startups Act. The Act, discussed in the chapter on "Crowdfunding and Taxation of Virtual Currencies," facilitated new ventures by removing many of the onerous filing requirements of the securities laws and provided a framework for the regulation of registered funding portals and broker-dealers that issuers are required to use as intermediaries in the offer of sale of securities. The DAO, during the "Offering Period" of April 30, 2016, through May 28, 2016, offered and sold "pseudonymously" 1.15 billion DAO tokens in exchange for a total of approximately 12 million Ether, a virtual currency based on the Ethereum blockchain. Holders of the DAO tokens had unrestricted rights to resell them.

The DAO initially sought to create a crowdfunding smart contract using the blockchain to execute and record the contracts. The purchase of DAO tokens with Ether entitled participants to vote on projects funded by the purchases and to "rewards" which were akin to dividends. Funds raised from investors were held at an Ethereum blockchain address associated with DAO. Promotion of the DAO was through its website "The DAO Website" which described its intended purpose, how it operated, and provided a link through which purchase of tokens could be made. The company also posted almost daily updates through the media and conducted online forums. Ether raised and future profits were to be maintained in the DAO's Ethereum blockchain address. Individuals seeking funding from the DAO were to submit a proposal for projects, which involved a smart contract published on the Ethereum blockchain, and had to provide details of the proposal which would be reviewed and published on the DAO Website and required approval by a majority of holders of the DAO tokens. The proposals were to be initially reviewed by one or more of the DAO's "Curators" who had the ultimate power to decide whether to submit a proposal for a vote.

The SEC conducted an investigation to determine whether the DAO violated U.S. securities laws by failing to register the purchase and sale of tokens as securities. In its Report of Investigation dated July 25, 2017, the SEC concluded that DAO Tokens are securities under the Securities Act of 1933 and the Securities Exchange Act of 1934. It stated that the foundational principles of the securities laws apply to organizations or capital-raising entities making use of distributed ledger technology. Citing the Howey seminal case and other precedents, it noted that the DAO Tokens sale is an investment in a common enterprise premised on a reasonable expectation of profits to be derived from the entrepreneurial or managerial efforts of others. The definition of a security, the SEC noted, is based on a flexible rather than static principle. In the DAO offerings, investors invested money which need not take the form of cash. Investors used Ether to make their investments in exchange for DAO Tokens. There is a reasonable expectation of profits inasmuch as investors who purchased DAO Tokens were investing in a common enterprise and reasonably expected to earn a profit from the enterprise in the form of dividends, other periodic payments, or the increased value of their investments. The profits were derived from the managerial efforts of others, specifically from the decisions and activity of Slock.it, its co-founders, and the DAO's Curators. Investors were urged to make their investments by the marketing of the DAO and active engagement of the company's co-founders with token holders. Control was centered on Slock. it, a German corporation, and the co-founders and the Curators who made the fundamental decisions whether or not to submit proposals for a vote by the token holders. The token holders' voting rights were limited and dependent on the efforts of the Curators, etc.

The SEC concluded that issuers must register offers and sales of securities unless a valid exemption exists. The SEC defines issuer to include "every person who issues or proposes to issue any security" and persons to include "any incorporated organization." It also includes issuers who "devise new ways to issue their securities and the definition of a security itself expands." Thus, the DAO, an unincorporated organization, was an issuer of securities and was responsible for the success or failure of the enterprise, for which concern investors needed information materials to make their investment decisions. Section 5 of the Securities Exchange Act of 1934 makes it unlawful for any broker, dealer, or exchange, directly or indirectly, to effect any transaction in security, or to report any such transaction, in interstate commerce, unless the exchange is registered as a national securities exchange under 6 of the Exchange Act, or is exempted from such registration. The DAO Platforms that traded DAO Tokens, according to the SEC, appear to fully meet the criteria of Rule 3b-16(a) which recites a functional test for determining whether a trading system meets the definition of an exchange. The test includes any organization, association, or group of persons bringing together the orders of multiple purchasers and sellers of securities and uses established, non-discretionary methods under which such orders interact with each other, and the sellers and buyers agree to the terms of the trade. The SEC concluded that the platforms that traded DAO Tokens satisfied the Rule and were not within the exemptions.

Nevertheless, the SEC decided not to institute enforcement action at this time and advised the issuers of distributed ledger or blockchain technology, as well as investors in the DAO, to comply with the appropriate registration requirements. The SEC apparently was keen to foster the new technology, and, as stated by SEC chairperson, Jay Clayton, "We seek to foster innovative and beneficial ways to raise capital, while ensuring first and foremost that investors and our markets are protected." In addition, a problem arose in June 2016 when a DAO that was built on Ethereum started with $150 million in crowdfunding but a third of the virtual currency (Ether), some $50 million to 55 million, was hacked but later restored on the Ethereum blockchain. The identity of the thief has not been discovered although it is believed that there was no actual loss.

SEC v. Munchee Inc.

In an administrative proceeding that has caused noteworthy comments concerning the expansion of SEC authority, the agency issued a cease and desist order and commencement of proceedings against Munchee pursuant to 8A of the Securities Act of 1933 that requires registration of certain securities offerings and which order was consented to by the respondent. Munchee commenced a business in California that created an iPhone application allowing users to review restaurant meals. In October and November, 2017, the company offered and sold digital tokens to be issued on a blockchain in order to raise $15 million for the purpose of buying advertisements, writing reviews, selling food, and other related applications. The company alleged that it was anticipated the tokens would increase in value and later be traded on secondary markets. The SEC, in an Order dated December 11, 2017, based on the Howey three-pronged analysis of what constitutes an investment and its actions, and findings in the DAO report, concluded that Munchee's efforts constituted investment contracts that required registration with the SEC under the 1933 Act. It determined that the three-pronged requirements were met in that purchasers of the tokens would have a reasonable expectation of a future profit based on the efforts of others (Munchee) that included the app's revision and creation of the MUN "ecosystem" with the proceeds from sales of the tokens. The company complied with the Order by not delivering the tokens and returning the proceeds received for them.

There were a number of commentators concerning the significance of the Munchee Order. The action highlights the position of the SEC in that offerings of blockchain-related tokens may be regulated as securities and are subject to registration and other Securities Acts requirements. The SEC stated that even if the tokens had a practical use, this did not preclude them from being a security. Characterizing the ICO as involving a "utility token" is not conclusory by its labelling but rather requires an assessment of the economic realities underlying the transaction. There were no findings or indications of fraud as is the usual basis in SEC rulings and no "bright-line" rules (clearly defined rules) expressed to guide future compliance of companies making similar offerings. In addition to a lack of fraudulent conduct, there were no claims made by Munchee that investors would participate in the company's profits; rather, the "utility tokens" could be used to purchase goods and services once the com- pany had raised sufficient capital to build the intended "ecosystem." Therefore, the case appears to symbolize the fact that the SEC will broaden its perspective concerning what constitutes security under the Howey analysis and its intent to prosecute firms that fail to file registration requirements under the Securities Acts of 1933 and 1934.

In another commentary, the lessons to be drawn are the need to consult counsel in making offerings which may draw SEC scrutiny where the emphasis, in addition to being a current utility, is that future development plans may materially enhance the value of the token; where the emphasis is on growth and profit or completion of a product rather than its utility; and where the marketing of the product or service is concentrated less on the utility and more on expansion. Thus, the offering should be strongly biased towards the existing practical application of the product, rather than the expectation of profit by future developments, to avoid SEC scrutiny.

SEC Chairman's Commentary

Jay Clayton, the Chairman of the SEC, in a public statement on December 11, 2017 at the same time as the issuance of the Munchee Order, offered his personal views concerning cryptocurrency and ICOs. He commented on the legality of a cryptocurrency offering and persons making the offerings, the fairness of the trading markets to date including manipulation and attendant risks, market professionals, and their impact, and related issues. He noted that the offerings present substantially less protection for the investor coupled with much greater opportunities and risks of fraud and manipulation. To date, no ICO has been registered with the SEC, nor has the SEC approved for listing and trading any exchange-traded products related to cryptocurrencies. Therefore, the public is warned about making investments and before doing so should consider several questions stated in the Public Statement and answered from those offering the ICOs. Among the risks faced by investors, and which the SEC has limited or no ability to assist with, are offerings that are trans-border with money paid deflected to foreign entities.

Clayton cautioned market professionals, including their attorneys, accountants, and consultants, that a change in the structure of the offerings by recording through a blockchain ledger does not change the substance of the transaction, which may entail an offering of security coupled with registration requirements. By calling a token a "utility" token does not remove it from consideration as security. When the offered tokens incorporate features that place an emphasis on making profits through the managerial efforts and expertise of others, then the appropriate legislative and regulatory requirements are to be met. Those persons who sell securities ordinarily are required to be licensed. Excessive promotion of thinly traded securities may be an indication of scalping (recommendation of the sale of securities to investors while simultaneously selling them), pump and dump (artificial inflation of stock usually by heavy promotion and then selling the shares where cheaply purchased), and other possible fraudulent activities.

For offerings that allege they are currencies or concern currency-related products not subject to securities regulations, the persons making the offers should either be able to demonstrate that the product is not a security or that it complies with the applicable registration and filing requirements. Brokers and dealers permitting payments in cryptocurrencies or purchases of cryptocurrencies on margin, or who use them to facilitate securities transactions, should exercise caution in doing so, including assuring that the cryptocurrency activities do not violate anti-money laundering laws and "know-your-customer" obligations. They are to treat cryptocurrencies as cash obligations. Whether or not these currencies will be treated as securities will be dependent on the particular facts of each offering.

SEC Warnings to Social Media

The enormous run up and partial collapse of Bitcoin had caused the SEC to issue warnings, particularly about celebrity endorsements that may sway unsophisticated investors to engage in high-risk involvement. In its Guidance Update of 2014, it noted that 206(4) of the Investment Advisers Act of 1940 generally prohibits an investment adviser from engaging in any act, practice, or course of business that is fraudulent, deceptive, or manipulative. It is a violation of the Act for an investment adviser to publish, circulate, or distribute any advertisement which refers, directly or indirectly, to any testimonial of any kind about the investment adviser or concerning any advice, analysis, report or other service rendered by such investment adviser. It is misleading to emphasize the positive aspects of the cryptocurrency and provide deceptive implication, or mistaken inference, while ignoring the known negative views. The prohibition covers not only investment advisers but also third parties with the endorsement of the adviser.

With respect to virtual currencies, both the SEC and the Federal Trade Commission (FTC) have been critical of endorsements particularly those stated on online gambling services, and concerning cryptocurrencies. Paid celebrities, such as Floyd Mayweather, Paris Hilton, and Mike Tyson, have lent their names to tout Bitcoin and cryptocurrencies. As a result, the SEC warned that celebrities and others using social media to encourage the public to purchase stocks and other investments may be acting unlawfully unless they disclose the nature, source, and amount of any compensation received. It further warned that any celebrity or other individual who promotes a virtual token or coin that is a security must disclose the compensation received. Failure to do so may violate the antitouting provisions of the Securities Acts. The FTC has similarly warned celebrities about false advertising that may be in violation of the Federal Trade Commission Act.41 After reviewing numerous Instagram posts by celebrities, athletes, and other influencers, it sent out more than 90 letters reminding celebrities and their marketers that they should clearly and conspicuously disclose their relationships to brands when promoting or endorsing products through social media.

SEC and Crypto Co.

SEC temporarily suspended trading of the shares of Crypto Co. until January 6, 2018 when its shares rose by 2700 percent in one month having gone public after its acquisition of a sport bra company. The SEC was concerned that the company's shares rose due to manipulative transactions in November 2017. According to a former SEC chairperson, Harvey Pitt, the SEC and the Financial Industry Regulatory Authority (FINRA) are increasing their surveillance and enforcement rules with respect to cryptocurrencies and companies engaged in their use and exchange.

SEC Disapproval of NYSE Proposed Rule Change

The New York Stock Exchange (NYSE) proposed a rule change to list and trade shares of SolidX Bitcoin Trust as Commodity-Based Trust Shares under the Exchange's Equities Rule which permits such listing of a security issued by a trust in a specified aggregate minimum number in return for a deposit of a quantity of the underlying commodity that could be redeemed at a holders' request by the Trust. The Trust would hold bitcoins as its primary asset together with smaller sums of cash which would be in the custody of and secured by the Trust's Bitcoin custodian, SolidX Management LLC, which is also the Sponsor. The Bank of New York Mellon would serve as the cash custodian and its administrator. Insurance would be procured to cover the potential loss of the Trust's bitcoins against loss or theft. The investment objective would be to track the price of bitcoins as measured by the TradeBlock XBX Index. The shares would be redeemable only in baskets of 100,000 shares and only to authorized participants.

In summary, the SEC, disapproved the requested change stating that it did not find the proposal consistent with 6(b)(5)45 of the Securities Exchange Act of 193446 which requires that the rules of a national securities exchange be designed to prevent fraudulent and manipulative acts and practices and to protect investors and the public interest. The reasons given are that the significant markets for bitcoins are unregulated and that the Exchange has not entered into or has been unable to enter into the type of surveillance-sharing agreement that addresses concerns about the potential for fraudulent or manipulative acts and practices in the markets for the shares.

Commodity Futures Trading Commission (CFTC)

The CFTC, which overseas and regulates all commodities and futures trading in accordance with the statutory requirements of the Commodity Exchange Act (CEA),47 defines a commodity under 1a(9) quite broadly to include not only wheat, corn, other crops, livestock, and the like but also includes "all services, rights, and interests…in which contracts for future delivery are presently or in the future dealt in." It had determined in 2015 that Bitcoin and other virtual currencies are included under the definition. Its jurisdiction includes oversight of futures, options, and derivatives contracts and comes into play when a virtual currency is used in a derivatives contract or in cases of fraud or manipulation involving a virtual currency traded in interstate commerce.

Prohibited Activities

The CFTC has indicated those activities that will call into play its enforcement. They include:

- Price manipulation of a virtual currency traded in interstate commerce;
- Pre-arranged or wash trading in an exchange-traded virtual currency swap or futures contract;

- A virtual currency futures or option contract or swap traded on a domestic platform or facility that has not registered with the CFTC as a SEF (Swap Execution Facility) or DCM (Designated Contract Markets); and
- Certain schemes involving virtual currency marketed to retail customers such as off-exchange financed commodity transactions with per- sons who fail to register with the CFTC.

Coinflip, Inc.

The seminal case wherein the CFTC asserted jurisdiction over Bitcoin trades is In re Matter of Coinflip, Inc., d/b/a Derivabit, wherein the CFTC charged the company and its controlling person, Francisco Riordan, with violation of the provisions of the Commodity Exchange Act (CEA) by conducting activity related to commodity options and by operating a facility for the trading or processing of swaps without being registered as a swap execution facility or designated contract market. The company operated an online facility named Derivabit which offered to connect buyers and sellers of Bitcoin option contracts. It advertised itself as a "risk management platform…that connects buyers and sellers of standardized Bitcoin options and futures contracts." It designated numerous put and call options contracts as eligible for trading on the Derivabit platform, listed Bitcoin as the asset underlying the option, and denominated the strike and delivery prices in U.S. dollars. The customer would register as a user and deposit Bitcoin into an account in that particular user's name. The customer would receive premiums and payments of settlement of the options contracts payable using Bitcoin at a spot rate determined by a designated third-party Bitcoin currency exchange.

In a consent offer and order, the respondents were ordered to cease and desist from conducting the facility, and to comply with applicable rules and regulations including making any public statements denying the allegations in the consent order. The legal basis for the complaint is the violation of 4c(b) of the CEA which makes it unlawful for any person to "offer to enter into, enter into or confirm the execution of, any transaction involving any commodity…which is of the character of, or is commonly known to the trade as, an 'option'…, 'bid', 'offer', 'put', [or] 'call'…contrary to any rule, regulation, or order of the Commission prohibiting any such transaction." The company also violated 5h(a)(1) of the CEA forbidding such conduct without registration consisting of matching competitive bidding with a counterparty to execute a contract to exchange U.S. dollars for bitcoins at a predetermined price and date. The Commission noted that bitcoins is a commodity rather than a currency under §1a (9) of the Act which defines "commodity" to include, among other things, "all services, rights, and interests in which contracts for future delivery are presently or in the future dealt in."

CFTC v. Bitfinex

In a consent order, the CFTC fined BFXNA Inc. d/b/a/ BITFINEX, a Hong Kong company, the sum of $75,000. The order stated that the company operated an online platform for exchanging and trading cryptocurrencies, mainly bitcoins, which permitted ineligible contract participants or commercial entities to borrow funds from other users on the platform in order to trade bitcoins on a leveraged, margined, or financed basis. The company was not registered with the Commission. From April 2013 through August 2015, it did not actually deliver bitcoins purchased on a leveraged, margined, or financed bases to the traders who purchased them but rather held them in an omnibus wallet account under its own private key for the customers who could not access the bitcoins until they were released by the company. The failure to "actually deliver" the commodity violated the CEA, notwithstanding that a book entry was noted on behalf of the customer.

Section 4d(a) of the Act requires all persons acting as futures commission merchants to register with the Commission, which the company failed to do. Bitfinex accepted orders for retail commodity transactions and received funds from those customers in connection with retail commodity transactions. Bitfinex was not, however, registered with the Commission in any capacity which violated §4d(a) of the Act. Accordingly, the company was deemed to have engaged in illegal, off-exchange commodity transactions and failed to register as a futures commission merchant, in violation of 4(a) and 4d of the Act, 7 U.S.C. 6(a) and 6(d).

CFTC v. LedgerX, LLC and TeraExchange

The CFTC has given recognition to cryptocurrency by its order granting LedgerX, LLC registration as a derivative clearing organization under the CEA. It was granted an Order of Registration as a Swap Execution Facility on July 6, 2017, and authorized to provide clearing services for collateralized digital currency swaps. It initially intends to clear Bitcoin options. It is expected that swaps of other cryptocurrencies will follow. The founder of Ledger X, Paul Chou, envisions a co-existence with fiat currency, such as the U.S. dollar and the Euro, by the ease of transfer from one currency to the other irrespective of where a person resides and engages in financial transactions. Derivatives in these currencies will be required to manage the volatility attendant to the various currencies. The CFTC had previously approved the registration of TeraExchange in May, 2016, which was the first facility to offer NDF (non-deliverable forward) with underlying Bitcoin. A year prior to the grant of registration, the CFTC had sanctioned TeraExchange, which agreed to cease-and-desist without the imposition of a fine for having engaged in a Bitcoin swap that constituted wash trading (the same person sells and buys shares of the same security to simulate market activity) and pre-arranged trading in violation of its regulations.

CME, CBOE, and Cantor Exchanges

On December 1, 2017, the CFTC gave recognition to three exchanges, namely, the Chicago Mercantile Exchange Inc. (CME) and the CBOE Futures Exchange (CFE) after both exchanges self certified new contracts for Bitcoin futures products, and to the Cantor Exchange after it self certified a new contract for Bitcoin binary options. The Chairman of the CFTC, J. Christopher

Cyptocurrency: The Next Level for Banking Reform

Giancarlo, after noting the CFTC's limited statutory authority to oversee the cash market for Bitcoin, stated that the three exchanges agreed to significant enhancements to protect customers and maintain orderly markets. The major concerns are that of volatility and trading practices of participants and their potential impact on the futures contracts' price discovery process, including market manipulation and market dislocations due to flash rallies and crashes and trading outages.

Given the sudden increase of interest in the creation of new technological currencies, the Commission intends to participate in risk monitoring activities including the monitoring and analysis of the size and development of the market, positions and changes in positions over time, open interest, initial margin requirements, variation margin payments, and stress testing positions. It will work closely with the National Futures Association (NFA) to conduct reviews of designated contract markets, derivatives clearing organizations, clearing firms, and individual traders involved in trading and clearing Bitcoin futures. If the Commission determines that the margins the Digital Clearing Organization (DCO) hold are inadequate, then it will require the margins held be increased. The recognition given to the exchanges has met opposition. In an open letter from President Walt (Walter) Lukken of the Futures Industry Association (FIA), on December 6, 2017, to the CFTC Chairman, Christopher Giancarlo, he criticized the self-certification process of the exchanges commenting that the risks posed by cryptocurrency products require "a healthy dialogue between regulators, exchanges, clearinghouses, and the clearing firms who will be absorbing the risk of these volatile, emerging instruments during a default. The one-day self-certification process and launch the following day, although adequate for standardized products, is highly inadequate because it does not align with the potential risks posed by the underlying trades. The fear is that clearing houses will bear a great risk associated with their guarantee fund contributions and assessment obligations. There should be a public discussion whether a separate guarantee fund for this product should be created and whether exchanges should increase their contributions to the clearing member guarantee fund. There should be a more thorough discussion among clearing member firms, clearinghouses, and exchanges to ascertain margin levels, trading limits, stress testing, and other protections and procedures in the event of excessive price movements."

The Economist magazine was also critical of futures contracts in Bitcoin stating: "The CBOE's price is set by an auction on just one modestly size bitcoin exchange, Gemini," whereas the CME's price will be based on data compiled from four exchanges. Whereas most futures margins are from 5 to 15 percent, the margins for CBOE and CME are 44 percent and 47 percent respectively. It quoted the head of Interactive Brokers, Thomas Peterffy, who warned of the risk to clearing houses due to the high volatility of Bitcoin prices which could cause clients to be unable to meet margin calls thereby leaving brokers to bear the costs, resulting in their financial ruin and, in the end, leaving clearing houses to unwind the contracts.

Cyptocurrency: The Next Level for Banking Reform

In contrast to the FIA letter, in a keynote address, Chairman Giancarlo gave his views concerning the future treatment of virtual currencies. In it, he stated initially to do no harm and then proposed a five-step process: "

1. Putting Our Best Foot Forward –Financial regulators should designate dedicated, technology savvy teams to work collaboratively with FinTech companies – both new and established – to address issues of how existing regulatory frameworks apply to new, digital products, services and business models derived from innovative technologies, including DLT;
2. Allowing Breathing Room – Financial regulators should foster a regulatory environment that spurs innovation similar to the FCA's sandbox, where FinTech businesses, working collaboratively with regulators, have appropriate "space to breath" to develop and test innovative solutions without fear of enforcement action and regulatory fines;
3. Getting Involved – Financial regulators should participate directly in FinTech proof of concepts to advance regulatory understanding of technological innovation and determine how new innovations may help regulators do their jobs more efficiently and effectively;
4. Listening and Learning – Financial regulators should work closely with FinTech innovators to determine how rules and regulations should be adapted to enable 21st Century technologies and business models; and

5. Collaborating Globally – Financial regulators should provide a dedicated team to help FinTech firms navigate through the various state, federal and foreign regulators and regimes across domestic and international jurisdictions. In summary, the Chairman stated that he plans to make FinTech a priority."

Authority Over Bitcoin Interpretation

On December 15, 2017, the CFTC announced a Proposed Interpretation concerning its authority over retail commodity transactions involving virtual currency such as Bitcoin. The proposed Interpretation provides for an exception that sets out the CFTC's view regarding the "actual delivery" exception that may apply to virtual currency transactions. Section 2(c)(2)(D) of the CEA grants the CFTC jurisdiction over retail commodity transactions which are defined as agreements, contracts or transactions in any commodity that are entered into with, or offered to, retail market participants on a leveraged or margined basis, or financed by the offeror, the counterparty, or a person acting in concert with the offeror or counterparty on a similar basis.

The exception to the exercise of jurisdictional authority is for contracts of sale that result in "actual delivery" within 28 days from the date of the transaction. The CFTC proposes that the exception will be granted for actual delivery of retail commodity transactions in virtual currency when:

1. a customer has the ability to (i) take possession and control of the entire quantity of the commodity, whether it was purchased on margin, or using leverage, or any other financing arrangement, and (ii) use it freely in commerce (both within and away from any particular platform) no later than 28 days from the date of the transaction; and
2. the offeror and counterparty seller (including any of their respective affiliates or other persons acting in concert with the offeror or counterparty seller on a similar basis) does not retain any interest in or control over any of the commodity purchased on margin, leverage, or other financing arrangement at the expiration of 28 days from the date of the transaction. The net import of the Proposed Interpretation is to exempt Bitcoin and other virtual currencies from heightened supervision although the CFTC will retain authority to investigate anti-fraud and manipulation in virtual currency cash markets as a commodity in interstate commerce.

CFTC Self-Certification Announcement

The CFTC, in an announcement dated January 4, 2018, discussed how it intends to extend its oversight over virtual currencies. It asserted a five-pronged approach namely: "

1. Consumer Education—a greater understanding of the wild assertions, bold headlines, and extreme hyperbole;

2. Assertion of Legal Authority—over virtual currency derivatives to support its efforts to combat fraud and manipulation;
3. Market Intelligence—to gain the ability to monitor virtual currency derivatives markets and underlying reference rates by gathering trade information and counterparty data for regulatory and enforcement insights into those markets;
4. Robust Enforcement—police fraud and manipulation in cash or spot markets and enforce the law and prosecute fraud, abuse, manipulation, or false solicitation in markets for virtual currency derivatives and underlying spot trading; and
5. Government-wide Coordination— coordination with the SEC, FBI, Justice Department, the U.S. Treasury's Financial Stability Oversight Council (FSOC), state agencies, and with Congressional and executive policy-makers."

In accordance with Congressional and administrative authorizations to DCMs as a self-regulatory organization to certify new products and the CFTC's principle-based approach, the CME and CBOE as stated above, commencing on December 1, 2017, were permitted to and did self-certify, and the Cantor Exchange also self-certified, for Bitcoin binary options. The CFTC has few powers to stay a self-certification except for a false statement filing which did not occur with the above-stated self-certifications. Even if the CFTC was desirous of blocking self-certification of Bitcoin futures products, it would not have prevented the spectacular and volatile nature of Bitcoin and other virtual currencies. Its role is thus to continue regulatory surveillance to ensure that the virtual currency spot markets continue to operate lawfully. Currently, it has gained experience in virtual currency derivatives such as TeraExchange swaps, Nadex binary options, and LedgerX options. Additional issues raised included whether Bitcoin futures qualify as systemically important derivatives that would cause it to comply with the enhanced requirements of the Systemically Important Derivatives Clearing Organization (similar to the FSOC's powers over systemically important financial institutions) that are determined to materially affect the overall U.S. economy.

The CFTC has undertaken a heightened review of DCMs concerning the terms and conditions of Bitcoin futures products. The review will focus on the extensive visibility and monitoring of markets for virtual currency derivatives and their underlying settlement reference rates. The heightened reviews will enable the CFTC to have the means to police certain underlying spot markets for fraud and manipulation. The heightened review will consist of the following:

- DCMs setting a substantially high initial and maintenance margin for cash-settled Bitcoin futures;
- DCMs setting large trader reporting thresholds at 5 bitcoins or less;
- DCMs entering direct or indirect information-sharing agreements with spot market platforms to allow access to trade and trader data;

- DCM monitoring of data from cash markets with respect to price settlements and other Bitcoin prices more broadly, and identifying anomalies and disproportionate moves in the cash markets compared to the futures markets;
- DCMs agreeing to engage in inquiries, including at the trade settlement level when necessary;
- DCMs agreeing to regular coordination with CFTC surveillance staff on trade activities, including providing the CFTC surveillance team with trade settlement data upon request; and
- DCMs coordinating product launches so that the CFTC's market surveillance branch can carefully monitor minute-by-minute developments.

The chairman of the CFTC, J. Christopher Giancarlo, indicated that the Commission's Market Risk Advisory Committee would hold a meeting at the end of January 2018 to consider the process of self-certification of new products and operational rules by DCMs under the CEA and CFTC regulations, as well as the risks, challenges, and market developments of virtual currencies. Giancarlo recited the inherent risks of virtual currencies, in addition to the nascent stage of the technology itself. Risks associated with virtual currencies include: operational risks of unregulated and unsupervised trading platforms; cybersecurity risks of hackable trading platforms and virtual currency wallets; speculative risks of extremely volatile price moves; and fraud and manipulation risks through traditional market abuses of "pump and dump schemes," insider trading, false disclosure, Ponzi schemes, and other forms of investor fraud and market manipulation. He emphasized that responsible innovation and development are consistent with the Commission's role in preventing fraud and manipulation. The key is consumer education coupled with regulation and enforcement.

Consumer Protection Resource Page

The CFTC has launched a virtual currency resource web page (cftc.gov/ bitcoin) that will act as a repository for its resources concerning virtual currency. The resource is intended to educate and inform the public about the virtual currency commodities including potential risks, particularly when investing or speculating in them, especially Bitcoin futures and options. It also released a Customer Advisory "Understanding the Risks of Virtual Currency Trading" that highlights the risks.

Financial Crimes Enforcement Network (FinCEN)

FinCEN's Guidance to Persons Administrating, Exchanging, or Using Virtual Currencies

The U.S. Treasury Department's FinCEN has taken an active role in its guidance and administrative rulings particularly with respect to the application of regulations under the Bank Secrecy Act (BSA) as they apply to virtual currencies with respect to persons who engage in their creation, acquisition, distribution, exchange, acceptance, or transmission. In essence, the purpose of the Act is to ensure that banks have in place the necessary controls for access to law enforcement authorities to detect money laundering, terrorist financing, and other criminal acts. Accordingly, there are record-keeping and registration requirements under the Act. In regulations pursuant to the Act, "money services businesses" (MSBs) are subject to the Act's requirements.

The question that arises is whether users and dealers of convertible virtual currencies are subject to the Act's provisions and regulations. FinCEN states that persons obtaining such currencies are not subject to the registration, reporting, and record-keeping requirements for MSBs but administrators or exchanges who accept and transmit such currency or buy or sell it for any reason are money transmitters under the regulations. The regulation does not differentiate between real and virtual currency but specifies that a money transmitter is one who provides money transmission services (acceptance of currency, funds, or other value as substitutes for them from one person and transmission to another) in the transfer of funds.

In its Guidance, FinCEN defines persons who participate in generic virtual currency arrangements as follows: a user is a person who obtains virtual currency to purchase goods or services; an exchanger is a person engaged as a business in the exchange of virtual currency for real currency, funds, or other virtual currency; and an administrator is a person engaged as a business in issuing (putting into circulation) a virtual currency and who has the authority to redeem (to withdraw from circulation) such virtual currency The Guidance states that a user who obtains convertible virtual currency and uses it to purchase real or virtual goods or services is not an MSB under its regulations inasmuch as the said use, in and of itself, does not fit within the definition of "money transmission services."

It is unclear how to characterize a person who neither purchases goods nor services but rather makes a gift of the virtual currency. He or she does not appear to fall within the ambit of an exchanger because such use is not in pursuance to a business. On the other hand, an administrator or exchanger that;

1. accepts and transmits a convertible virtual currency, or
2. buys or sells convertible virtual currency for any reason, is a money transmitter under the regulations unless a limitation to or exemption from the definition applies to the person. It is a money transmitter to the extent that it allows persons to transfer value to another or between one location to another location. It includes the allowance of payment to a third party for virtual goods and services.

With respect to de-centralized convertible virtual currency (e.g., Bitcoin), a person who creates (mines) units of the currency to purchase real or virtual goods is not a transmitter but is characterized as a user and is thus exempt from the FinCEN regulations. On the other hand, if the said user who creates units of convertible virtual currency and sells them to another person for real money or equivalent, or accepts the said currency as part of the acceptance and transfer of funds, then he or she is considered to be a money transmitter engaged its transmission. Money service businesses have additional requirements that include the maintenance of transaction records and, if a transaction is $3000 or more, the parties are to obtain information about the transmitter, the recipient, and the transaction between the parties, and relay the information to other intermediary financial institutions in subsequent fund transmissions. They are required to monitor transactions for any suspicious activity and report customer transactions involving cash of $10,000 or more. This is one of the means by which anonymous Bitcoin and other virtual currencies may be investigated.

FinCEN's Ruling Concerning Virtual Currency Software Development January 30, 2014

In a later opinion letter, FinCEN further elaborated upon its position vis-à-vis the application of its regulations to virtual currency development and virtual currency trading platforms. The following query was posed to FinCEN: the Company stated it intends to produce a piece of software that will facilitate the Company's purchase of a virtual currency from sellers by automating the collection of virtual currency and the payment of the equivalent in currency of legal tender. The potential sellers, using the Company's software interface, would initiate the process of offering virtual currency to the Company choosing among several options for receiving the equivalent in a currency of legal tender. The software remains private between the parties. The Company intends to invest in convertible virtual currency for its own account by buying the virtual currency from sellers and reselling the currency when it so chooses at a virtual currency exchange.

FinCEN's response is that based on the facts presented, and in accordance with its Final Rule of July 21, 2011 which defined a "money service business" as "a person wherever located doing business, whether or not on a regular basis or as an organized business concern, wholly or in substantial part within the United States, in one or more of the capacities listed [therein]...," so a "money transmitter" is one that provides money transmission services which includes the transmission of currency funds, or other value that substitutes for currency. The production of the Company's software does not in itself constitute acceptance and transmission of value making the Company a money transmitter; however, an administrator or exchanger of convertible virtual currencies that (1) accepts and transmits a convertible virtual currency, or (2) buys or sells convertible virtual currencies for any reason including acting as an intermediator between the user and a seller of goods or services the user is purchasing on the user's behalf, is a money transmitter under FinCEN's regulations. If the Company is buying and selling the said currency exclusively as investments for its own account it is not engaged in the exchange of the currency but if it provides services to others including investment related or brokerage services that involves the acceptance and transmission of convertible virtual currencies, then it will come within the ambit of being a money transmitter requiring registration with FinCen and related obligations.

FinCEN's Ruling Concerning Convertible Virtual Currency Trading and Booking Platform

FinCEN issued a ruling as to whether a company's convertible virtual currency trading and booking platform caused it to be a money transmitter requiring compliance with registration requirements with the agency. The platform would consist of a trading system to match offers to buy and sell convertible virtual currency for the currency of legal tender and a set of book accounts in which prospective buyers or sellers of one type of currency or the other can deposit funds to cover their exchanges. Each account would be segregated separately in U.S. dollars and a virtual wallet and protected from seizure by the company's creditors. The customer submits an order with the company to purchase or sell the currency deposited at a given price. The platform to be created would automatically attempt to match each purchase order of one currency to one or more sell orders of the same currency. If the company finds a match, it will then purchase the virtual currency from the customer and sell it to the prospective buyer. If no match is found, the customer may either retain the funds in the company's account or have the funds returned to him or her.

FinCEN ruled that, based on the given facts, the company would be a money transmitter. After reciting the definition of a money transmitter, it stated its disagreement with the company's position that that there is no money transmission when the instructions of the customers are issued subject to the condition of finding an offsetting match. The said definition does not contain any element of conditionality before it applies. A person that accepts currency, funds, or any value that substitutes for currency, with the intent and/or effect of transmitting currency, funds, or any value that substitutes for currency to another person or location, if a certain pre-determined condition established by the transmitter is met, is a money transmitter under FinCEN's regulations. The fact that the transmission is subject to finding a willing buyer, which may not occur, does not constitute an exception to the definition. Neither does a key feature of the Platform, that customers are never identified to each other, alter the ruling. Each trade conducted through the Platform results in two money transmission transactions, one between the company and the customer wishing to buy virtual currency, and another between the company and the customer wishing to sell such virtual currency at the same exchange rate.

FinCEN has concluded that the money transmission that takes place within the system does not qualify for the exemption as claimed by the company. FinCEN stated that there are three fundamental conditions that must be met for the exemption to apply:

1. the money transmission component must be part of the provision of goods or services distinct from money transmission itself;

2. the exemption can only be claimed by the person that is engaged in the provision of goods or services distinct from money transmission; and
3. the money transmission component must be integral (that is, necessary) for the provision of the goods or services. The company's intended platform facilitates the transfer of value, both real and virtual, between third parties. The money transmission is the sole purpose of the company's system and is not a necessary part of another, non-money transmission service being provided by the company. Therefore, it must register as a money transmitter.

FinCEN's Application of Money Transmission to Virtual Currency Mining

FinCEN responded to an inquiry from a company which requested a ruling whether certain ways of disposing of the bitcoins mined by it would make it a money transmitter under the BSA. The company alleged that it mined bitcoins that have not yet been used or transferred but rather would be used in the future to purchase goods or services by converting the virtual currency into legal tender and using the legal tender currency to purchase goods and services, or to transfer the virtual currency to the owner of the company. FinCEN stated that it understands the mining of Bitcoin imposes no obligation on a Bitcoin user to send the mined bitcoins to anyone or any place for the benefit of another but rather the user is free to use the mined currency for the user's own benefit to purchase real or virtual goods and services.

Such use does not cause the use to be a money transmission under the regulations because it is neither an "acceptance" nor a "transmission" within the meaning of the Rule.

Similarly, if the use is to pay debts incurred in the ordinary course of business or where a corporate user makes distributions to shareholders, these also do not come within the Rule. The key element is whether the person is engaging in the business of money transmission. Thus, if on occasion the person needs to convert the mined Bitcoin into real currency or other convertible virtual currency as, for example, where the person from whom goods or services are requested refuses to accept Bitcoin or where the user wishes to diversify currency holdings in anticipation of future needs for investment purposes, neither one is deemed to be a money transmission provided that the user is doing so for the user's own purposes and not as a business service for others. The said conversion of currencies does not, in itself, constitute a money transmission making the person a money transmitter.

After reciting the regulations and definitions as stated in the Guidance above, FinCEN concluded that the company would be deemed a "user" of Bitcoin but is not a money service business to the extent that it uses bitcoins it has mined:

1. to pay for the purchase of goods or services, pay debts it has previously incurred (including debts to its owner(s)), or make distributions to owners; or

2. to purchase real currency or another con- vertible virtual currency, so long as the real currency or other convertible virtual currency is used solely in order to make payments or for the company's own investment purposes. In the event that the company were to engage in any transfer to third parties on behalf of sellers, creditors, owners, or counterparties, or should it engage in any other activity constituting acceptance and transmission of either currency of legal tender or virtual currency, then such activity should be carefully scrutinized in as much as the company may be engaged in money transmission activities that would be subject to the requirements of the BSA.

Requirements When Designated as a Money Services Business

Once a business has been designed as a "money services business" a panoply of requirements follows. Under the regulations issued pursuant to the BSA, each money services business must develop, implement, and maintain an effective anti-money laundering program. As defined by the regulations, an effective anti-money laundering program is one that is reasonably designed to prevent the money services business from being used to facilitate money laundering and the financing of terrorist activities. The written program is to be commensurate with the risks posed by the location, size, nature, and volume of the financial services provided by the MSB. Copies of the program is to be made available to the Treasury Department upon request.

At a minimum, the program is to incorporate policies, procedures, and internal controls reasonably designed to assure compliance and shall include provisions:

1. verifying customer identification;
2. filing reports;
3. creating and retaining records; and
4. responding to law enforcement requests. The said business is to have an automated data processing system that integrates compliance procedures with such systems. It is to designate a person to assure day-to-day compliance with the program; that the money services business properly files reports and creates and retains records; provides appropriate training of appropriate personnel concerning their responsibilities under the program; includes training in the detection of suspicious transactions; and provides for independent review to monitor and maintain an adequate program.

U.S. v. Lord

An example, in addition to other cases cited in the chapter on "Criminal Prosecutions and Civil Litigations Concerning Virtual Currencies" on the prosecution of crimes and civil offenses, is U.S. v. Lord. Randall Lord, a chiropractor, and his son, Michael Lord, attempted to withdraw their plea of "Guilty" which plea was denied by the court. They began operating a business called localbitcoins.com in which they posted advertisements for Bitcoin exchange services wherein they exchanged cash, credit card payments, and other forms of payments for bitcoins. Interested persons would transfer money to the defendants' account and the defendants would then purchase bitcoins from Coinbase, which would then be transferred to the said interested persons less a commission for the services rendered. The defendants used a number of bank accounts for the transactions. Coinbase, an online Bitcoin broker, contacted the defendants after it noted the volume of their activity and told them that as Bitcoin exchanges they were required to register with FinCEN as per the Guidance of March 2013. The defendants stated to Coinbase that they were registered although they had not done so until months after the earlier transactions in which they had exchanged over $2.5 million for bitcoins for customers. Federal agents were made aware of the exchange when investigating Michael Lord for alleged drug dealing with a purchaser of bitcoins from the defendants. After an indictment of the defendants on various counts concerning the operation of the Bitcoin exchange business, Randall Lord pleaded guilty to Count 1 of the indictment which charged the defendants with conspiracy to operate and the actual operation of an unlicensed money service business. Michael Lord pleaded guilty to being a member of a drug conspiracy.

The court denied Michael Lord's request to withdraw his plea to the drug charge stating that he presented no arguments that constitute a "fair and just" reason for withdrawing his guilty plea on this counts, and does not claim innocence of that count. With respect to the operation of a money transmission business without a license, the defendants had argued that a license was not required under Louisiana law, which the court agreed.

Nevertheless, the court found the defendants were properly charged under federal law. The court noted that the statute sets forth two separate methods by which the government may prove that a defendant is an "unlicensed money transmitting business":

1. failure to obtain a state license where such a license is necessary (conceded by the government and not shown herein), or
2. failure to comply with separate federal registration requirements.

The court did find that the guilty plea for violation of the federal regulations regarding the unlicensed money transmission business appeared sufficiently to have a basis in fact and in law as presented by the prosecution. The court defined "money service business" and "money transmitter" and found there was sufficient evidence to so charge and permit the plea given to the violations. To allow a withdrawal of the pleas given the delay in doing so, the court applied a multi-factor test for making the determination whether to allow the withdrawal. The court examined each of the factors provided in the Federal Rules of Criminal Procedure and found, in essence, that the withdrawal would be highly inconvenient to the court and its resources which would have to try a 15-count indictment. The court had extensively questioned the defendants at the time of the pleas whether they were competent to enter a guilty plea and determined that the pleas were knowingly and voluntarily made with their free and voluntary waiver of their constitutional rights.

Additional Agencies That May Regulate Virtual Currencies

Federal Reserve Board

The Governor and Vice-Chair for Supervision of the FED, Randal K. Quarles, stated that although digital currencies did not presently pose major concerns to the financial stability of the United States, nevertheless, issues may arise in the future if they attain wide-scale coverage. The problem is that if the central asset of the U.S. payment system cannot be predictably redeemed for the U.S. dollar at a stable exchange rate when the economy is faced with a financial crisis, the risk and potential liquidity resulting therein could raise fundamental concerns. Private-sector and non-banks can potentially face liquidity demands that cannot be attained which then may have significant spill-over effects on the entire economy. Issues may be raised as to whether Bitcoin and/or other cryptocurrencies may come within the jurisdiction of the Financial Stability Oversight Council (FSOC), created under the Dodd-Frank Act, which oversees "systemically important" financial institutions whose demise or downturn may harm the entire U.S. economy. Under such circumstances, there may be instituted onerous rules and regulations that could hinder the development of the new technologies.

The Federal Reserve Board has refrained from pursuing the regulation of virtual currencies. Janet Yellen, the former Chairperson of the Board of Governors of the Federal Reserve System, stated that the Fed does not have the authority to supervise or regulate Bitcoin in any way and requested Congress for authority to enhance its supervision.

Consumer Financial Protection Bureau (CFPB)

According to its website, the Bureau is responsible for making financial markets work for consumers, providers, and the economy as a whole, by affording protection from unfair, deceptive, or abusive tactics, and can initiate enforcement against violators of its provisions. Companies must ensure that consumers are made aware of the prices, risks, and terms of agreements so that they may make responsible financial decisions. Created under the Dodd-Frank Act, the Bureau has become the proverbial whipping-boy of the political parties that began with the attempt by President Obama to name Elizabeth Warren as its first head but which was not consented to by the Senate thus leading her to successfully become elected as U.S. Senator for Massachusetts. With respect to virtual currency, the Bureau issued a consumer advisory alerting consumers to the risks associated with hackers, lack of protection that other fiat currencies possess, costs that may substantially exceed that of other currency transactions, and the scams that inevitably are attempted. It advised consumers to know whom they are dealing with and that, if using exchanges, they should consult the FinCEN website to ascertain whether the exchanges being dealt with are properly registered. It further warned of the use of Bitcoin kiosks which are unlike other ATMs and the protection afforded by the latter; the volatility of the price of bitcoins; the consequences of losing a private key (which may cause a total loss of the investment); and the lack of government insurance that is accorded to fiat bank and credit union deposits.

Office of Comptroller of the Currency (OCC)

Although not directly addressing virtual currency, the OCC clearly is aware of the implications of the new technology. In accordance with recommendations for the implementation of innovative technologies, the OCC created the Office of Innovation to Implement the Framework to address new and different consumer preferences for financial products and services. The rise in non-banks (shadow banks) and their increased importance rivaling that of traditional banks and, inferentially, the advent and greatly increased DLT, call for new banking models. Accordingly, the OCC commenced a study in 2015 focused on innovation in order to better understand the new, evolving, regulatory landscape. Accordingly, it arrived at a number of recommendations. The first is "responsible innovation" to meet the needs of consumers, businesses, and communities with sound risk management and aligned with the banks' business strategy. Its guiding principles are support responsible innovation; foster an internal culture receptive to responsible innovation; leverage agency experience and expertise; encourage responsible innovation that provides fair access to financial services and fair treatment of consumers; further safe and sound operations through effective risk management;

encourage banks of all sizes to integrate responsible innovation into their strategic planning; promote ongoing dialogue through formal outreach; and collaborate with other regulators.

The newly created Office of Innovation would provide internal and external visibility whose functions would be: to serve as a central point of contact and facilitate responses to inquiries and requests; conduct out-reach and provide technical assistance; enhance awareness, culture, and education; monitor the evolving financial services landscape; and collaborate with domestic and international regulators. The principles guiding the Office of Innovation are ensure efficient and effective execution of core functions; leverage OCC expertise; preserve existing decision-making functions; develop resources on innovation for internal and external shareholders; and provide credible evidence to processes and decision-making.

Federal Trade Commission (FTC)

The FTC was created under the Federal Trade Commission Act of 1914.99 Originally, its mandate was to prevent unfair methods of competition in commerce and this was later amended to prevent unfair or deceptive acts or practices which, in effect, is to protect consumers. Its enforcement in Bitcoin and blockchain activity has been negligible other than issuing warnings but it did participate in an action affecting consumers who purchased Bitcoin mining machines and services.

FTC v. BF Labs, Inc. In an action against BF Labs, Inc. d/b/a Butterfly Labs,100 the FTC sought equitable relief consisting of injunctive relief, rescission or reformation of contracts, restitution, the refund of monies paid, and disgorgement of ill gotten monies for alleged misrepresentations. It was alleged that the defendants operated Butterfly Labs, which sold Bitcoin mining machines and services that consumers purportedly could use to generate bitcoins. The defendants charged consumers upfront between $149 and $29,899 for the machines and services with the latter sum charged for the highest powered machines. It was later alleged that, in many instances, consumers who purchased the machines or services, about 20,000 in number, were not able to use them to generate bitcoins because the machines and services were never provided. In other instances, the delivery of the machines was greatly delayed for up to a year, making them obsolete, or the machines were otherwise damaged or defective. Butterfly Labs' advertising on Facebook and elsewhere was allegedly misleading as well as its claim to provide mining services at a set upfront price. No refunds were made although at times promises of refunds were assured.

The action resulted in an agreed settlement whereby Butterfly Labs and two of its operators consented that they will be prohibited from misrepresenting to consumers whether a product or service can be used to generate bitcoins or any other virtual currency, on what date a consumer will receive the product or service, and whether the product is new or used. The company and a senior officer were prohibited from taking up- front payments for Bitcoin machines and other products used to mine for any virtual currency unless those products are available and will be delivered within 30 days. If the product is not actually delivered within 30 days, the defendants must provide a refund. Damaged or defective machines are to result in prompt refunds and lateness in delivery will require a consumer's permission to so deliver. The orders included partially suspended monetary judgments conditioned upon the surrender of the cash value of all bitcoins obtained for the machines.

North American Securities Administrators Association (NASAA)

Non-governmental organizations also warn investors for reasons comparable to those previously stated. Thus, NASAA is particularly concerned about investors succumbing to the headlines and hype that has garnered so much attention with the seemingly extraordinary rise in value of cryptocurrencies. Joseph P. Borg, NASAA's President and Director of the Alabama Securities Commission, warned about the lack of a safety net via insurance or control by central banks and that cryptocurrencies cannot be exchanged for other commodities. NASAA's research shows that 94 percent of regulators believe there is a risk of fraud involving cryptocurrencies and were unanimous in their view that more regulation is needed to provide greater investor protection. It compared ICOs with IPOs whereby the latter sell shares of stock to raise capital but ICOs sell tokens which often have no value to fund a project. The concerns replicate those previously stated including common red flags of alleged guaranteed high investment returns, unsolicited offers, pressure to buy immediately, unlicensed sellers, and a "sounds too good to be true" fault line.

In the chapter on "States' Regulation of Virtual Currencies," we will discuss how U.S. states, in addition to federal regulation, have begun to enter the fray inasmuch as their citizens' investments have been compromised by unscrupulous entrepreneurs who take advantage of people's lack of knowledge about the technical aspects of making transactions in cryptocurrencies. Each state, as a sovereign entity, adapts such regulations, if any, to its perceived best interests in protecting the public.

International Regulation

The advent and speed of financial innovations brought about initially by the Internet that serves as a basis for the transformation of global payment systems inevitably has raised significant concerns among law enforcement agencies about criminal activity. Among the issues are concerns voiced by national central banks about the incorporation of new currencies into the global financial network and governmental apprehensions in their endeavor to protect their citizens from harmful investments. We discuss some of the ongoing efforts by nations and by international agencies to understand and promulgate measures to encourage innovative financial endeavors and thwart inevitable harmful activities.

International Organizations And Entities

The Bank for International Settlements.

The Bank for International Settlements (BIS), through its Committee on Payments and Market Infrastructures, issued a report on digital currencies in November, 2015. In the report, BIS set forth the supply-side factors that may influence the currencies' future development which primarily are fragmentation due to the numerous digital currencies in circulation; scalability and efficiency, which at the time of this report, was smaller than traditional payment systems; pseudonymity (not anonymity) in as much as the distributed ledger is usually publicly available; technical and security concerns by malicious actors using falsified ledgers; and business model sustainability that will be difficult to achieve. It also noted the demand-side issues of security, cost, usability, volatility, risk of loss, irrevocability, processing speed, cross-border reach, data privacy, and marketing and reputational effects.

The regulatory issue BIS addresses is the degree of regulation that should occur both on a global and national level. It recommends five categories of actions to be addressed, namely:

1. information/moral suasion whereby users are made aware of the risks of partaking in the currencies;
2. regulation of specific entities such as exchanges, merchant acceptance facilities, and digital wallet applications;

3. interpretation of existing regulations to ascertain whether they need updating due to the rise of the new technologies;
4. broader regulation to enlarge regulations applicable to traditional payment methods and intermediaries to cover the new currencies; and
5. prohibition by the various national states.

BIS also addressed the implications of virtual currencies for central banks and their role in acclimating to virtual currencies. BIS' emphasis is on consumer protection and the basis for its value predicated on the user's perception of value. With the decentralized nature of virtual currencies, it will be difficult for central banks to anticipate possible disruptions. There are legal risks due to the lack of a legal structure to govern their use. There are implications for financial stability and monetary policy owing to their impact on retail payment systems, liquidity for central banks, and the degree of interconnection between users of traditional and non-traditional currencies. A future course of action may include banks' investigations of the distributed ledgers in payment systems.

European Union

European Central Bank (ECB)

The ECB, as early as October 2012, was concerned about virtual currencies shortly after their issuance. It referred to them as "virtual currency schemes," because of the two aspects of resembling money and possessing their own retail payment systems. After reciting the characteristics of the currencies, it noted the business reasons for their creation and growth, namely, for virtual community users to participate in them; to generate revenue for their owners; to have control over them in accordance with their business model and strategy; and to compete with traditional currencies such as the euro and the dollar.

After reciting case studies, risks to central banks, and other considerations, the ECB's conclusion was that at the time of the report (October, 2012), virtual currencies did not pose a risk to price stability provided they remained at a relatively low level; they tend to be inherently unstable and low risk because of their low volume and lack of wide acceptance; are not currently regulated when the report was issued; could pose a challenge to public authorities due to use by criminal elements, money launderers, and persons committing fraud; could impact central banks if the public perceives their abuses as due to a lack of central bank intervention; and do come within central banks' authority to the extent that they become part of the payment system.

In a later report in 2015, the ECB noted the dramatic increase in the number of decentralized virtual currencies and the increased dangers to the payment system and, perhaps, more importantly, to the users who are exposed to risks of exchange rate, volatility, counterparty relating to the anonymity of the payee, investment fraud, and other risks. It expressed concern over the lack of co-ordinated governmental efforts from national authorities to mitigate these risks which range from warnings, statements, and clarification of the legal status of the currencies, to licensing, and supervision of their activities. It thus recommended a co-ordinated response by the legislative, regulatory, and supervisory frameworks to the various schemes discussed in its earlier report.

EU Directive on Money Laundering

The EU enacted the Fourth Anti-Money Laundering Directive on May 20, 2015—its mission is twofold,

1. to counter money laundering used for criminal purposes and
2. to combat the financing of terrorist activities. Member states were required to bring the requirements of the Directive into force at the end of December, 2016. The European Union Commission thereafter proposed, among other changes, amendments that virtual currency exchange platforms be incorporated into the Directive. It distinguished virtual currency exchange platforms, which are currency exchange offices that trade virtual currencies for real (fiat) currencies, from virtual currency custodian wallets in which providers hold virtual currency accounts on behalf of customers wherein payments can be made or received.

Virtual currency exchange platforms can be considered as "electronic" currency exchange offices that trade virtual currencies for real currencies (or so-called "fiat" currencies, such as the euro). On the other hand, virtual currency custodian wallet providers hold virtual currency accounts on behalf of their customers by providing virtual wallets from which payments in virtual currencies can be made or received. In the "virtual currency" world, they are the equivalent of a bank or payment institution offering a payment account. "Member states are to ensure that providers of exchange services between virtual currencies and fiat currencies, custodian wallet providers, currency exchange and check cashing offices, and trust or company service providers, are licensed or registered…."

Interestingly, a report of the European Commission appears to conclude that virtual currencies seem rarely to be used by criminal organizations, even with the characteristics of anonymity, due mainly to the lack of sophistication in their use. Other initiatives, especially after the ransomware attack on May 12, 2017, include the project TITANIUM (Tools for the Investigation of Transactions in Underground Markets) whereby researchers from four law enforcement agencies have gathered together to develop and implement tools to combat money laundering schemes and other criminal activities while safeguarding individual privacy and other fundamental rights. It aims to analyze legal and ethical requirements and put in place guidelines for storing and processing data, information, and knowledge required for criminal investigations.

The European Parliament in a resolution of May 26, 2016 on virtual currencies called for a proportionate regulatory approach that does not stifle the innovation or add to costs in setting forth the regulatory challenges created by the widespread use of virtual currencies and Distributed Ledger Technology (DLT). It calls for the creation of a

Dynamic Coalition on Blockchain Technologies at the Internet Governance Forum and requests the EU Commission to promote a shared and inclusive governance of DLT so as to avoid the problems that the EU had in regulating the Internet. It suggests that the major EU legislation, including EMIR (European Market Infrastructure Regulation), CSDR (Central Securities Depositories Regulation), SFD (Social Fund for Development), MiFID/ MiFIR (Markets in Financial Instruments Directive and Regulation), UCITs (Undertakings for Collective Investments Securities), and AIFMD (Alternative Investment Fund Managers Directive), could provide a regulatory framework for the governance of virtual currencies and DLTs in line with the activities carried out, irrespective of the underlying technology. Even as virtual currencies and DLT-based applications expand into new markets and extend their activities, more tailor-made legislation might be needed. With respect to the Anti-Money Laundering Directive that seeks to end the anonymity associated with such platforms, the European Parliament expects that any proposal in this regard will be targeted, justified by means of a full analysis of the risks associated with virtual currencies, and based on a thorough impact assessment.

European Securities and Markets Authority (ESMA)

"ESMA is an independent EU authority that contributes to safeguarding the stability of the EU's financial system by enhancing the protection of investors and promoting stable and orderly financial markets." It had undertaken

Cyptocurrency: The Next Level for Banking Reform

in 2015 a study of virtual currency entitled "Call for Evidence." It noted that virtual currency investment products consist of two different types, namely, collective investment schemes (CISs), and exchange platforms that offer different types of virtual currency derivatives. It identified 12 collective investment schemes, two regulated companies based in Europe that offer financial contracts for difference (CFDs) in bitcoins and litecoins; active platforms that offer CFDs or binary options for bitcoins or litecoins; and a number of exchange platforms that offer futures and other derivatives that are unregulated and their locations unknown.

ESMA's focus was on three issues:

1. investment products which have virtual currency as an underlying funding platform;
2. investment in virtual currency-based assets/securities, and the transfer of those assets/securities; and
3. other uses of the distributed ledger in relation to investment. The document, while raising the issues, asked for comments from investors and other participants. Specifically, ESMA noted that, with respect to the first issue, there are traditional investments that may have exposure to virtual currencies such as collective investment schemes or potentially non-registered derivatives such as options and contracts for difference. For the second issue, wherein traditional assets are exchanged for virtual currencies, and the third issue concerning other uses beyond virtual

currency that may be applicable to investors, ESMA asked for comments and responses to a series of questions illustrating its concern about the size and volume of DLT-based uses; the profile of investors; and other related issues.

A number of months thereafter, in June 2016, ESMA published the responses to the questions raised in April, 2015. It described the benefits and risks of DLT to securities markets within the EU. The benefits noted were:

- Clearing and settlement—increased speed, efficiency, elimination of multiple third parties, and possible one-step process for clearing and settlement;
- Record of ownership and safekeeping of assets—promote a unique database, remove contractual ambiguities through smart contracts, increased automation, directly issue digital securities, track ownership, and act as a trusted source;
- Reporting and oversight—facilitate the collection, consolidation, and sharing of data by use of a singular source;
- Counterparty risk—shorten the settlement cycle of the transaction and possibly remove the need for a central clearing facility because of the immediacy of the settlement;
- Efficient collateral management—reduce and/or remove counterparty risk for cash/spot transactions, and improve processing or reduce the need for collateral movements;

- Availability—permit transactions on a seven-day, 24-hour basis;
- Security and reliance—DLT is highly secure and resistant to cyberattacks;
- Costs—major benefit of significant reduction of costs by reducing the need for individual ledgers and business continuity plans; and
- Additional benefits—enhanced pre-trade information, ease of advertising, matching of buyers and sellers, and verification of ownership.

The key challenges, according to the 2016 discussion paper are:

- Technological issues—interoperability with existing systems and between different networks; the need to settle in central bank money and a recourse mechanism; position netting; and margin finance and short selling;
- Governance and privacy issues—the need for rules for the non-permissioned and the permissioned systems to validate transactions, minimum capital requirements, focus on the prevention of fraud or error, correction mechanisms and penalties, and possible intellectual property violations; privacy invasion may occur with Know Your Customer requirements, and storage of private data;
- Regulatory and legal issues—fitting the DLT into the existing regulatory framework, legality and

enforceability of the records kept on DLT, and supervision of the DLT network;
- Key risks—cyber risk, fraud, and money laundering; operational risks; market volatility, interconnectedness, and new pockets of risks; fair competition and orderly markets;
- Other risks—complexity of encryption techniques, and uncertainty that may arise with the migration of the DLT to a new environment.

European Union's New Blockchain Initiative

The EU Commission with support from the EU Parliament launched the E.U. Blockchain Observatory and Forum whose purpose is to "highlight key developments of the blockchain technology, promote European actors and reinforce engagement with multiple stakeholders involved in blockchain activities." Having recognized the technology as a "major breakthrough" that will inevitably transform how business models in the numerous areas of financial activity will be transformed, it noted that the benefits accruing will reduce costs while increasing trust, traceability, and security. The Observatory and Forum will monitor blockchain develop- ments, fund projects, cooperate with existing EU states' and businesses' initiatives, ensure transnational co-operation, consolidate expertise, and address challenges arising from the use of blockchain. It will partner with ConsenSys, which has established itself as a global leader in the blockchain ecosystem.

European Court of Justice Ruling

Does the exchange of fiat currencies for comparable value Bitcoin virtual currency and vice versa constitute a transaction subject to VAT (Value Added Tax) under Article 2 of the VAT Directive which imposes the tax on the supply of goods and/or services for a consideration within the territory of a member state of the EU? The European Court of Justice rendered a judgment on October 22, 2015 in response to a request for a preliminary ruling from the Supreme Administrative Court of Sweden. The Court noted that Article 14(1) of the Directive states that supply of goods shall mean the transfer of the right to dispose of tangible personal property as owner and Article 24(1) defines supply of services to mean any transaction that does not constitute a supply of goods.

The Court stated: "first, that the 'bitcoin' virtual currency with bidirectional flow, which shall be exchanged for traditional currencies in the context of exchange transactions, cannot be characterized as 'tangible property' within the meaning of Article 14(1) of the Directive, given that virtual currency has no purpose other than as a means of payment" comparable to traditional currencies inasmuch as it is money which is legal tender. Therefore, transactions which involves the exchange of the currencies do not constitute a "supply of goods" under Article 14(1). With respect to "supply of services" to be subject to VAT, there must be a direct link between the services supplied and the consideration received by the taxable person. The court further determined that the transaction is a supply of services within Article 24(1); however, the said exchange of currencies falls within the exemptions stated in Article 135(1)e of the Directive which exempts means of payment from VAT. Bitcoin is neither security conferring a property right nor a security of comparable nature, nor is it a current account or a deposit account that would have caused it to come within the ambit of the tax.

The implications of the decision is that services that provide exchange services for bitcoins are exempt from VAT as are other exchange services that exchange foreign currencies. One commentator suggested that the exemption may be open to examination due to the anonymity afforded Bitcoin users and persons participating in the exchange of Bitcoin.

Organisation For Economic Co-operation And Development (OECD)

The OECD does not appear to have taken an official or recommended position regarding virtual currencies but its views have been expressed in several authorized articles by OECD staff. In a Working Paper, the OECD Chief of Staff discussed the nature and valuing of cryptocurrencies, their risk events, market volatility, fraud, substitutes for Bitcoin, and the diverse regulatory measures being taken by governmental entities. He noted a paradox in that the more unlawful and wrongful the anonymous use of cryptocurrencies, the more likely government are incentivized to intervene. In concluding remarks, he observed that the generic policy issues to be addressed include a discussion of whether to ban cryptocurrencies; grant recognition of the technology; best practices of registration for consumer protection; a level playing field for all players in the financial field; governmental backing for the currencies; and remedies for non-compliance of regulations.

United Nations (UN)

he UN expressed its concern about virtual currency in the context of terrorism. In addition, to resolutions condemning terrorism, it has commenced a joint project between the UN Counter-Terrorism Committee Executive Directorate and the Swiss non-governmental organization ICT Peace entitled "Tech against Terrorism." The public-private endeavor is directed towards the prevention of the spread of terrorism through the use of the Internet. Included is the restraint of use of virtual currencies by the groups.

G20

It appears that virtual currency, in particular, Bitcoin, will be on the agenda for the next G20 to take place on November 30–December 1, 2018, in Buenos Aires, Argentina. The French Finance Minister, Bruno Le Maire, proposed that the regulation of Bitcoin, and presumably other virtual currencies, will be on the agenda indicating international concern about the effect the new technology and currencies have on national and international economies.

IOSCO

The International Organization of Securities Commissions (IOSCO) has commenced a study on the effects and consequences of the technologies underlying virtual currencies. In international meetings of the heads of national securities commissions, the benefits and risks of DLT and FinTech were discussed together with the challenges and regulatory efforts that national governments should consider and undertake. On January 18, 2018, the IOSCO Board issued a communication warning wherein it stated that there are clear risks posed by Initial Coin Offerings (ICOs), generally in exchange for Bitcoin or Ether and even for fiat currency. The concern is that the offerings are often outside the legal jurisdiction of the customers thereby raising investor apprehensions. It made reference to a meeting of the IOSCO Board on October 17–19, 2017 that discussed the growing usage of ICOs to raise capital as an area of concern.

Many other international organizations are beginning to discuss and offer possible suggestions and commentaries on the development of virtual currencies and their effect upon the relevant spheres of concern. It appears that only effective co-operation among the various governmental and non-governmental entities will diminish ICOs' and virtual currency exchanges' wrongdoings in the foreseeable future.

CHAPTER 7

Actions Taken By Uk Authorities And The Government

Since the Cryptoassets Taskforce's 2018 report, the government and UK authorities have taken a number of actions to address risks and support innovation arising from cryptoassets, including (but not limited to):

- communicating minimum policy expectations for stablecoins (BoE, HMT) - these have been communicated through speeches and international reports, including the Financial Stability Board (FSB) report on stablecoin regulation and the G7's global stablecoin working group report which stated that 'no global stablecoin project should begin operation until the legal, regulatory and oversight challenges and risks... are adequately addressed, through appropriate designs and by adhering to regulation that is clear and proportionate to the risks'. They have also been set out by the UK's Financial Policy Committee (see box 3A)
- clarifying the regulatory perimeter (FCA) – this sets out when tokens are likely to be a specified

investment under the Financial Services and Markets Act 2000 Regulated Activities Order 2001 (RAO), including those that are a financial instrument under the second Markets in Financial Instruments Directive (MIFID II), or e-money captured under The Ministry of Justice are also funding the Law Commission to carry out a project exploring the legal status of digital assets. Primarily, the Commission will consider the issue of possession, and will provide recommendations for reform to ensure the law is capable of accommodating digital assets. They aim to publish a consultation paper in the first half of 2021. "Reinventing the wheel (with more automation)", speech given by Andrew Bailey at the Brookings Institution virtual event, September 2020; "It's time to talk about money", speech given by Jon Cunliffe at the LSE, February 2020; "Seizing the opportunities from digital finance", speech given by Andy Haldane at TheCityUK, November 2020; "Payments after the COVID crisis" speech given by Christina Segal-Knowles at the LSE, June 2020. G7 Working group report on "Investigating the impact of global stablecoins", CPMI October 2019; and FSB report on "Regulation, Supervision and Oversight of Global Stablecoin Arrangements", October 2020. The Bank of England's August 2020 Financial Stability Report. The EMRs. Depending on the activity that will be undertaken, FCA authorisation or registration may be required

- implementing the Fifth Anti-Money Laundering Directive (HMT, FCA) – bringing custodian wallets providers and cryptoasset exchange providers into anti-money laundering (AML) and counter-terrorist financing (CTF) regulation
- consulting on bringing a broader subset of cryptoassets within the FCA financial promotions regime (HMT) – if taken forward, this would apply to the promotion of relevant activities in relation to qualifying cryptoassets
- banning the sale, marketing and distribution of derivatives and exchange traded notes that reference certain types of cryptoasset to retail consumers (FCA) – finalised rules come into force 6 January 2021, restricting the sale, marketing and distribution of contracts for difference, futures, options and exchanged-traded notes referencing unregulated, transferable cryptoassets
- consumer warnings about cryptoasset scams (FCA) – as well as providing guidance on how consumers can protect themselves, the FCA also publishes a warning list of known firms running scams. In May 2019, the FCA (in conjunction with Action Fraud) reported that the number of reports of cryptoasset and forex investments scams tripled in 2018/19 (note, however, rising cryptoasset usage during this period)
- support for DLT-based services through the FCA sandbox (FCA) - the FCA continues to support innovative financial services firms through its various initiatives. This includes its Direct Support

function, which provides regulatory feedback to firms, and its Regulatory Sandbox, which offers the opportunity to test products in a live environment with FCA oversight. Particularly in the Regulatory Sandbox, DLT has been, and continues to be, the most popular technology tested, with roughly a third of all firms using it to facilitate their products and services. DLT-based solutions tested in the Sandbox include payments, tokenisation of financial instruments, Digital ID and insurance intermediation. Building on these actions, the government judges that further regulatory adjustments are required to enable the government and authorities to meet objectives discussed below.

Policy Approach

Objectives, Principles And UK Initiatives

HM Treasury and other Cryptoassets Taskforce authorities have identified a series of objectives and principles to guide the government's approach to regulating cryptoassets. These are as follows:

Objectives;

Protecting financial stability and market integrity. This includes maintaining the appropriate regulatory standards, ensuring infrastructure is operationally resilient and that safeguards are in place to mitigate any risks to financial stability. Delivering robust consumer protections. This means ensuring consumers benefit from the same of level of protection they would when other regulated instruments are being used for the same purpose (e.g. payments). Promoting competition, innovation and supporting UK competitiveness. This means continuing to encourage and support UK fintech firms, and ensuring consumers and businesses have access to a variety of high-quality services and products.

Principles

Maintaining the current division of UK regulator responsibilities as far as possible and applying the principle of 'same risk, same regulatory outcome'. In doing so, the government will remain technology agnostic, while also considering whether the technology used gives rise to additional risks or equally where its use may mitigate risks. This supports the government's desire to ensure a level playing field and reduce opportunities for arbitrage. In practice, it means drawing on existing regulations and requirements insofar as they are applicable, with adjustments or additional requirements where needed to address specific characteristics or risks. The government will also seek to maintain as far as possible the current delineation of UK regulator responsibilities with respect to regulation of activities, including across the Bank of England, FCA and Payments System Regulator (PSR).

Ensuring the approach is proportionate, focussed on where risks and opportunities are most urgent or acute. UK authorities should avoid applying disproportionate or overly burdensome regulation to entities particularly where end users are aware of risks or the activities do not give rise to financial stability risks. The government is therefore proposing to take an incremental, phased approach to regulatory adjustments.

Ensuring the approach is agile, able to reflect international discussions and aligned to the future government approach to financial services and payments regulation. Given the cross-border nature of cryptoassets, the UK is committed to working with other jurisdictions and through the international standard-setting bodies to support harmonization of treatment as far as is feasible. In doing so, the approach should allow for changes to reflect international discussions, including on equivalence where relevant.

The government will also seek to ensure that the regulatory approach to cryptoassets coheres with the outcomes of the Payments Landscape Review and Future Regulatory Framework (FRF) Review, which are considering how the regulatory framework for financial services and payments need to adapt to be fit for the future. The government recognises that there may be cases in which there is tension between different principles, and they will need to be prioritised or balanced against each other.

Overarching Approach And Related UK Initiatives

The government is proposing an approach to cryptoasset regulation under which firm requirements are designed and implemented by the independent regulators. This would involve the independent regulators using agile powers to issue rules or codes of practice, within a framework of objectives and broader considerations set by HMT and Parliament.

This has two key benefits: first, cryptoasset models continue to develop and evolve rapidly, and this approach allows the regime to respond to developments. The government wants to ensure the regime can keep pace and adapt as new models or innovations emerge. Second, international work is in progress to develop appropriate global regulatory standards and review existing guidance. For example, international work is underway to assess the application of Principles for Financial Market Infrastructures (PFMIs) to stablecoins. The PFMIs are standards issued by the Bank of International Settlements' (BIS) Committee on Payments and Market Infrastructures (CPMI) and the International Organization of Securities Commissions (IOSCO). The government wants to ensure it has the flexibility to update regulation to take account of the outcomes of this work.

In practice, this means that HMT will not seek to specify detailed firm requirements through legislation (and therefore has not done so in this consultation). Instead, the government aims to define the scope of the regulatory perimeter and the objectives and principles applicable under that new regime. Reflecting this, the government is seeking views on those areas only in this consultation. The UK's financial services regulators will consult on detailed firm requirements should the government adopt this approach. This could be subject to enhanced scrutiny requirements to ensure the regulators are appropriately accountable when setting firm requirements.

In July 2020 the government published a Call for Evidence to support a review of the UK payments landscape. The Payments Landscape Review (PLR) is taking a holistic stocktake of the payments landscape and is considering changes needed to keep pace with new innovations. The government will set out more detail in response to the PLR call for evidence shortly. Changes under consideration through this consultation on cryptoassets are intended to support and align with the government's broader approach to payments through the PLR.

HM Treasury and the Bank of England are continuing analytical work to evaluate the possible opportunities and risks associated with a UK central bank digital currency (CBDC), and of CBDC initiatives being undertaken elsewhere. The government welcomed the Bank of England's discussion paper in March 2020, as well as its important work with overseas central banks to share valuable experience related to CBDCs. HM Treasury and the Bank of England are now working together to consider next steps. The UK is taking a leading role in exploring this topic to understand the wide-ranging opportunities and challenges it could bring.

A number of other jurisdictions are considering or have implemented legislative changes to bring cryptoassets and stablecoins into regulation. Approaches across different jurisdictions vary in terms of scope and substance. HMT and UK authorities are closely monitoring developments in this space, including the European Commission's Market in Cryptoassets (MiCA) proposed regulation, which introduces a bespoke regulatory regime and applies it to a wide set of issuers and service providers. Other international approaches include outright bans or amendments to existing legislation (e.g. securities legislation) to bring tokens, and the service providers around them (e.g. exchanges, wallets), into scope.

Expanding The Regulatory Perimeter

The First Phase Of Legislative Changes

Inline with the government's aim to ensure the approach to regulating cryptoassets is proportionate, and to focus on where risks and opportunities are most acute, the government has considered how best to sequence any changes. This chapter sets out the government's proposal and rationale.

At present, many cryptoassets and unregulated exchange tokens remain highly volatile and cannot be reliably used as a means of payment or store of value. The FCA's latest consumer research suggests that the dominant retail use case for cryptoassets is speculative investment: at present 47% of UK cryptoasset consumers said they bought cryptocurrencies 'as a gamble that could make or lose money' and 89% understood that they are not subject to regulatory protections.1 This suggests that at present consumer awareness of risks associated with the purchase of cryptoassets is relatively high.

The size of the UK cryptoassets market is still relatively small, but rapidly growing. The government recognises that many firms engaging in cryptoasset activities are SMEs and start-ups. The government wants to ensure that any approach enables responsible innovation to occur, particularly where risks are well-communicated and understood. The government also wants to ensure that their use does not threaten stability and safeguards are in place to avoid their use in illicit activities.

The government is, therefore, considering an approach in which the use of currently unregulated tokens and associated activities primarily used for speculative investment purposes, such as Bitcoin, could initially remain outside the perimeter for conduct and prudential purposes. At the same time, these would be subject to more stringent regulation in relation to consumer communications via the financial promotions regime (if adopted) and AML/CTF regulation. Utility tokens - those used to access a service - would also remain outside the authorisation perimeter.

At the same time, the use of stablecoins is rising; in June 2020, it was reported that there was more value in transactions using stablecoins than in Bitcoin for the first time.2 Stablecoins aim to hold their value, typically against a reference asset, meaning they can be more reliably used as a means of exchange or store of value, though they may also be used to facilitate investment or trading activities. This is supported by FCA research which found that stablecoins are the most likely to be used as a means of payment; 27% of stablecoin owners have used them to purchase goods and services.

Cyptocurrency: The Next Level for Banking Reform

The government believes that if appropriate standards and regulation can be met, certain stablecoins would have the potential to play an important role in retail and cross-border payments (including settlement). This means they would have the potential to deliver benefits of DLT such as speed, efficiency and resilience. Some initiatives may have the potential to support financial inclusion and economic growth both domestically and on a cross-border basis. The Covid-19 pandemic has accelerated the use of digital forms of payments, which could increase the uptake of stablecoins for transactions and remittances in the future.

The government believes that appropriately designed regulation can promote innovation and industry growth, enabling responsible industry actors to innovate and supporting consumer confidence. However, in the absence of appropriate regulation and oversight, stablecoins could pose a range of risks. These include:

- risks to financial stability and market integrity: were stablecoins are used widely as a means of payment, they may pose risks to financial stability and the real economy. The ability of individuals and businesses to make and receive payments safely and smoothly with confidence is critical to financial stability. Disruption or outage within the stablecoin chain could lead to consumers being unable to access their money and make payments. Stablecoins could also be used to store value and, by design or use, constitute money-like instruments. Uncertainty about, or large fluctuations in, the value of the asset could give rise to similar risks to financial stability associated with the operational or financial failure of traditional payments systems. Reflecting this risk, in modern economies, private assets that function as money-like instruments are subject to high levels of protections that ensure that consumers can use them with confidence and exchange them seamlessly with other forms of privately issued money in widespread use. Most stablecoin arrangements seek to provide stability via some form of referenced asset such as a commodity or fiat currency. Depending on the nature of the reference assets and how the reserve is held and managed, the ability to provide stability and redeemability could come with additional risks.

- risks to consumers: these include, in the first instance, the risk that consumers could lose money through volatility of the value of the stablecoin or firm failure. Risks are likely to be increased where consumer protections are limited for example, due to an absence, uncertainty or failure of a claim for redemption. Consumers may also not understand the product or service they are being offered and consumer data could be lost or misused. Consumer harm may also derive from models being too complex, or excessive prices, fees and charges. In addition, there are risks of fraud, financial crime, cyber-attacks or maladministration, with potential for consumer harm if services are vulnerable to operational and

security risks leading to inaccessibility or inefficiencies.
- risks to the competition: some initiatives could increase competition by challenging the market dominance of incumbent financial institutions. However, due to their ability to scale, and plug into existing online services, some stablecoin arrangements could quickly achieve market dominance, providing a similar service to a regulated service despite not yet not having the same regulatory and compliance obligations. This would create an unlevel playing field.

The FSB's report 'Addressing the regulatory, supervisory and oversight challenges raised by "global stablecoin" arrangements' sets out ten recommendations. This includes the recommendation that authorities have the necessary tools and powers in place to comprehensively regulate stablecoin arrangements. The FPC has also communicated two regulatory expectations for systemic stablecoins and its views on the need to adjust the UK regulatory framework to support appropriate regulation of these arrangements (see box below). It is within this context, and in light of the risks and opportunities discussed above, that the government judges that there is a strong case for bringing stablecoins into the regulatory perimeter.

The government therefore proposes to first introduce a regulatory regime for stable tokens used as a means of payment. This would cover firms issuing stable tokens and firms providing services in relation to them, either directly or indirectly to consumers.

To a longer timetable, the government will consider the case for bringing a broader set of cryptoasset market actors or tokens into an authorisation regime. UK authorities and the government will continue to actively monitor the market, focusing on how services and products are used and the risks they may pose to consumers. The government will also seek to ensure its approach provides flexibility to enable new activities to be brought into the perimeter in the future in an agile way, subject to appropriate consultation and scrutiny. Should new risks emerge or if presented with evidence of significant consumer harm, the government will take further action.

Scope Of Regulation And Requirements

The activities around tokens used for payments may be similar to existing payment services such as the execution of payment transactions. However, the government also recognizes that these tokens may also be used for other purposes than payments. For instance, today many are used as temporary stores of stable value for investors moving funds between cryptoassets without transitioning into fiat money.

Rules and requirements under the proposed regime would take relevant aspects of the UK's current approach to e-money and payments regulation, drawing on existing rules as far as possible. The main pieces of UK legislation governing payments regulation are the Electronic Money

Cyptocurrency: The Next Level for Banking Reform

Regulations 2011 and Payments Services Regulations 2017. These provide powers to the FCA and PSR to regulate and supervise firms engaged in relevant payment activities.

In addition, the Banking Act 2009 and Financial Services (Banking Reform) Act 2013 provide the Bank of England with power and responsibility for regulation of systemically important payment systems and service providers to those payment systems, and the Payments Systems Regulator (PSR) with power and responsibility for regulation of payment systems, respectively. HM Treasury anticipates both organizations would need powers over any system widely used for payments, and that their approaches will follow their respective remits.

In addition, the approach will draw on broader elements of financial services regulation, for instance in relation to the protection of client assets, as well as specific requirements for stablecoins, such as safeguarding of the stablecoin and the means of accessing the stablecoin wallet with the associated private key.

The government's priority is to ensure that tokens which could reliably be used for retail or wholesale transactions are subject to appropriate regulation. The government considers that at present tokens that maintain a stable value based on their reference assets (e.g. fiat currency) are most likely to maintain a stable value and fulfill this function. Depending on legal structure and specific backing arrangements these tokens may have similar characteristics to e-money, which is subject to comprehensive requirements in UK financial services regulation.

The government proposes to seek therefore to ensure that tokens which could be reliably used for retail or wholesale transactions are subject to minimum requirements and protections as part of a UK authorisation regime. The government is considering whether those tokens deemed out of scope from these minimum requirements should be subject to restrictions with respect to marketing or promotion for use in retail or wholesale payments activity.

Some tokens may not neatly fall within this category. For example, so-called 'algorithmic stablecoins' seek to maintain a stable value through the use of algorithms to control supply, without any backing by a reference asset. The government judges that these tokens more closely resemble unbacked exchange tokens and may pose similar risks in relation to their ability to maintain stability of value, so may not be suitable for retail or wholesale transactions. For this reason, algorithmic stablecoins are outside the scope of the proposals for stable tokens set out in the remainder of this chapter. The government invites views on this assessment and will consider this position based on responses received.

Actors, Activities And Requirements

As set out a range of market actors can be involved in facilitating the use and issuance of stable tokens. Key participants or entities are likely to include:

- issuers or systems operators, responsible for managing the rulebook of a system, the infrastructure, burning and minting coins (among others).
- cryptoassets exchanges, enabling consumers to exchange tokens for fiat money or other tokens.
- wallets, which may provide custody of tokens and/or manage private keys. Along with exchanges, these are often the main consumer interface.

The government's view is that regulation would apply to the firms undertaking the following functions or activities, either in terms of establishing the rules governing the activities or operating the infrastructure in relation to these activities.

- issuing, creating or destroying asset-linked tokens

The activity of the token issuer in minting and burning tokens

- issuing, creating or destroying single fiat-linked tokens

The activity of the token issuer in minting and burning tokens

- value stabilisation and reserve management

The activity of managing the reserve assets that are backing the value of a stable token and providing custody/trust services for those assets to ensure stabilization of the stable token

- validation of transactions

The activity of authorising or verifying the validity of transactions and records

- access

The activity of providing services or support to facilitate access of participants to the network or underlying infrastructure

- transmission of funds

The activity of ensuring the correct and final settlement of transactions while limiting counterparty and default risk

- providing custody and administration of a stable token for a third party

The activity of managing tokens on behalf of owners, including the storage of private keys

- executing transactions in stable tokens

The activity of conducting transactions on behalf of another

- exchanging tokens for fiat money and vice versa

The Activity Of Purchasing/Exchanging A Stable Token With Fiat Money.

These are partly aligned with the stablecoin activities identified by the FSB, adding further granularity and aligning activities with those used under UK law. The government considers that many of these activities bear similarity to currently regulated payment or e-money activities (for example executing payment transactions). However, others do not currently form part of traditional payment chains and may not be captured by analogous rules under existing payments regulation but could still pose risks to consumers and stability. This includes providing custody and administration of the token, the main aspect of which is the storing and protection of the private key.

Considering the objective to manage the risks of tokens being used as a means of payment whilst supporting innovation and competition, and reflecting the activities outlined above, the government judges that the following high-level requirements would be necessary.

- authorisation requirements with associated threshold conditions The requirement to be authorized prior to operating
- prudential requirements, including capital and liquidity requirements, accounting and audit requirements

Requirements relating to effective management of capital and liquidity, to protect consumers and financial stability

- Requirements for the maintenance and management of a reserve of assets obligation to have reserve assets underlying the token's value and requirements to ensure the quality and safekeeping on those assets
- orderly failure and insolvency requirements

Requirements to ensure issuers and service providers are prepared for modified resolution or administration, or insolvency

- safeguarding the token

Requirements principally on wallets and exchanges to ensure those entities are appropriately protecting users' tokens and the privacy and security of keys to those tokens

- systems, controls, risk management and governance

Requirements relating to effective overall management of an issuer or service provider

- notification and reporting

Requirements relating to firms' disclosures to regulators and customers

- record keeping

Requirements relating to firms' internal record keeping processes

- conduct requirements

Requirements relating to the rights that firms must provide toward customers

- financial crime requirements

Requirements relating to proper implementation of anti-money laundering and counter-terrorist financing rules, among others

- outsourcing requirements

Requirements relating to safe outsourcing of key services to ensure continuous and adequate functioning

- operational resilience, service reliability and continuity requirements Requirements to ensure

> business continuity in the event of physical, electronic, governance or other business failures

- security requirements (including cyber and cloud)

Requirements relating to safeguards against cyber security risks related to the technology and infrastructure used.

UK authorities are considering requirements in relation to the reserves held for stable tokens (and related innovations), particularly where they operate at systemic scale. This includes, for example, how to ensure that regulation and requirements are appropriate for the risks taken in the reserve assets where stable tokens are intended for widespread use in retail or wholesale transactions. This also involves exploring what regulation might be necessary to enable issuers of systemic stable tokens to hold reserve assets in central bank accounts, commercial bank deposits or high-quality liquid assets to meet the FPC's expectations. UK authorities will consult in due course on the impact of these options and how these options would be applied across systemic and non-systemic firms.

As set out, a subsection of tokens already falls within the existing e-money regime (e.g. where, among other criteria within the EMRs, they provide users with a claim on the issuer and funds are redeemable at any time at par value). The government's view is that where such tokens are subject to existing regulation, these requirements should continue to apply.

In practice, this means that some tokens, where they meet the criteria for e-money, will be subject to e-money regulation and must be authorised by the FCA as such. To avoid scope for arbitrage and avoid confusion for consumers, the government is also considering whether stable tokens that are linked to a single fiat currency should meet the requirements applicable to e-money. Any stable tokens treated as e-money, which has significant potential to become systemic (see criteria below), would likely require enhanced regulation to meet the FPC's stablecoin expectations. The government is considering how to ensure that this can be applied in a manner that provides an appropriate and clear framework to support innovation.

In line with other regulation, the proposed authorization regime would also allow for exclusions where, although an activity may fall within scope, the firm conducting that activity would not need to be authorised. This may occur where the activity does not give rise to the same risks. For instance, services based on stable tokens used within a limited network of service providers (closed loop) or for acquiring a very limited range of goods or services (e.g. store payment cards) could be excluded. A lighter regime is being considered for smaller firms below a certain turnover, also akin to current payments regulation.

Stable Token Payment Systems

The Payment Systems Regulator (PSR) is an economic regulator that regulates payment systems designated to it by HM Treasury to achieve objectives in relation to protecting interests of users, promoting competition and innovation. A payment system is defined within the

Financial Services (Banking Reform) Act 2013 (the FSBRA 2013), as a system that enables persons to make transfers of funds.

The government judges that stable token arrangements which play a similar function to existing payments systems may be appropriate candidates for regulation by the PSR and is considering whether legislative adjustments are required to clarify this. Designation of a system for regulation by the PSR gives the PSR powers to place requirements or take action on the participants in that system. Participants are defined as system operators, infrastructure providers or payment service providers in relation to that system.

Systemic Stable Token Payment Systems

Where stable token arrangements reach systemic scale, the government judges that existing systemic payments regulation which applies to the system and service providers in relation to the system should also apply. In the UK this is enforced by the Bank of England under powers contained within part 5 of the Banking Act 2009 (the BA 2009), following a recognition decision made by HM Treasury.

The government judges that a systemic stable token arrangement could be assessed for Bank of England regulation in the same way that current payment systems and service providers are (i.e. when potential disruption could lead to financial stability risks). Criteria under the BA 2009 for systemic payment systems includes consideration of their ability to disrupt the UK financial system and businesses based on current or likely volume and value of transactions, nature of transactions and links to other systems, as well as substitutability and use by the Bank of England in its role as monetary authority.

The government's proposal is that these criteria should also extend to stable tokens arrangements that perform a retail or wholesale payment system function. This would mean that a stable token with significant potential to be systemic at launch would need to be captured from launch by such regulation. Appropriate triggers for treatment in this manner would include likely user base, likely transaction volumes and likely avenues for the acquisition of customers (e.g. through widely used platform).

Issuers or system operators that reach systemic status, as well as critical service providers as defined under the BA 2009, would be subject to regulation by the Bank of England and enhanced requirements grounded in the PFMIs against which they would be required to produce an annual compliance self-assessment. In line with powers to issue codes of practice and rules within current payments system and service provider legislation, the Bank of England would be given powers to specify enhanced requirements.

The Bank of England will be required to consult on the proposed supervisory approach and enhanced requirements to be applied to systemic stable token systems and service providers. This will build on the PFMI and be grounded in the FPC's expectations set out in Box 3A. To meet the FPC's expectations, a systemic stable token arrangement would need to provide holders with a robust legal claim, ensure stability of value and enable users to redeem tokens at par into fiat. For asset-linked tokens, this would imply significant capital and prudential requirements and other protections.

Stable tokens bring together payment system activity, the issuance of a new, money-like asset and the storage of reserve assets. Current regulation for systemic payment systems applies to the recognized payment system operator as well as designated critical service providers in relation to a recognised system – for example information technology services or infrastructure providers.

The government's view is that it is possible other service providers or core entities that form part of a stable token chain could pose systemic risks (e.g. wallets). It is therefore considering, for stable token arrangements, whether Bank of England systemic regulation grounded in the PFMIs and FPC expectations should also apply to service providers or entities within a chain where these pose systemic risks. For example, the government judges that certain wallets used to safeguard or exchange customer funds could pose systemic risks if used at scale because of the potential wider impact of any disruption (e.g. of consumers' ability to withdraw funds) and their potential role in fulfilling critical functions in the chain.

In applying, this assessment approach, the bar for systemic importance and Bank regulation would remain high, as it is for payment systems and service providers to those systems at present. Within a competitive and diverse landscape, it is not clear that many service providers will attain systemic importance to require such enhanced regulation. However, the dynamic and nascent nature of the market requires ensuring the adequate powers are in place, subject to the recognition process, should they be needed now or in the future.

Location Requirements

For firms carrying on payment services, the requirement to be authorized or regulated by the FCA applies in relation to activities that are carried on by way of regular occupation of business activity in the UK. Whereas, powers in relation to recognised payment systems under BA2009 apply on an extra- territorial basis. Due to the digital, decentralised and cross-border nature of stable tokens, the government and UK authorities are considering whether firms actively marketing to UK consumers should be required to have a UK establishment and be authorized in the UK. Options include: requiring UK presence and UK authorization for stable token issuers, system operators and service providers when marketed in the UK; defining the activity conducted in the UK and determining whether UK authorization is required as a result; or no location requirements.

The government and UK authorities are also considering the case for location requirements for systemic stable token arrangements under BA2009.

Authorizations Regime For Token Issuers And Service Providers

As set out, the government's proposal is the FCA would authorise and supervise firms both stable token issuers and relevant service providers where they carry on certain regulated activities, an indicative list of which is set out below. The table also indicates where firms undertaking certain activities may be subject to BoE and/or PSR regulation.

Call for evidence on investment and wholesale uses

Security Tokens

The use of tokens to facilitate securities transactions is an important development for the financial sector. The representation of traditional securities, such as equities or debt, on a distributed ledger (the 'tokenisation' of assets) could have substantial implications for the way assets are traded or capital is raised. Security tokens that exist and are traded exclusively on the distributed ledger (and are therefore 'digitally native') are also playing an increasing role across markets. Existing examples of security tokens include Santander's 'blockchain bond' issued on the Ethereum blockchain.

Security tokens can sometimes be distributed through initial coin offerings (ICOs) which enable businesses to raise capital for their projects, by issuing digital tokens in exchange for fiat currencies or other cryptoassets, e.g. Bitcoin or Ether. ICOs are viewed as high risk, but where used safely could be used as an alternative funding tool for new and innovative business models, products and services, while the use of DLT could make the capital raising process more streamlined, faster and cheaper and facilitate global interconnectedness of markets.

As part of the FCA's Regulatory Sandbox programme, firms have compliantly issued equities, bonds and structured products on the Ethereum blockchain. These small-scale tests showed the potential of DLT-based systems to deliver securities issuances more efficiently; faster and cheaper when compared to traditional issuances, while increasing the transparency of ownership.

However, the government recognises that existing regimes were not originally intended to support the use of cryptoassets or DLT-based innovations. It would therefore like to understand what changes may be necessary to remove obstacles and enable the use of these new technologies.

For instance, there is no legal definition of a security token or tokenised security in the UK. The FCA has described them as providing rights and obligations akin to specified investments, like a share or a debt instrument or units in a collective investment scheme this would mean that in the UK such tokens meet the relevant definitions in the RAO. If a token is negotiable on the capital markets (for example because it can be transferred from one person to another who then acquires legal title of the token), then it might be considered a transferable security under this framework.

The government would like to understand whether further legal clarification is required in the future, or whether the application of existing rules under this regime leads to specific obstacles, costs or barriers for participants.

DLT-Based Financial Market Infrastructures

Distributed ledger technology (DLT) could potentially transform financial markets and the infrastructures that underpin them. The representation of assets on distributed ledgers could in theory deliver benefits such as more efficiency, improved liquidity, enhanced transparency and greater security. It may fundamentally alter the structure of the current market ecosystem, which is currently characterized by several different financial market infrastructures (FMIs) and intermediaries performing separate functions, from trade management processes, through to clearing and settlement, and on to post settlement activities such as custody and asset servicing.

However, the adoption of DLT across financial markets may face several challenges and hurdles. The ability to overcome these challenges, and the way in which they are overcome, could be important in determining whether the benefits of DLT will be realised. This section of the consultation therefore aims to gather views about the potential of DLT to transform financial markets, what steps would need to be taken to fully realise this potential, and what barriers stand in the way of adoption.

In the first instance, the government wants to understand more about what the benefits of DLT may be to financial markets. In particular, the government would like to understand what the specific advantages are to adopting DLT in different parts of market value chains including whether DLT could lead to more efficient trading, clearing or settlement, and if so what the nature of the efficiencies realised would be (for example reduced settlement times or lower costs). The government would also appreciate views on where the benefits of DLT may go beyond efficiency and cost-and the term 'FMI' includes multilateral systems across all parts of the market value chain, including at the trading level as well as clearing and settlement, effectiveness, particularly to security and transparency, and where it may spur innovation by changing the way markets operate.

Conversely, the government also invites industry views on the possible drawbacks of DLT if adopted across financial markets. For example, the creation of new intermediaries could create greater fragmentation within the existing FMI ecosystem, particularly if new DLT FMIs are not interoperable with each other or existing FMIs. This could potentially result in more complexity, less efficiency, and a reduction in the ability of supervisors to ensure regulatory compliance. It is possible that DLT FMIs make markets less, rather than more, transparent to market participants, depending on how they are specified.

Views would also be welcome regarding areas where the benefits of DLT for FMIs may be overstated- for example, it may be that incremental reform of existing market practices, or the further development of existing technology, will improve the performance of existing FMIs, rather than the adoption of DLT. Consideration should also be given to whether the optimal route is for increased take-up of DLT by existing FMIs, rather than DLT solely being utilised by new entrants.

The government is also seeking feedback regarding what regulatory or legal barriers exist that currently limit the adoption of DLT in UK financial markets. In particular, the government would like views as to whether existing UK legislation is adequate for capturing DLT-based FMIs, and whether the current legislation or regulation makes creating and operating a DLT excessively burdensome. It would be useful to hear feedback regarding how DLT will interact with existing rules around transfer of title, settlement finality, financial collateral, shareholder rights, and corporate actions, and whether there is a need to optimize legislation across these areas to better accommodate DLT FMIs while safeguarding stability and security.

More broadly, industry views around the wider incentives and challenges in adopting DLT across financial markets and the potential solutions to these, would be valuable. Feedback could cover technical challenges, but also issues around industry incentives to implement DLT in a way that benefits UK markets collectively.

It is possible that a degree of coordination/collective action by market participants is required to achieve the benefits of DLT FMIs, while ensuring that innovation is not stifled. An example of where this may be needed is to ensure DLT FMIs are interoperable either with each other or with existing FMIs, so as to avoid or mitigate the new layers of intermediation and fragmentation that may otherwise be created, as noted above. The outcome in this instance could be the development of a basic set of standards that ensure the interoperability of DLT FMIs. Feedback to this consultation could consider other areas where it may be useful for the market to develop standards (such as cybersecurity, transparency, confidentiality and governance arrangements), as well as other approaches for overcoming barriers to adoption across markets.

The government is also seeking views over where government or regulator intervention may be useful. For instance, the government would welcome industry feedback regarding initiatives that could be taken forward for trialing or testing DLT FMIs. This could entail making use of existing schemes, such as the FCA Sandbox, or developing new propositions, such as an initiative for testing the operation of a DLT FMI in the market. The government would have to carefully consider the impact of any proposals given the systemic importance of FMIs to the financial system and would need to work closely with the Bank of England given their role in regulating and supervising FMIs.

As noted above, market coordination may be required to deliver the benefits of DLT in the FMI space. The government would therefore appreciate views on whether regulators or government has a role to play in convening market participants. Alternatively, respondents may feel that any initiatives should be best left to the market. Given FMIs are important for international markets, specific UK rules could create conflicts with rules in other jurisdictions, meaning it may be preferable to take forward rules at global level first before adoption in the UK.

CHAPTER 8

A Central Bank Issuing Digital Currency

People trust that the existing fiat currency issued by a centralised authority has stable value because of stable monetary policies, because the currency can be used to pay taxes to government, and because it is impossible for anyone to spend the same piece of currency more than once.

According to Cukierman (2019), in order to preserve the effectiveness of monetary policy in a world increasingly flooded by private digital currencies, central banks will eventually have to issue their own digital currencies. Although a non-negligible number of central banks (CBs) are actively considering the pros and cons of a central bank digital currency (CBDC) there is yet no CB that has issued such a currency on a full scale.

Thus, the feasibility and desirability of central banks issuing their own fiat versions of digital currencies has been the focus of a growing debate in recent years. Numerous central banks around the world are researching the topic, including the Bank of Canada (2017), the European Central Bank (Mersch, 2017), the People's Bank of China (Qian, 2017), the Sveriges

Riksbank (2017) and the Bank of England (2017). For instance, Gupta et. al. (2017) conclude their case in favour of issuing a digital currency by the Fed. They claim that a "Fedcoin" would have many advantages because it would mitigate the risk of attacks and it would be based on the assumptions that the central bank is honest, the protocol's cryptography is secure, and that each transaction is processed by a set of nodes with an honest majority.

Meaning et al. (2018) provide a definition for CBDC as "any electronic, fiat liability of a central bank that can be used to settle payments, or as a store of value." As such, CBDC can be viewed as electronic narrow money and in some senses already exists in the form of central bank reserves. It is also confusing to think about whether CBDC is a cryptocurrency or not. Cryptocurrencies, in principle, make use of DLT technology. The central bank does not necessarily need to use the same technology because it has its own. This kind of CBDC would not be a cryptocurrency, but would remain a central bank digital currency. Currently, whether central banks should issue CBDCs is a question open to debate. On the one hand, it would be efficient because it could make use of the new technology. However, it could be the case that CBDCs interfered with the private banking system, especially if the public can hold deposits within the central bank.

Another concern is that if these currencies are not issued by the central bank, at some point these currencies, will become the alternative of legal tender. But abstaining from providing a public alternative to privately produced digital currencies carries the risk that sooner or later those currencies will largely replace legal tender. Recognizing this risk, most central banks currently research the various options for eventually adopting some form of CBDC. Some like the Dutch central bank and the central bank of Uruguay have started to limitedly use this currency. The Federal Reserve Bank is also thinking about issuing a "Fedcoin."

Based on traditional modelling, Barrdear and Kumhof (2016) assess the potential impact CBDC may have on the macroeconomy. They build a dynamic stochastic general equilibrium model and find that the introduction of a CBDC via purchases of government bonds could increase real GDP by as much as 3%. Bordo and Levin (2017) also analyse the design of CBDC and its implication. They conclude that CBDC could act as a highly effective form of money and promote true price stability, as the real value of CBDC could be easily held stable over time.

Public Sector Mandates For CBDC And Stablecoin Governance

Central banks, finance ministries and regulatory or oversight bodies have multiple mandates that relate to stablecoins and CBDC, both directly and indirectly. Generally, central banks are tasked to maintain certain levels of employment and price stability using monetary policy. Their purview often extends to areas related to the oversight and management of monetary, financial and payment systems. In the words of the European Central Bank (ECB): "By pursuing its tasks of maintaining monetary and financial stability and the smooth operation of payment systems, [the ECB] ensures that money and payments serve European society. We have always been committed to maintaining confidence in our currency, which has meant adapting the form of money and payment services we provide to the changing ways in which people spend, save and invest."

In a speech in August 2020, US Federal Reserve Governor Lael Brainard expanded on this concept: "The introduction of Bitcoin and the subsequent emergence of stablecoins with potentially global reach, such as Facebook's Libra [now Diem], have raised fundamental questions about legal and regulatory safeguards, financial stability, and the role of currency in society. This prospect has intensified calls for CBDCs to maintain the sovereign currency as the anchor of the nation's payment systems."

Regulatory and oversight bodies, meanwhile, have mandates that apply more directly to private stablecoin initiatives. For example, the US Securities and Exchange Commission (SEC) is charged with protecting investors, maintaining fair, orderly and efficient markets, and facilitating market integrity and capital formation. Looking at Europe, the

European Securities and Markets Authority (ESMA) is responsible for "enhancing the protection of investors and promoting stable and orderly financial markets."

Mandates For Public Sector Financial Institutions

Consumer protection

Consumer protection in the financial space generally falls to a country's financial regulator. For example, in Australia, the Australian Securities and Investments Commission (ASIC) regulates "corporate, markets, financial services and consumer credit…It also licenses and regulates individuals and businesses that engage in consumer credit activities.

In addition, ASIC's market regulation role makes it responsible for supervising financial market operators and participants, including real-time trading on Australia's domestic licensed markets."

Financial stability

Financial stability is a goal shared across many government bodies. Those institutions that touch the financial sector often have a mandate to maintain financial stability. For example, the Financial Stability Oversight Council (FSOC) is a collaborative body chaired by the US Treasury Secretary that creates "collective accountability for identifying risks and responding to emerging threats to financial stability." It is made up of representatives from the Federal Reserve, Office of the Comptroller of the Currency, Consumer Financial Protection Bureau, Securities, and Exchange Commission, Federal Deposit Insurance Corporation, Commodity Futures Trading Commission, Federal

Housing Finance Agency, and National Credit Union Administration.

Monetary stability

Central banks commonly adhere to core mandates centred on price stability, often in tandem with mandates related to high employment. As expressed by the Swiss National Bank (SNB), "Article 99 of the Federal Constitution entrusts the SNB, as an independent central bank, with the conduct of monetary policy in the interests of the country as a whole. The mandate is explained in detail in the National Bank Act (art. 5 para. 1), which requires the SNB to ensure price stability and, in so doing, to take due account of economic developments."

Competitive markets

Most countries have opted to create governmental bodies solely responsible for maintaining competition. For example, Canada has its Competition Bureau, "an independent law enforcement agency, [which] ensures that Canadian businesses and consumers prosper in a competitive and innovative marketplace." Finland has its competition and consumer protection authority in one body: the Finnish Competition and Consumer Authority. The US relies on the Federal Trade Commission and the US Department of Justice's Antitrust Division.

Market integrity

Market integrity is a broad mandate that falls under the remit of numerous regulators. In the context of regulation, it is generally understood to mean the elimination of market abuse activities, creation of non-discriminatory access to the market, transparent and accurate information about the prices of securities and accurate information about issuers of securities.

Prevention of illicit activity

Countries regulate their financial and professional sectors for anti-money laundering and combating the financing of terrorism (AML/CFT) based on the Financial Action Task Force (FATF) Recommendations. These include requirements for financial institutions to apply risk-based preventive measures against money laundering and terrorist financing (e.g. customer due diligence/KYC, sanctions screening and reporting suspicious transactions to authorities). These actions need to be supported by supervising compliance with these obligations and building law enforcement capacity to investigate suspected illicit activity. The FATF Recommendations were amended in 2019 to explicitly require regulation of digital currencies and those providing digital currency services; the guidance was updated in October 2021, specifying how FATF standards apply to stablecoins and definitions for virtual assets, among other issues.

Bitcoin Questions

With the economic basics of the operation of Bitcoin explained, and the main potential use cases of Bitcoin discussed, a few of the most salient questions surrounding Bitcoin's operation are examined here.

Is Bitcoin Mining A Waste?

Anyone who joins the Bitcoin network generates a public address and a private key. These are analogous to an email address and its password: people can send your bitcoins to your public address while you use your private key to send bitcoins from your balance. These addresses can also be presented in Quick Response (QR) code format.

When a transaction is made, the sender broadcasts it to all other network members (nodes), who can verify the sender has enough bitcoins to fulfill it, and that he has not spent these coins on another transaction. Once the transaction is validated by a majority of the CPU behind the network, it is inscribed onto the common ledger shared by all network members, allowing all members to update the balance of the two transacting members. While it is easy for any network member to verify the validity of a transaction, a system of voting based on giving each member one vote could be gamed by a hacker creating a lot of nodes to vote to validate their fraudulent transactions. Only by making accuracy based on CPU cycles expended by members, in other words, employing a proof-of-work system, can Bitcoin solve the double-spending problem without a trusted third party.

In its essence, proof-of-work involves network members competing to solve mathematical problems that are hard to solve but whose solution is easy to verify. All Bitcoin transactions verified in a ten-minute interval are transcribed and grouped together into one block. Nodes compete to solve the PoW math problems for a block of transactions, and the first node to produce the correct solution broadcasts it to network members, who can very quickly verify its correctness. Once the validity of the transactions and PoW are verified by a majority of the network nodes, a set quantity of bitcoin is issued to reward the node that correctly solved the PoW. This is known as the block subsidy, and the process of generating the new coins has been referred to as mining, because it is the only way that the supply of coins is increased, in the same way that mining is the only way to increase the supply of gold. On top of the block subsidy, the node that correctly solved the PoW also gets the transaction fees included by senders. The sum of the transaction fees and the block subsidy is the block reward.

Although solving these problems might initially seem a wasteful use of computing and electric power, proof-of-work is essential to the operation of Bitcoin.1 By requiring the expenditure of electricity and processing power to produce new bitcoins, PoW is the only method so far discovered for making the production of a digital good reliably expensive, allowing it to be a hard money. By ensuring that finding the solution to the mathematical problem consumes large quantities of processing power and electricity, nodes who expend that processing power have a very strong incentive to not include any invalid transactions in their blocks to receive the block reward. Because it is far cheaper to verify the validity of transactions and the PoW than it is to solve the PoW, nodes attempting to enter invalid transactions into a block are almost certainly doomed to failure, ensuring that their expended processing power goes unrewarded.

PoW makes the cost of writing a block extremely high and the cost of verifying its validity extremely low, almost eliminating the incentive for anyone to try to create invalid transactions. If they tried, they would be wasting electricity and processing power without receiving the block reward. Bitcoin can thus be understood as a technology that converts electricity to truthful records through the expenditure of processing power. Those who expend this electricity are rewarded with the bitcoin currency, and so they have a strong incentive to maintain its integrity. As a result of attaching a strong economic incentive for honesty, Bitcoin's ledger has been practically incorruptible for the period of its operation so far, with no example of a successful double-spend attack on a confirmed transaction. This integrity of the bitcoin ledger of transactions is achieved without having to rely on any single party being honest. By relying entirely on verification, Bitcoin dooms fraudulent transactions to failure and obviates the need for trust in anyone for transactions to be completed.

For an attacker to try to insert fraudulent transactions into the Bitcoin ledger, he would need to have a majority of the processing power behind the network to accept his fraud. Honest nodes that are part of the network would have no incentive to do so, because it would undermine the integrity of Bitcoin and devalue the rewards they are receiving, wasting the electricity and resources they have expended on it. So an attacker's only hope would be to mobilize a quantity of processing power that constitutes more than 50% of the network to verify his fraud and build on it as if it was valid. Such a move could have been possible in the early days of Bitcoin when the total processing power behind the network was very small. But because the economic value held in the network at the time was nonexistent or insignificant, no such attacks materialized. As the network continued to grow and more members brought processing power to it, the cost to attack the network rose.

The reward to nodes for verifying transactions has proven to be a profitable use of processing power. In January 2017, the processing power behind the Bitcoin network is equivalent to that of 2 trillion consumer laptops. It is more than two million times larger than the processing power of the world's largest supercomputer, and more than 200,000 times larger than the world's top 500 supercomputers combined. By monetizing processing power directly, Bitcoin has become the largest single-purpose computer network in the world.

Another contributing factor in this growth in processing power is that the verification of transactions and the solving of the PoW problems has moved from being conducted by personal computers to specialized processors built specifically to be optimally efficient at running the Bitcoin software. These Application Specific Integrated Circuits (ASICs) were first introduced in 2012, and their deployment has made adding processing power to the Bitcoin network more efficient, because no electricity is wasted on any irrelevant computing processes that would be present in any other, non-Bitcoin-specific computing unit. A global distributed network of independent dedicated miners now protects the integrity of the Bitcoin ledger. All of these miners have no conceivable purpose but verifying Bitcoin transactions and solving proof-of-work. Should Bitcoin fail for whatever reason, these ASICs would be rendered useless and their owners' investment would be lost, so they have a strong incentive to maintain the honesty of the network.

For someone to alter the record of the network they would need to invest hundreds of millions, if not billions, of dollars building new ASIC chips to alter it. Should an attacker succeed in altering the record, he would be highly unlikely to gain any economic benefit from it, as compromising the network would probably reduce the value of bitcoins to close to nothing. In other words, to destroy Bitcoin, an attacker needs to expend very large sums of money with no return at all. And in fact, even if such an attempt succeeded, the honest nodes on the network can effectively go back to the record of transactions before the attack and resume operation. The attacker would then need to continue incurring significant running costs to keep attacking the consensus of the honest nodes.

In its early years, Bitcoin users would run nodes and use them to carry out their transactions and to verify each other's transactions, making each node a wallet and a verifier/miner. But with time, these functions have been separated. ASIC chips are now specialized only in verifying transactions to receive reward coins (which is why they are commonly referred to as miners). Node operators can now generate unlimited wallets, allowing businesses to offer convenient wallets for users who can send and receive bitcoins without operating a node or spending processing power on verifying transactions. This has moved Bitcoin away from being a pure peer-to-peer network between identical nodes, but the main functional importance of the decentralized and distributed nature of the network has arguably remained intact, as a large number of nodes still exists and no single party is relied on to operate the network. Further, specialized mining has allowed for the processing power backing the network to grow to the astoundingly large size it has reached.

In its early days, when the tokens had little or no value, the network could have been conceivably hijacked and destroyed by attackers, but as the network had little economic value, nobody seems to have bothered. As the economic value held on the network increased, the incentive to attack the network may have increased, but the cost of doing so rose much more, resulting in no attacks materializing. But perhaps the real protection of the Bitcoin network at any point in time is that the value of its tokens is entirely dependent on the integrity of the network. Any attack that succeeds in altering the blockchain, stealing coins, or double-spending them would be of little value to the attacker, as it would become apparent to all network members that it is possible to compromise the network, severely reducing demand for using the network and holding the coins, crashing the price. In other words, the defense of the Bitcoin network is not just that attacking it has become expensive, but that the attack succeeding renders the attacker's loot worthless. Being an entirely voluntary system, Bitcoin can only operate if it is honest, as users can very easily leave it otherwise.

The distribution of the Bitcoin processing power, and the strong resistance of the code to change, combined with the intransigency of the monetary policy, are what has allowed Bitcoin to survive and grow in value to the extent to which it has today. It is hard for people new to Bitcoin to appreciate just how many logistical and security challenges Bitcoin has had to endure over the years to arrive at where it is today. Bearing in mind that the Internet has created opportunities for hackers to attack all sorts of networks and websites for fun and profit, this achievement becomes more startling. The ever-growing number of security breaches that happen to computer networks and email servers across the world on a daily basis have occurred to systems which offer the attackers not much more than data or opportunities to score political points. Bitcoin, on the other hand, contains billions of dollars of value, but continues to operate safely and reliably because it was built, from day one, to operate in a highly adversarial setting, subject to relentless attack. Programmers and hackers worldwide have tried to tear it apart using all sorts of techniques, and yet it has continued to operate according to the exact essence of its specification.

Sir Patrick Bijou

Out of Control: Why Nobody Can Change Bitcoin

"The nature of Bitcoin is such that once version 0.1 was released, the core design was set in stone for the rest of its lifetime." —Satoshi Nakamoto, 6/17/2010

Bitcoin's resilience has so far not been restricted to successfully repelling attacks; it has also ably resisted any attempt at changing it or altering its characteristics. The true depth of this statement and its implications has not yet been fully realized by most skeptics. If Bitcoin's currency were to be compared to a central bank, it would be the world's most independent central bank. If it were to be compared to a nation-state, it would be the most sovereign nation-state in the world. The sovereignty of Bitcoin is derived from the fact that, as far as anyone can tell, the way its consensus rules operate makes it very resistant to alteration by individuals. It is no exaggeration to say nobody controls Bitcoin, and that the only option available to people is to use it as it is or not use it.

This immutability is not a feature of the Bitcoin software, which is trivial to change for anyone with coding skills, but rather is grounded in the economics of the currency and network, and stems from the difficulty of getting every member of the network to adopt the same changes to the software. The software implementation that allows an individual to run a node that connects to the Bitcoin network is open source software, which was initially made available by Satoshi Nakamoto in collaboration with the late Hal Finney and some other programmers. Since then, any person has been free to download and

Cyptocurrency: The Next Level for Banking Reform

use the software as he or she pleases, and to make changes to it. This creates a freely competitive market in Bitcoin implementations, with anyone free to contribute changes, or improvements to the software and present them to users for adoption.

Over time, hundreds of computer programmers from around the world have volunteered their time to improve the node software and in the process improve the capabilities of individual nodes. These coders have formed several different implementations, the largest and most popular of which is known as "Bitcoin Core." Several other implementations exist, and users are free to alter the source code at any point. The only requirement for a node to be a part of the network is that it follows the consensus rules of the other nodes. Nodes which break the consensus rules by altering the structure of the chain, the validity of the transaction, the block reward, or any one of many other parameters in the system end up having their transactions rejected by the rest of the nodes.

The process of what defines the parameters of Bitcoin is an example of what Scottish philosopher Adam Ferguson called "the product of human action, and not of human design." Although Satoshi Nakamoto and Hal Finney and others had produced a working model of the software in January 2009, the code has evolved significantly since then through the contributions of hundreds of developers as chosen by thousands of users who run nodes. There is no central authority that determines the evolution of the Bitcoin software and no single programmer is able to dictate any outcome. The key to running an implementation that gets adopted has proven to be the adherence to the parameters of the original design. To the extent that changes have been made to the software, these changes can be best understood as improvements to the way in which an individual node interacts with the network, but not alterations to the Bitcoin network or its consensus rules. While it is outside the scope of the book to discuss which parameters these are, suffice it to specify this criterion: a change that puts the node who adopts it out of consensus with other nodes requires all other nodes to update in order for the node initiating the change to remain on the network. Should a number of nodes adopt the new consensus rules, what emerges is referred to as a hard fork.

Bitcoin's coders, then, for all their competence, cannot control Bitcoin, and are only Bitcoin coders to the extent that they provide node operators with software the node operators want to adopt. But coders aren't the only ones who cannot control Bitcoin. Miners, too, for all of the hashing power they can marshal, also cannot control Bitcoin. No matter how much hashing power is expended on processing blocks that are invalid, they will not be validated by a majority of Bitcoin nodes. Therefore, if miners attempted to change the rules of the network, the blocks they generate would simply be ignored by the network members who operate the nodes, and they would be wasting their resources on solving proof-of-work problems without any reward. Miners are only Bitcoin miners to the extent that they produce blocks with valid transactions according to the current consensus rules.

It would be tempting here to say that node operators control Bitcoin, and that is true in an abstract collective manner. More realistically, node operators can only control their own nodes and decide for themselves which network rules to join and which transactions they deem valid or invalid. Nodes are severely restricted in their choice of consensus rules because if they enforced rules inconsistent with the consensus of the network, their transactions would be rejected. Each node has a strong incentive to maintain network consensus rules and to stay compatible with nodes on these consensus rules. Each individual node is powerless to force other nodes to change their code, and that creates a strong collective bias to remain on the current consensus rules.

In conclusion, the Bitcoin coders face a strong incentive to abide by consensus rules if they are to have their code adopted. The miners have to abide by the network consensus rules to receive compensation for the resources they spend on proof-of-work. The network members face a strong incentive to remain on the consensus rules to ensure they can clear their transactions on the network. Any individual coder, miner, or node operator is dispensable to the network. If they stray away from consensus rules, the most likely outcome is that they will individually waste resources. As long as the network provides positive rewards to its participants, it's likely that replacement participants will come up. The consensus parameters of Bitcoin can thus be understood as being sovereign. To the extent that Bitcoin will exist, it will exist according to these parameters and specifications. This very strong status-quo bias in

Bitcoin's operation makes alterations to its money supply schedule, or important economic parameters, extremely difficult. It is only because of this stable equilibrium that Bitcoin can be considered hard money. Should Bitcoin deviate from these consensus rules its value proposition as hard money would be seriously compromised.

To the best of this author's knowledge, there have been no significant coordinated attempts to alter the monetary policy of Bitcoin,[3] but even far simpler attempts at altering some of the technical specifications of the code have so far failed. The reason that even seemingly innocuous changes to the protocol are extremely hard to carry out is the distributed nature of the network, and the need for many disparate and adversarial parties to agree to changes whose impact they cannot fully understand, while the safety and tried-and-tested familiarity of the status quo remains fully familiar and dependable. Bitcoin's status quo can be understood as a stable Schelling point,[4] which provides a useful incentive for all participants to stick to it, while the move away from it will always involve a significant risk of loss.

If some members of the Bitcoin network decided to change a parameter in the Bitcoin code by introducing a new version of the software that is incompatible with the rest of the network members, the result would be a fork, which effectively creates two separate currencies and networks. For as long as any members stay on the old network, they would benefit from the infrastructure of the network as it exists, the mining equipment, the network effect, and name recognition. In order for, the new fork to succeed it would need an overwhelming majority of users, mining hashing power, and all of the related infrastructure to migrate at the same time. If it doesn't get that overwhelming majority, the likeliest outcome is that the two Bitcoins would trade versus one another on exchanges. Should the people behind the fork hope for their fork to succeed, they will have to sell their coins on the old fork and hope everyone else does the same, so that the price of it collapses and the price of the new fork rises, thus driving all the mining power and economic network to the new network. But because any change in any parameter in Bitcoin's operation is likely to have beneficial effects on some network members at the expense of others, it is unlikely that a consensus would form to shift to the new coin. More broadly, the majority of Bitcoin holders only hold it because they were attracted to the automated nature of its rules and their imperviousness to direction by third parties. Such individuals are highly unlikely to want to risk giving discretion for fundamental changes to the network to a new group proposing a new incompatible codebase. Whether such a majority exists or not is a moot point; what matters is that enough of them exist to make it always certain that they will continue with the current system parameters unless their operation is compromised for some reason.

Barring such catastrophic failure in the current design, it is a safe bet that there will be a significant percentage of nodes choosing to stay with the old implementation, which automatically makes that choice far safer for anyone considering going onto a fork. The problem with deciding to go onto a fork is that the only way to help it succeed is by selling your coins on the old chain. Nobody wants to sell their coins on the old network to move to the new network, only to find that not everybody moved and the value of the coins on the new network collapses. In summation, no move to a new implementation with consensus rules can take place unless the vast majority is willing to shift together, and any shift without the majority shifting is almost certain to be economically disastrous for everyone involved. Because any such move to a new implementation likely gives the party proposing the change significant control over the future direction of Bitcoin, bitcoin holders, who are needed for this shift to succeed, are to a large extent ideologically opposed to any such group having authority over Bitcoin and are highly unlikely to support such a move. The existence of this group makes supporting a fork highly risky for everybody else. This analysis may help explain why Bitcoin has resisted all attempts to change it significantly so far. The coordination problem of organizing a simultaneous shift among people with adversarial interests, many of whom are strongly vested in the notion of immutability for its own sake, is likely intractable barring any pressing reason for people to move away from current implementations.

For instance, an edit to increase the issuance rate of the currency to raise the coins that reward miners might appeal to miners, but it would not appeal to current holders, and so they are unlikely to go with such a proposal. Similarly, an edit to increase the size of the Bitcoin network blocks would likely benefit miners by allowing them to run more transactions per block and possibly collect more transaction fees to maximize return on their investment in their mining equipment. But it would likely not appeal to long-term holders of Bitcoin, who would worry that larger blocks would cause the size of the blockchain to grow much bigger, and thus make running a full node more expensive, thereby dropping the number of nodes in the network, making the network more centralized and thus more vulnerable to attack. The coders who develop software to run Bitcoin nodes are powerless to impose changes on anybody; all they can do is propose code, and users are free to download whichever code and version they like. Any code that is compatible with the existing implementations will be far more likely to be downloaded than any code that is not compatible, because the latter would only succeed if the overwhelming majority of the network also ran it.

As a result, Bitcoin exhibits extremely strong status-quo bias. Only minor and uncontroversial changes to the code have been implemented so far, and every attempt to alter the network significantly has ended with resounding failure, to the delight of long-term Bitcoin stalwarts who like nothing more about their currency than its immutability and resistance to change. The highest-profile of these attempts have concerned increasing the size of individual blocks to increase transaction throughput. Several projects have gathered the names of some very prominent and old-time Bitcoiners, and spent a lot on trying to gain publicity for the coin. Gavin Andresen, who was one of the faces most publicly associated with Bitcoin, has pushed very aggressively for several attempts to fork Bitcoin into having bigger blocks, along with many stakeholders, including some skilled developers and deep-pocketed entrepreneurs.

Initially, Bitcoin XT was proposed by Andresen and a developer by the name of Mike Hearn in June 2015, aiming at increasing the size of a block from 1MB to 8MB. But the majority of nodes refused to update to their software and preferred to stay on the 1-megabyte blocks. Hearn was then hired by a "blockchain consortium of financial institutions" to bring blockchain technology to the financial markets and published a blogpost to coincide with a glowing profile of him in the New York Times which hailed him as desperately trying to save Bitcoin while painting Bitcoin as now being doomed to failure. Hearn proclaimed "the resolution of the Bitcoin experiment", citing the lack of growth in transaction capacity as a lethal roadblock to Bitcoin's success and announcing he had sold all his coins. The bitcoin price on that day was around $350. Over the following two years, the price was to increase more than forty-fold while the "blockchain consortium" he joined is yet to produce any actual products.

Undeterred, Gavin Andresen immediately proposed a new attempt to fork Bitcoin under the name of "Bitcoin Classic," which would have raised the blocksize to 8 megabytes. This attempt fared no better, and by March 2016 the number of nodes supporting it began to fizzle. Yet, supporters of increasing the blocksize regrouped into Bitcoin Unlimited in 2017, an even wider coalition that included the largest maker of Bitcoin mining chips, as well as a wealthy individual who controls the bitcoin.com domain name and has spent enormous resources trying to promote larger blocks. A lot of media hype was generated and the sense of crisis was palpable to many who follow Bitcoin news on mainstream media and social media; yet the reality remained that no fork was attempted, as the majority of nodes continued to run on the 1MB-compatible implementations.

Finally, in August 2017, a group of programmers proposed a new fork of Bitcoin under the name of "Bitcoin Cash," which included many of the earlier advocates of increasing the block size. The fate of Bitcoin Cash is a vivid illustration of the problems with a Bitcoin fork that does not have consensus support. Because a majority chose to stay with the original chain, and the economic infrastructure of exchanges and businesses supporting Bitcoin is still largely focused on the original Bitcoin, this has kept the value of Bitcoin's coins much higher than that of Bitcoin Cash, and the price of Bitcoin Cash continued to drop until it hit a low of 5% of Bitcoin's value in November 2017. Not only is the fork unable to gain economic value, it is also dogged with a serious technical problem that renders it almost unusable. Seeing as the new chain has the same hashing algorithm as Bitcoin, miners can utilize their processing power on both chains and receive rewards in both. But because Bitcoin's coins are far more valuable than Bitcoin Cash, the processing power behind Bitcoin remains far higher than that of Bitcoin Cash, and Bitcoin miners can shift to Bitcoin Cash any time the rewards get high. This leaves Bitcoin Cash in an unfortunate dilemma: if the mining difficulty is too high, then there will be a long delay for blocks to be produced and transactions to process. But if the difficulty is set too low, the coin is mined very quickly and the supply increases quickly. This increases the supply of the Bitcoin Cash coins faster than the Bitcoin chain, and would lead to the coin reward for Bitcoin Cash running out very quickly, thus reducing the incentive for future miners to mine it. Most likely, this will have to lead to a hard fork that adjusts the supply growth to continue offering rewards to miners. This problem is unique to a chain breaking off from Bitcoin, but was never true for Bitcoin itself. Bitcoin mining was always utilizing the largest amount of processing power for its algorithm, and the increase in processing power was always incremental as miners employed more mining capacity. But with a coin that breaks off from Bitcoin, the lower value of the coin and the lower difficulty makes the coin constantly vulnerable for quick mining by the much larger mining capacity of the more valuable chain.

After the failure of this fork to challenge Bitcoin's prime position, another attempt at a fork to double the blocksize, negotiated between various startups active in the Bitcoin economy, was canceled in mid-November as its promoters realized they were highly unlikely to achieve consensus for their move and would instead most likely end up with another coin and network. Bitcoin stalwarts have learned to shrug at such attempts, realizing that no matter how much hype is generated, any attempt to change the consensus rules of Bitcoin will lead to the generation of yet another Bitcoin copycat, like the altcoins which copy Bitcoin's incidental details but do not have its only important characteristic: immutability. From the discussion above it should be clear that Bitcoin's advantages lie not in its speed, convenience, or friendly user experience. Bitcoin's value comes from it having an immutable monetary policy precisely because nobody can easily change it. Any coin that begins with a group of individuals changing Bitcoin's specification has with its creation lost arguably the only property that makes Bitcoin valuable in the first place.

Bitcoin is straightforward to use, but virtually impossible to alter. Bitcoin is voluntary, so nobody has to use it, but those who want to use it have no choice but to play by its rules. Changing Bitcoin in any meaningful way is not really possible, and should it be attempted will produce another pointless knock-off to be added to the thousands already out there. Bitcoin is to be taken as it is, accepted on its own terms and used for what it offers. For all practical intents and purposes, Bitcoin is sovereign: it runs by its own rules, and there are no outsiders who can alter these rules. It might even be helpful to think of the parameters of Bitcoin as being similar to the rotation of the earth, sun, moon, or stars, forces outside of our control which are to be lived, not altered.

Antifragility

Bitcoin is an embodiment of Nassim Taleb's idea of antifragility, which he defines as gaining from adversity and disorder. Bitcoin is not just robust to attack, but it can be said to be antifragile on both a technical and economic level. While attempts to kill Bitcoin have so far failed, many of them have made it stronger by ending up allowing coders to identify weaknesses and patch them up. Further, every thwarted attack on the network is a notch on its belt, another testament and advertisement to participants and outsiders of the security of the network.

A global team of volunteer software developers, reviewers, and hackers have taken a professional, financial, and intellectual interest in working on improving or strengthening the Bitcoin code and network. Any exploits or weaknesses found in the specification of the code will attract some of these coders to offer solutions, debate them, test them, and then propose them to network members for adoption. The only changes that have happened so far have been operational changes that allow the network to run more efficiently, but not changes that alter the essence of the coin's operation. These coders can own Bitcoin tokens, and so have a financial incentive to work on ensuring Bitcoin grows and succeeds. In turn, the continued success of Bitcoin rewards these coders financially and thus allows them to dedicate more time and effort to the maintenance of Bitcoin. Some of the prominent developers working on maintaining Bitcoin has become wealthy enough from investing in Bitcoin that they can make it their prime occupation without receiving pay from anyone.

In terms of media coverage, Bitcoin appears to be a good embodiment of the adage "all publicity is good publicity." As a new technology that is not easy to understand, Bitcoin was always going to receive inaccurate and downright hostile media coverage, as was the case with many other technologies. The website 99bitcoins.com has collected more than 200 examples of prominent articles announcing the death of Bitcoin over the years. Some of these writers found Bitcoin to be a contravention to their worldview—usually related to the state theory of money or Keynesian faith in the importance of an elastic supply of money—and refused to consider the possibility they might be wrong. Instead, they concluded that it must be Bitcoin whose existence is wrong, and therefore they predicted it would die soon. Others believed strongly in the need for Bitcoin to change to maintain its success, and when they failed to get it to change in the way they desired, they concluded it must die. These people's attacks on Bitcoin led them to write about it and bring it to the attention of ever-wider audiences. The more obituaries intensified, the more its processing power, transactions, and market value grew. Many Bitcoiners, this author included, only came around to appreciating the importance of Bitcoin by noticing how many times it had been written off, and how it continued to operate successfully. The Bitcoin obituaries were powerless to stop it, but they seem to have helped it gain more publicity and awaken the public's curiosity to the fact that it continues to operate in spite of all the hostility and bad press it gets.

A good example of Bitcoin's antifragility came in the fall of 2013, when the FBI arrested the alleged owner of the Silk Road website, which was a truly free online market allowing users to sell and buy anything they wanted online, including illegal drugs. With Bitcoin's association in the public's mind with drugs and crime, most analysts predicted the closing of the website would destroy

Bitcoin's utility. The price on that day dropped from around the $120 range to the $100 range, but it rebounded quickly and began a very fast rise, reaching $1,200 per bitcoin within a few months. At the time of writing, the price had never again dropped to the level it was at before the closing of the Silk Road website. By surviving the closing of the Silk Road unscathed, Bitcoin demonstrated that it is far more than a currency for crime, and in the process it benefited from the free publicity from the Silk Road media coverage.

Another example of Bitcoin's antifragility came in September 2017, after the Chinese government, announced the closure of all Chinese exchanges that traded Bitcoin. Whereas the initial reaction was one of panic that saw the price drop by around 40%, it was only a matter of hours before the price started recovering, and within a few months the price had more than doubled from where it was before the government's ban. While banning exchanges from trading Bitcoin could be viewed as an impediment to Bitcoin's adoption through a reduction in its liquidity, it seems to have only served to reinforce Bitcoin's value proposition. More transactions started happening off exchanges in China, with volume on websites like localbitcoins.com exploding. It may just be that the suspension of trading in China caused the opposite of the intended effect, as it drove Chinese to hold onto their Bitcoin for the long term rather than trade it for the short term.

Can Bitcoin Scale?

At the time of writing, one of the most high-profile debates surrounding Bitcoin concerns the question of scaling, or increasing the transaction capacity. Bitcoin's 1-megabyte blocks mean that the capacity for transactions as it stands is around less than 500,000 transactions per day. Bitcoin has already approached these levels of transactions, and as a result, transaction fees have risen significantly over the past few months. The implementation of a technology called Segwit could result in a quadrupling of this daily capacity, but it is nonetheless becoming clear that there will be a hard limit to how many transactions can be processed over the Bitcoin blockchain, due to the decentralized and distributed nature of Bitcoin. Each Bitcoin transaction is recorded with all network nodes, who are all required to keep a copy of the entire ledger of all transactions. This necessarily means that the cost of recording transactions will be far higher than for any centralized solution which only needs one record and a few backups. The most efficient payment processing systems are all centralized for a good reason: it is cheaper to keep a central record than to keep several distributed records and have to worry about them updating in sync, a process which so far can only be achieved using Bitcoin proof-of-work.

Centralized payment solutions, such as Visa or MasterCard, employ one centralized ledger to which all transactions are committed, as well as a backup that is entirely separate. Visa can process around 3,200 transactions per second or 100.8 billion transactions per year.5 Bitcoin's current 1-megabyte blocks are able to process a maximum of four transactions per second, 350,000 transactions per day, or around 120 million transactions per year. For Bitcoin to process the 100 billion transactions that Visa processes, each block would need to be around 800 megabytes, meaning every ten minutes, each Bitcoin node would need to add 800 megabytes of data. In a year, each Bitcoin node would add around 42 terabytes of data, or 42,000 gigabytes, to its blockchain. Such a number is completely outside the realm of possible processing power of commercially available computers now or in the foreseeable future. The average consumer computer, or the average external hard drive, has a capacity in the order of 1 terabyte, about a week's worth of transactions at Visa volumes. For some perspective, it is worth examining the sort of computing infrastructure that Visa employs to process these transactions.

In 2013, a report showed that Visa owns a data center described as a "digital Fort Knox" containing 376 servers, 277 switches, 85 routers, and 42 firewalls.6 Granted, Visa's centralized system is a single point of failure, and so it employs very large amounts of redundancy and spare capacity to protect from unforeseen circumstances, whereas in the case of Bitcoin, the presence of many nodes would make each one of them non-critical, and so requiring less security and capacity. Nonetheless, a node that can add 42 terabytes of data every year would require a very expensive computer, and the network bandwidth required to process all of these transactions every day would be an enormous cost that would be clearly unworkably complicated and expensive for a distributed network to maintain.

There are only a handful of such centers in existence worldwide: those employed by Visa, MasterCard, and a few other payment processors. Should Bitcoin attempt to process such a capacity, it could not possibly compete with these centralized solutions by having thousands of distributed centers on a similar scale; it would have to become centralized and employ only a few such data centers. For Bitcoin to remain distributed, each node on the network must cost something reasonable for thousands of individuals to run it on commercially available personal computers, and the transfer of data between the nodes has to be at scales that are supported by regular consumer bandwidth.

It is inconceivable that Bitcoin could run the same scale of transactions on-chain that a centralized system can support. This explains why transaction costs are rising, and in most likelihood, will continue to rise if the network continues to grow. The biggest scope for scaling Bitcoin transactions will likely come off-chain, where many simpler technologies can be used for small and unimportant payments. This ensures there can be no compromise of Bitcoin's two most significant properties for which using extensive processing power is justified: digital sound money and digital cash. There are no alternative technologies that can offer these two functions, but there are many technologies that can offer small payments and consumer spending at low costs, and the technology for these choices is very simple to implement relatively reliably with current banking technologies. Bitcoin mass use for merchant payments is not even very feasible given that it takes anywhere from 1 to 12 minutes for a transaction to receive its first confirmation. Merchants and customers cannot wait that long on payments, and even though the risk of a double-spend attack is not significant enough for one small payment, it is significant enough for merchants who receive large numbers of transactions as in the example of the attack on Betcoin Dice, discussed later in the section on attacks on Bitcoin.

For people who want to use bitcoin as a digital long-term store of value, or for people who want to carry out important transactions without having to go through a repressive government, the high transaction fees are a price well worth paying. Saving in Bitcoin by its very nature will not require many transactions, and so a high transaction fee is worth paying for it. And for transactions that cannot be carried out through the regular banking system, such as people trying to get their money out of a country suffering inflation and capital controls, Bitcoin's high transaction fees will be a price well worth paying. Even at current low levels of adoption, the demand for digital cash and digital sound money has already raised transaction fees to the point where they cannot compete with centralized solutions like PayPal and credit cards for small payments. This has not stalled Bitcoin's growth, however, which indicates that the market demand for Bitcoin is driven by its use as a digital cash and digital store of value, rather than small digital payments.

If Bitcoin's popularity continues to grow, there are some potential scaling solutions that do not involve creating any changes to the structure of Bitcoin, but which take advantage of the way transactions are structured to increase the number of payments possible. Each Bitcoin transaction can contain several inputs and outputs, and using a technique called CoinJoin, several payments can be grouped together into one transaction, allowing several inputs and outputs for only a fraction of the space that would have been needed otherwise. This could potentially raise the transaction volume of Bitcoin to the millions of payments per day, and as the transaction costs rise higher, this is more and more likely to become a popular option.

Another possibility for scaling Bitcoin is digital mobile USB wallets, which can be made to be physically tamper-proof and can be checked for their balance at any time. These USB drives would carry the private keys to specific amounts of Bitcoins, allowing whoever holds them to withdraw the money from them. They could be used like physical cash, and each holder could verify the value in these drives. As fees have been rising on the network, there has been no respite in the growth of demand for Bitcoin, as evidenced by its rising price, indicating that users value the transactions more than the transaction costs they have to pay for them. Instead of the rising fees slowing Bitcoin's adoption, all that is happening is that the less important transactions are being moved off-chain and the on-chain transactions are growing in importance. The most important use cases of Bitcoin, as a store of value and uncensorable payments, are well worth the transaction fees. When people buy Bitcoin to hold it for the long-term, a one-off small transaction fee is to be expected and is usually dwarfed by the commission and the premium placed by the sellers. For people looking to escape capital controls or send money to countries facing economic difficulties, the transaction fee is well worth paying considering Bitcoin is the only alternative. As Bitcoin adoption spreads, and transaction fees rise high enough that they will matter to the people paying them, there will be economic pressure to utilize more of the above scaling solutions which can increase transaction capacity without making changes that compromise the rules of the network and force a chain split.

Beyond these possibilities, the majority of Bitcoin transactions today are already carried out off-chain, and only settled on-chain. Bitcoin-based businesses, such as exchanges, casinos, or gaming websites, will only use Bitcoin's blockchain for customer deposits and withdrawals, but within their platforms, all transactions are recorded on their local databases, denominated in Bitcoin. It is not possible to make accurate estimates of the number of these transactions due to the very large number of businesses, the lack of public data on the transactions taking place in their proprietary platforms, and the quickly shifting dynamics of the Bitcoin economy, but a conservative estimate would put them as being more than 10 times the number of transactions carried out on the Bitcoin blockchain. In effect, Bitcoin is already being used as a reserve asset in the majority of the transactions in the Bitcoin economy. Should Bitcoin's growth continue it is only natural to see the number of off-chain transactions increase faster than the on-chain transactions.

Such an analysis may contradict the rhetoric that accompanied the rise of Bitcoin, which promotes Bitcoin as putting an end to banks and banking. The idea that millions, let alone billions, could use the Bitcoin network directly for carrying out their every transaction is unrealistic as it would entail that every network member needs to be recording every other member's transactions. As the numbers grow, these records become larger and constitute a significant computing burden. On the other hand, Bitcoin's unique properties as a store of value are likely to continue to increase demand for it, making it hard for it to survive as a purely peer-to-peer network. For Bitcoin to continue to grow there will have to be payment processing solutions handled off the Bitcoin blockchain, and such solutions are emerging out of the grind of competitive markets.

Another important reason why banking as an institution is not going away is the convenience of banking custody. While many Bitcoin purists value the freedom accorded to them by being able to hold their own money and not rely on a financial institution to access it, the vast majority of people would not want this freedom and prefer to not have their money under their responsibility for fear of theft or abduction. In the midst of the very common antibank rhetoric that is popular these days, particularly in Bitcoin circles, it is easy to forget that deposit banking is a legitimate business which people have demanded for hundreds of years around the world. People have happily paid to have their money stored safely so they only need to carry a small amount of money on them and face little risk of loss. In turn, the widespread use of banking cards instead of cash allows people to carry small sums of money on them at all times, which likely makes modern society safer than it would be otherwise, because most potential assailants these days realize they are not likely to come across a victim carrying significant amounts of cash, and theft of banking cards is unlikely to yield significant sums before the victim is able to cancel them.

Even if it were possible for Bitcoin's network to support billions of transactions per day, obviating the need for second-layer processing, many, if not most, Bitcoiners with significant holdings will eventually resort to keeping them in one of the growing number of services for safe custody of Bitcoin. This is an entirely new industry and it is likely to evolve significantly to provide technical solutions for storage with different degrees of safety and liquidity. Whatever shape this industry takes, the services it provides and how it evolves will shape the contours of a Bitcoin-based banking system in the future. I make no prediction as to what shape these services will take, and what technological capabilities they will have, except to say that it will likely utilize cryptographic proof mechanisms on top of establishing market reputation in order to operate successfully. One possible technology for how this might be achieved is known as the Lightning

Network, a technology under development that promises increasing transaction capacity significantly by allowing nodes to run payment channels off-chain, which only use the Bitcoin ledger for verification of valid balances rather than transfers.

In 2016 and 2017, as Bitcoin approached the maximum number of daily transactions, the network continued to grow, as is clear from the data in Chapter 8. Bitcoin is scaling through an increase in the value of on-chain transactions, not through a rise of their number. More and more transactions are being carried out off-chain, settled on exchanges or websites that handle Bitcoin, turning Bitcoin into more of a settlement network than a direct payment network. This does not represent a move away from Bitcoin's function as cash, as is commonly believed. While the term cash has come to denote the money used for small consumer transactions today, the original meaning of the term refers to money that is a bearer instrument, whose value can be transferred directly without resort to settlement by, or liability of, third parties. In the nineteenth century, the term cash referred to central bank gold reserves, and cash settlement was the transfer of physical gold between banks. If this analysis is correct, and Bitcoin continues to grow in value and off-chain transactions while on-chain transactions do not grow as much, Bitcoin would be better understood as cash in the old meaning of the term, similar to gold cash reserves, rather than the modern term for cash as paper money for small transactions.

In conclusion, there are many possibilities for increasing the number of bitcoin transactions without having to alter the architecture of Bitcoin as it is, and without requiring all current node operators to upgrade simultaneously. Scaling solutions will come from node operators improving the way they send data on Bitcoin transactions to other network members. This will come through joining transactions together, off-chain transactions, and payment channels. On-chain scaling solutions are unlikely to be enough to meet the growing demand for Bitcoin over time and so second-layer solutions are likely to continue to grow in importance, leading to the emergence of a new kind of financial institution similar to today's banks, using cryptography, and operating primarily online.

Is Bitcoin For Criminals?

One of the very common misconceptions about Bitcoin from its inception is that it would make a great currency for criminals and terrorists. A long list of press articles have been published with unsubstantiated claims that terrorists or criminal gangs are using Bitcoin for their activity. Many of these articles have been retracted, but not before they have imprinted the idea into the minds of many people, including misguided criminals.

The reality is that Bitcoin's ledger is globally accessible and immutable. It will carry the record of every transaction for as long as Bitcoin is still operational. It is inaccurate to really say Bitcoin is anonymous, as it is rather pseudonymous. It is possible, though not guaranteed, to establish links between real-life identities and Bitcoin addresses, thus allowing the full tracking of all transactions by an address once its identity is established. When it comes to anonymity, it is useful to think of Bitcoin as being as anonymous as the Internet: it depends on how well you hide, and how well the others look. Yet Bitcoin's blockchain makes hiding that much more difficult on the Web. It is easy to dispose of a device, email address, or IP address and never use it again, but it is harder to completely erase the trail of funds to one bitcoin address. By its very nature, Bitcoin's blockchain structure is not ideal for privacy.

All of this means that for any crime that actually has a victim, it would be inadvisable for the criminal to use Bitcoin. Its pseudonymous nature means that addresses could be linked to real-world identities, even many years after the crime is committed. The police, or the victims and any investigators they hire, might well be able to find a link to the identity of the criminal, even after many years. The Bitcoin trail of payments itself has been the reason that many online drug dealers have been identified and caught as they fell for the hype of Bitcoin as completely anonymous.

Bitcoin is a technology for money, and money is something that can be used by criminals at all times. Any form of money can be used by criminals or to facilitate crime, but Bitcoin's permanent ledger makes it particularly unsuited to crimes with victims likely to try to investigate. Bitcoin can be useful in facilitating "victimless crimes," where the absence of the victim will mean nobody trying to establish the identity of the "criminal." In reality, and once one overcomes the propaganda of the twentieth-century state, there is no such thing as a victimless crime. If an action has no victims, it is no crime, regardless of what some self-important voters or bureaucrats would like to believe about their prerogative to legislate morality for others. For these illegal but perfectly moral actions, Bitcoin could be useful because there are no victims to try to hunt down the perpetrator. The harmless activity carried out shows up on the blockchain as an individual transaction which could have a multitude of causes. So one can expect that victimless crimes, such as online gambling and evading capital controls, would use Bitcoin, but murder and terrorism would more likely not. Drug dealing seems to happen on the Bitcoin blockchain, though that is likely more down to addicts' cravings than sound judgment, as evidenced by the large number of Bitcoin drug purchasers that have been identified by law enforcement. While statistics on this matter are very hard to find, I would not be surprised to find buying drugs with Bitcoin is far more dangerous than with physical government money.

In other words, Bitcoin will likely increase individuals' freedom while not necessarily making it easier for them to commit crimes. It is not a tool to be feared, but one to be embraced as an integral part of a peaceful and prosperous future.

One high-profile type of crime that has indeed utilized Bitcoin heavily is ransomware: a method of unauthorized access to computers that encrypts the victims' files and only releases them if the victim makes a payment to the recipient, usually in Bitcoin. While such forms of crime were around before Bitcoin, they have become more convenient to carry out since Bitcoin's invention. This is arguably the best example of Bitcoin facilitating crime. Yet one can simply understand that these ransomware crimes are being built around taking advantage of lax computer security. A company that can have its entire computer system locked up by anonymous hackers demanding a few thousand dollars in Bitcoin has far bigger problems than these hackers. The incentive for the hackers may be in the thousands of dollars, but the incentive for the firm's competitors, clients, and suppliers for gaining access to this data can be much higher. In effect, what Bitcoin ransomware has allowed is the detection and exposition of computer security flaws. This process is leading firms to take better security precautions, and causing computer security to grow as an industry. In other words, Bitcoin allows for the monetizing of the computer security market. While hackers can initially benefit from this, in the long run, productive businesses will command the best security resources.

CONCLUSION

The Bitcoin protocol is a clever mixture of technologies and concepts from different fields which in combination created something remarkable. Most of the used primitives, like chaining of cryptographic hash functions, asymmetric cryptography, or proof-of-work, were known and had been studied for a while before Bitcoin was conceived. The novelty of Bitcoin lies in the fusion of these building blocks with an incentive system based on game theory and a practical use case, namely a digital currency. This created a new type of probabilistic distributed consensus system dubbed Nakamoto consensus. The novelty of this mechanism is that it allows the "anonymous" participation in the consensus process through the process of mining without requiring any kind of trusted setup procedure in advance.

Bitcoin is not the answer to everything, but it has undoubtedly had an impact in a number of different areas and communities: It created a new class of randomized consensus systems and rekindled research in the field of distributed consensus and Byzantine fault-tolerant systems in general. It bootstrapped a vivid and diverse community that is driving the development of this set of technologies further. The original online publication, software implementation, and further development by the community in its early days outpaced traditional academic research and publishing cycles. It demonstrated that you can implement and run a decentralized digital currency system with a market capitalization in the billions of dollars before even having a sound theoretical model of why it works. It showcased that interdisciplinary thinking can lead to novel approaches and solutions with practical applications.

While Bitcoin and blockchains are hardly the answer to life, the universe and everything, as ideologists or advertising sometimes paint it, the fusion of its underlying technologies and methods has opened new pathways and outlined new possibilities in different areas of research. Furthermore, cryptographic currency technologies also have a sociological and practical dimension with disruptive potential. Never before was it this easy to create a currency that can be used worldwide without the absolute need for a trusted third party or the requirement to distribute physical coins and notes. This change of paradigm forces us to rethink the concept of money and currencies and enables us to envision a future in which a multitude of different cryptographic currencies exist, all of which encode their individual techniques and a set of rules accepted within the community of their users. As long as there are methods to easily use different cryptographic currencies and also exchange assets between them it is not necessary to rely on just one cryptocurrency for everything.

www.ingramcontent.com/pod-product-compliance
Lightning Source LLC
Chambersburg PA
CBHW072143100526
44589CB00015B/2069